TOTAL SYSTEM
DEVELOPMENT
FOR INFORMATION
SYSTEMS

TOTAL SYSTEM DEVELOPMENT FOR INFORMATION SYSTEMS

FRANK G. KIRK

A WILEY—INTERSCIENCE PUBLICATION

JOHN WILEY & SONS,   New York • London • Sydney • Toronto

Library of Congress Cataloging in Publication Data:

Kirk, Frank G   1933–
   Total system development for information systems.

   1. Management information systems.   I.   Title.

T58.6.K56   658.4'03   73–4359
ISBN 0–471–48260–9

Printed in the United States of America

10 9 8 7 6 5 4 3 2

To my wife

Judy

And to my children

Mark, Robin, and Maya

PREFACE

This book describes the process of developing computer-based man-machine information systems. Many books have already addressed parts of this subject. Few books, however, have attempted to discuss the entire subject in an orderly fashion and to maintain a balanced treatment of the human factors side of system development as well as the "computer science," "system engineering," and "operations research" aspects. The focus of this book is on a disciplined method of developing the total system.

For a variety of reasons, few systems have met their intended objectives. Some systems went awry because of technological difficulties with computer hardware, and others because of programming or language deficiencies. Many failed because people were improperly designed into the system. This book contends that the methodology for successful total system development exists and can be rationally explained.

The book has been written to meet a need often expressed by the users, developers, development managers, and buyers of information systems. The organization and language attempt to satisfy these varied needs. The book is written in a front-to-back style; that is to say, it is sequential, and the concepts, vocabulary, and developmental philosophy are introduced incrementally and are built on one another. Readers who attempt to start in the middle will probably be confused and receive an improper impression of system development. The sequence of the book reflects the total system development process from the initial idea to the operational system performing its defined functions in the intended environment.

This book not only reflects my own experiences but also includes all the techniques, language, concepts, and procedures that could be gained by reviewing hundreds of aerospace, industrial, and military research reports. In addition, dozens of individuals and books have contributed to the present understanding of the subject. Although this book does not purport to be the definitive or final work on the subject, my hope is that it will be a lasting contribution at this level of detail.

The book does not treat all aspects of the development of information systems at an even level of detail. Many facets of the subject, such as operations research, modeling, data base design, and programming techniques, have been treated in depth in other books. However, such subjects as design for human performance in information systems, characteristics of information systems, and project management have received too little attention. Therefore, this book offers more detail on subjects which have been inadequately described in the literature of today and less detail where good materials are available elsewhere.

Development of total systems suggests a vertical treatment of the subject, starting with the germ of an idea for a new system and continuing to where the system is designed and operational, and even beyond, to where the system is maintained or supported in a dynamic environment until it either is no longer needed or is replaced by another system. This is often referred to as the system life cycle. This book will discuss the entire life cycle. Also, the term "total system design" is sometimes used to denote a horizontal look at the development of a system. Specifically, "total system design" usually refers to equal design treatment of the human performance considerations with the computer and software considerations. This book will cover total system design in the context of total system development.

Finally, I wish to acknowledge the invaluable assistance of friends and colleagues who have contributed in some way to this book. In particular, I thank James Altman, Georgia Brown, John Gardner, Fredel Goodrich, Wayne Gustafson, Ralph Marion, George Purifoy, Jr., Spence Sawyer, Bill Thatcher, and Dixie Thierry.

It is my hope that the book can be used as a practical guide to the daily performance of system developers as well as a general tutorial introduction to the discipline. As a guide it contains activity-by-activity procedures for performing system design. Although it is not a handbook in the sense of being all inclusive, it discusses methods for designing the total system. How well I have succeeded in my aims the reader alone will judge.

FRANK G. KIRK

Kenilworth, Illinois
January 1973
viii

CONTENTS

ix

TOTAL SYSTEM
DEVELOPMENT
FOR INFORMATION
SYSTEMS

CHAPTER 1 SYSTEM DEVELOPMENT— DEFINITION AND SCOPE

Any discussion of system development necessarily begins with a definition of the term "system." In the broadest sense, a system is a combination of people, equipment, and procedures ordered for the accomplishment of a unified purpose or objective. Obviously, this definition covers systems of all types and complexities—from a woman's housecleaning system to the system used by the astronauts for a soft landing on the moon. The following chapters, however, are limited to a discussion of information systems. All are systems which involve informational output, whether this output takes the form of computer-printed documents or other machine-processed data.

Information systems have eleven identifiable, interrelated characteristics which describe them as precisely as anatomical characteristics describe an animal. These characteristics are people, equipment, procedures, objectives, communications media, dynamics, data base, input, output, limitations, and control. Each of these characteristics is discussed below.

PEOPLE

The most important characteristic of any information system is people. People recognize the need for a new system, develop the system, and implement it. The need for any business system springs from the problems and requirements of people within the business and should achieve for these people the results they desire. Because business problems are no respecters of organizational lines and departmental jurisdiction, the people involved in system development should be drawn from all departments and levels of an organization. They must work as a team, on an integrated basis, to achieve the results desired.

1

EQUIPMENT

The equipment involved in an information system includes far more than the computer and associated peripherals or auxiliaries. In the broad, system sense, the term "equipment" takes in all of the devices or machines that contribute to a stipulated end result. Equipment may include factory production units, typewriters, adding machines, delivery vehicles, and anything else, such as training equipment, directly related to achieving system objectives.

PROCEDURES

By definition, a system's structure presupposes that something will be done, according to set methods, with the information entered into the system. Procedures are all the methods necessary to accomplish the objectives of a system, whether they be manual or machine. In more technical terminology, procedures are the processes which combine and manipulate input and data base content to achieve specified results, or output. Procedures must be established to deal with both routine and anticipated but nonroutine occurrences.

Procedures may include programming, systems design, equipment setup, calculations, printing, clerical operations, and many types of automated and man/machine interactions.

UNIFIED PURPOSE OR OBJECTIVES

Essential to every system is a specific purpose, a set of objectives. In dealing with complex systems it is necessary to state these objectives formally, clearly defining the specific results to be achieved. The more precisely system objectives are stated, the more effective will be their implementation. Conversely, the vaguer the statement of objectives, the greater is the number of assumptions which will have to be made and the less likely a system development is to meet the "needs" which initiated the development effort.

The importance of clearly defined and stated system objectives is so obvious that their presence has tended to be assumed in published discussions on system development. In actual fact, however, the lack of clearly stated, clearly understood objectives has been a major cause for failure and/or misdirection of system development efforts. Part of the reason for this situation is that the top management of an organization is generally responsible for the statement of objectives. System development activities, however, are performed by people at lower organizational levels. There is a natural tendency, therefore, not to question, review, or refine statements handed down from above. When necessary procedural and technical enlargements are not made in general statements of objectives, opportunities for misunderstanding and inexactness occur. Hence, when objectives are not precisely defined, a system is far less likely to serve the desired end.

Furthermore, many system development efforts fall short of success because they are undertaken for the wrong reasons. Misdirected or inappropriate objectives stem from a variety of causes, including the following:

1. Vague expressions of desires to improve existing processes or procedures.
2. Desire to use a modern computer system for its own sake, with the goal of computerization overshadowing better organizational results.
3. Confusion between system objectives and system development objectives.

The last is a fine point which will be dealt with further in Chapter 7. However, in considering system elements, it is important to recognize that differences or conflicts can exist between the end results to be achieved by the system and the practical realities of system development. Objectives are one thing; the resources necessary to meet them can be something entirely different. For systems to achieve their objectives, harmony must exist between the objectives themselves and the skills, money, time, equipment, procedures, and people required for project implementation.

System development is a process for implementing change, which is a necessity in modern business and government organizations. Management of change in the form of new system development cannot be effectively launched until targets are clearly sighted. Formulation of objectives based on specific needs, therefore, is an initial requirement in system development.

COMMUNICATIONS MEDIA

For a comprehensive system to function effectively, communication is essential both internally and externally. A system must be capable of receiving communicated information at its point of inception. Communication is also essential between participants and, as required, between equipment elements. The end product, or output, of a system must also be communicated. The results of communication should be such that they can alter the course of activities or events.

Information may be communicated in a variety of forms, using any acceptable medium for making known the facts or conditions. For example, system outputs can be communicated via print or type, the spoken word, signals, bells, alarms, lights, or any other comprehensible medium which provides a satisfactory interface from and to the "outside" world relative to the system.

DYNAMIC NATURE

A system must be able to withstand and adapt to planned or predicted changes in environment or internal conditions and functions. The term "dynamic" reflects the ability of a system to alter itself or to be altered readily. Requirements for system revision may be *environmental*, resulting from changes in laws, regulations, climate, geography, or population size, or *internal*, reflecting the addition of new equipment, setting of new objectives, management decisions, changes in personnel, and so on.

DATA BASE

A data base is a logically organized arrangement of semipermanent, fairly frequently accessed information which can be made available in either or both of the following ways:

- Manually accessed, as is done with filing cabinets.
- Mechanically or electronically accessed, as is done with a cathode ray tube to a computer file.

An information processing system must be able to respond to and utilize data—source facts represented in system-compatible form——which are either entered externally or generated within the system itself. The composite data to which a system has access in the routine performance of its mission are generally known as the data base.

On occasion, the data base can provide input to the system. However, definite distinctions exist between input items and items within a system's data base. Generally, input tends to contain newly created, transaction or transitory type of information. A data base, on the other hand, consists of information of a reusable and a more static nature. For example, an input document for a long-distance telephone information system might indicate that a telephone subscriber in New York (212) had placed a call to Los Angeles (213) and talked for 5 minutes. The telephone numbers, area codes, and length of call would be input data (captured at the time of occurrence). But applicable rates, whether recorded manually or by a computer, would come from the data base. Furthermore, the toll for the call would be incorporated within the data base files for customer billing and possible later reference in answering inquiries.

INPUT

"Input," a term already used above, refers to all the external events and generated information relevant to the system. Input is more than the specific items fed to a computer; it covers all external stimuli associated with the system. The input process, in turn, calls for the coding and/or formatting of such stimuli for recognition and response by the system. However, the emphasis in identifying and evaluating input should be on the source, rather than on any intermediate processes involved in formatting, coding, or transmission.

OUTPUT

The informational results of a system are expressed as output. For example, typical information results of a payroll system would include such items as pay checks, payroll journals, payroll registers, labor cost information, deduction reports on social security, withholding taxes, and union dues.

LIMITATIONS

Every system must have defined areas of applicability, limits of interest and activity. These limits are referred to as boundaries or parameters. Even though a system may relate closely to another one and at times interlock with it, each system must have its own specific limits for specific situations. For example, output from a payroll system might logically become part of the input for a manufacturing cost system, but the development of the payroll system would not concern itself with problems of manufacturer cost. Similarly, output from an automobile manufacturing system could be input for a whole transportation system, but each system would function within specified, knowledgeably defined limits.

CONTROL

Interaction between men, machines, and procedures takes place constantly in any system, and this interaction must be checked frequently. Control, therefore, is one of the requisite features or characteristics of any effective system. To be effective, control must be exercised over many system characteristics. For example, processes to be controlled must generate some interim output. This, in turn, must be communicated, evaluated against control criteria, and then input as constraints or control elements over system operation. In effect, then, control is made up of a series of internal, predesigned criteria incorporated within the stated objectives and design of the system.

THE NATURE OF A SUBSYSTEM

With the eleven system characteristics in mind, it is worth while to consider briefly the existence of subsystems. Subsystems are often developed within information systems because of the complexity of current business and government problems.

A subsystem is an identifiable, self-contained, independently controllable section of a system. The distinction between systems and subsystems is made largely in terms of objectives, processing continuity, and scope. A subsystem has two chief characteristics:

1. Its objectives and limitations are ordered within the larger objectives of the system.
2. It is contained entirely within a system.

SYSTEM DEVELOPMENT—THE BUILDING OF SYSTEMS AND SUBSYSTEMS

Systems and subsystems do not come into being of their own accord; they must be built in an orderly fashion by a method known as system development. System development is the series of structured phases by which a team of individuals, from varying disciplines, creates and implements a system.

System development is best handled sequentially, in a series of phases which follow one another logically. Subdivision into phases makes it possible for people with specialized knowledge to work only on the sections of a development project to which their skills apply. As work on a new phase begins, the composition of a development team can be varied to fit the requirements of the particular phase. Phasing, or staging, a system development project also provides opportunity for progress reporting and evaluation. System development, because of its scope and the expenditures involved, is best checked and evaluated at several critical points between initiation and implementation.

Even though it is phased, system development should be considered a continuous, rather than a stop-and-go, process—a process in which one phase contributes to and overlaps the next. Nine separate phases will be dealt with in individual chapters of this book:

1. Formation of objectives phase.
2. Definition phase.
3. Preliminary design phase.
4. Detail design phase.
5. Testing phase.
6. Conversion phase.
7. Operational phase.
8. Evaluation phase and Maintenance phase.
9. Support phase

An interdisciplinary project team is as important to system development as is sequential phasing of the project. The personnel of a comprehensive team usually come from a full range of management, scientific, and technical pursuits and may include specialists in behavioral sciences, computer sciences, operations research, statistics, and other areas. Specific backgrounds for members of project teams developing information systems will be considered more fully in Chapter 3.

Early in any discussion of modern information systems, it is important to establish that a growing emphasis in system development is placed (in contrast to the earlier stress on computers and other technical skills) on management skills. This has occurred because the emphasis in system outputs is increasingly management oriented. Furthermore, management techniques themselves are tending toward a prescriptive rather than a conventional postscriptive approach.

The term "prescriptive" indicates the single most vital feature of modern management. Traditionally, management employees looked at historical operating data concerning the activities for which they were responsible. When the data indicated that problems existed, these people devised and implemented corrective measures. This postscriptive approach, although still in use, is giving way to the prescriptive approach.

Compelled by the size and pace of modern business, industrial, and governmental activity, management is developing techniques to antici- pate problems and correct them long before their presence is an- nounced by historical data. For example, department store wholesalers used to keep inventories at fixed levels, regardless of seasons. Invaria- bly, however, demands for various types of merchandise varied season- ally. With the advent of computers, seasonal demand could be anticipated and inventories prescribed to accommodate fluctuating trends.

Perhaps the dominant characteristic of a modern, large-scale system is the one which is least tangible. Management personnel, scientific specialists, and technicians working together as a team can develop a successfully designed, operational system that achieves and maintains an identity of its own. Systems continue. They outlast the people who create them. They survive changes in specific pieces of equipment or alterations in procedures. A well-developed system can be said to be greater than the sum of its parts.

CHAPTER 2 SYSTEM DEVELOPMENT— STRUCTURE, FUNCTIONAL CHARACTERISTICS, AND ENVIRONMENTAL FACTORS

NATURE OF SYSTEM DEVELOPMENT

There is nothing new, unique, or even unusual about the system development process. In its basic form, everyone practices some type of system development as part of his everyday life. In our youth, we plan for educational and/or working experience objectives and implement them. When we marry, we buy homes to accommodate growing families and provide for family experiences, education, vacations, and financial security. We develop hobbies for our spare time, and many of us think ahead extensively to a leisurely retirement program. Also, for most of his adult life, the average person plans for, reacts to, and works at the development of a satisfying, productive career.

Even at the individual or family level, conflicts arise and decision making is a continuing requirement. The desire for a new television set may be in conflict with the proposed purchase of both a dishwasher and a refrigerator and require a choice between them. The need for a new family car may be instrumental in reaching a decision for a motoring vacation rather than a flight to a distant area. The point is that, in all human endeavors, resources of time, money, and skill are limited and must be applied so as to achieve the most beneficial results from efforts expended within given circumstances.

The same principles, on an obviously larger scale, apply to the development and implementation of information systems for business and governmental organizations. Parts of this book will deal with the great and continually growing scope and depth of information system development and implementation. However, at the outset, the impor-

9

tant thing to realize is that intellectually there is nothing either mysterious or unusual about the system development process.

The other important point about the nature of system development which should be realized at an early stage is that there is a lot more to information systems than the mere manipulation of numbers. Systems deal with actions, behavior, interrelationships. Quantitative and mathematical skills are part of this picture, but they are not a totality. The really vital skill in systems analysis, design, and development is the understanding of interaction between people and processes in terms of functional and time relationships. This skill, in turn, calls for the application of basic reasoning and logical capabilities.

This point has been borne out by studies and analyses which show that successful systems analysts are just as likely to have backgrounds in social sciences, psychology, or even languages as in mathematics or other quantitatively oriented disciplines. The job of systems analysis involves identifying and devising solutions for problems.

The cycle of problem identification and solution development follows a logical pattern from the general to the specific. For example, the Apollo moon landing was a most successful system project. From the standpoint of system analysis and development, the development effort for such a project obviously moved from the general to the highly specific. The basic mission was to transport a team of men to the moon and bring them back safely. Application of reason and logic led to the subdivision of this overall project into a large number of separate, specifically related subsystems. One group, for example, studied the necessary structure of the launching vehicle. Another dealt with propulsion. A third was responsible for the landing craft. Others were involved with the medical and physical aspects of survival in space. Other teams studied the potential effect of meteorites on a space vehicle. Literally tens of thousands of separate reasoning and logic efforts were built into the totality of the Apollo program.

Because of the interrelated nature of all of the separate things necessary for development and implementation, system projects have been characterized as team efforts. Although the people and groups involved have individual specialties, they must all be related and directed toward the accomplishment of uniform, coherent objectives. For purposes of illustration, a modern football team can serve as an analogy for a modern system development team.

The initial objective for a team entering a new season is to win a championship by defeating all of its opponents. The components of victory are then broken down into offense and defense. Within these categories, they are further subdivided into the specialties of quarterbacks and running backs, blocking assignments for linemen, pass patterns, and so on. Similarly, defensive strategies are subdivided into assignments for linemen, linebackers, and corner men, safeties, punt return formations, and so on.

Anyone who has discussed or watched modern football games knows that a missed block by a lineman can result in a lost resource when a quarterback is injured by a defensive lineman who should have been stopped. Similarly, a bad snap from center can lead to temporary disaster.

The system development team is structured in much the same way as the football team and functions similarly. Just as an offensive tackle is expected not to score a touchdown himself, but to clear the way for others who specialize in this function, so also a team of system analysts may be assigned to a small, specialized unit of work of a supportive nature. For example, on the Apollo project, a team of specialists was put to work finding a plastic lining for the nozzle which fed liquid oxygen into the rocket engines of the left-off vehicle. These people were remote in their actions and thinking from the men who actually walked on the moon. But, without a material which could hold its dimension stability under cryogenic temperatures, the entire system could not have performed to the standards necessary to meet the mission objectives.

In a business-oriented information system project, the role of a specialist like a programmer can be likened to that of the football player who specializes in kicking field goals or returning punts. These athletic specialists are not called in at the beginning of a team endeavor. They are not involved in mapping strategy. Rather, they perform specialties in circumstances which result from the actions of others.

RELATIVE POSITION OF SYSTEM DEVELOPMENT EFFORTS

Just as a football team is part of a league or conference, so also a system development team is part of a larger organizational structure within which it functions. Here, too, a parallel exists. Fans are familiar with the many reorganizations and reorientations which have affected leagues and conferences for football, baseball, basketball, and other sports, particularly during the 1960s. The same type of thing has occurred with the information systems function within business and governmental organizations. Just about everyone familiar with information processing is aware of the tradition behind the emergence of computer-inclusive systems. For the better part of two decades, computers existed and computer systems were implemented largely as replacements for business machines. The great preoccupation of computer people in the business data processing environment was the conversion of systems from mechanized accounting or punched card machines to computers. With this background, data processing facilities operated almost entirely under accounting departments or the controller's function.

More important than the history of computer evolution is an analysis of the reasons why information processing could not realize its full potential under the aegis of accounting departments or controllers. Of the many reasons, three stand out:

1. By nature, accounting is an after-the-fact, postscriptive type of activity. In direct contrast, system development is prescriptive in nature.
2. Operational systems represent a service type of activity. They call for close interrelationships between departments and groups in every sector of the organization. The auditing and recordkeeping functions which comprise the chief duties of a conventional accounting department tend not to be compatible with the active relationships necessary to system development and operation.
3. Accounting and control groups tend to be too far removed from decision-level management to function effectively in the development of informational end products designed for management use.

In other words, the accounting-oriented heritage tended, for many years, to restrict the use of computers to bookkeeping-type functions. The real management values of computerized information systems emerged and came to the forefront only after the potential information and guidance values of the cumulative files created by computers effectively generated their own demands for management attention.

With the recognition of the separate value of informational results from computerized systems, a shifting of emphasis and responsibilities took place. Gradually, information systems departments began to emerge with charters and responsibilities independent of traditional accounting functions. Even in a company where the information systems department continued to report to the controller, a new emphasis was placed on interdisciplinary skills and on the establishment and use of communication channels between the systems group and all other departments within the organization with potential use for information systems. The common denominator, organizationally, for an effective information systems department today is that it has free access to all operational segments of its company or agency. It has reporting channels leading to a high management level and a built-in mechanism for responsiveness to its needs, activities, and findings.

Part of this organizational recognition resulted from the avalanche type of development which marked the information processing industry during the 1950s and 1960s. Expanding economies and growing competition made computerized systems virtually mandatory for all large organizations. The rate of demand far outstripped the availability of the skills necessary to design, develop, and implement information systems. The shortages of people and the hectic pace at which systems development projects were undertaken led to many disappointments and outright failures in the results of system development efforts.

Organizationally, a development which paralleled the establishment of a separate identity for the information systems department was the centralization of the function as a whole. In the early days, the tendency had been to decentralize computer installations and the responsibility for system development and implementation. Inevitably, many organizations found their decentralized groups duplicating each other's efforts in key problem areas, while other problems which needed attention were neglected because of shortages in people and budgets. Thus, centralization became a marked trend which paralleled the provision of a separate organizational identity for the information system function.

Another largely technical consideration also contributed to the organizational recognition and centralization of the information system function. As high-level management recognized the potential for organizing, processing, interpreting, and using computer-processed information on an overall, company-wide basis, considerable excitement was generated by the prospect of comprehensive data bases which would serve total management information needs. The idea of developing total systems which could, theoretically at least, answer any management requirements at any time led to considerable interest and planning activity aimed at the creation of "corporate data bases."

Although total, inclusive data bases proved, at least during the 1960s, to be too ambitious a concept for ready implementation, the impetus this prospect exerted on behalf of the creation of central, independently recognized information systems departments proved highly beneficial. Centralization of the information system function served, in itself, to provide a mechanism for coming to grips with realities where computers were concerned. By establishing one source for responsibility and control of all computer-inclusive projects, this trend forced the managements of many organizations to take their first long, hard look at the establishment of priorities and the allocation of resources, particularly for information systems projects. This, in turn, created an environment in which the money, time, and people assigned to the information systems function could be measured against potential results from commitments elsewhere within the organization. In effect, the information systems function was in a position to compete, in terms of results and potential benefits to the organization as a whole, with other areas or departments where management could also apply its money, people, or time. In other words, an environment was created where computerized systems had to be made attractive as a management investment.

The continuing comparison between investments in information systems and those in other areas within the organization serves, in itself, to restructure much of the thinking in regard to management emphasis and investment. With computerized information systems, businesses are, in effect, premanaged rather than postmanaged. In this type of situation, management funds are applied for positive results rather than against negative conditions. In other words, management information systems started as a tool for uncovering opportunities to anticipate requirements, rather than limiting management to the correction of problems after they have proved costly enough to merit special attention.

For the purposes of this discussion, it is assumed that the values of a separately identified information systems department with independent, high-level reporting responsibilities have been recognized in most large organizations and that steps have been taken or are in process for setting up the information systems function on such a basis.

ORGANIZATIONAL STRUCTURE FOR INFORMATION PROCESSING

Now that the relative position and function of the information systems department within the typical business or governmental organization have been identified, the next logical step is to describe the structural mechanism within which it interacts with the rest of its organization. Here, too, experience and evolution have played important roles in the way in which information systems are developed and implemented. By the late 1960s, as systems gained the scope to make them increasingly interdisciplinary, many organizations began to set up executive-level steering committees composed of prospective users. These committees, in general, were charged with management surveillance of the systems function and of projects selected for and carried into development. Typically, a committee of this type was responsible for communication with and surveillance of the information systems function. One of the major advantages behind the formation of high-level executive committees for this function was that they became a natural mechanism for consensus. Since key user department heads or vice presidents were represented on the committee, they could presumably thrash out priorities and coordination problems at a level high enough to ensure cooperation and compliance throughout the organization.

In practice, this was substantially the way things worked out for most organizations. Then the high-level committee approach developed its own symptomatic problems. Specifically, the group occupied such a high position within the overall organization that communication and presentations tended to occur at a high-order, summary level. This left too much room for misconceptions and small surprises in technical or user implementation areas within the systems under development.

By the 1970s, therefore, organizational structures tended to provide for multilevel user involvement in the system development process. Specifically, each system under development was made a responsibility of a specially established project team. User members were made regular and permanent components of each such team. If several departments would use a system under development, each was represented on the team. These user members were specifically selected from organizational levels where the implemented system would ultimately operate. In other words, system project teams were structured for full-scale user involvement. This involvement, in turn, became a key to the acceptability and practicality of new computer-inclusive systems. The user members contributed expertise on working conditions and problems within the areas to be impacted by new systems. Once a system was designed and developed to satisfy the convictions of the user members of the project team, it became the responsibility of these persons to "sell" the system to their peers. This, in essence, became a mechanism for certifying that the solutions incorporated within a new system for dealing with the problems defined in the statement of objectives did, in fact, meet the actual needs of the people and functions within the areas where the system would ultimately be installed.

The various organizational structure trends for dealing with the information systems function are shown graphically in Figures 2–1, 2–2, and 2–3. Figure 2–1 shows the traditional organizational structure approach, under which systems activities tended to be made a part of the controller's function. As the chart shows, in a typical case an assistant controller was placed in charge of activities which fell under a heading such as the one indicated: mechanized system development.

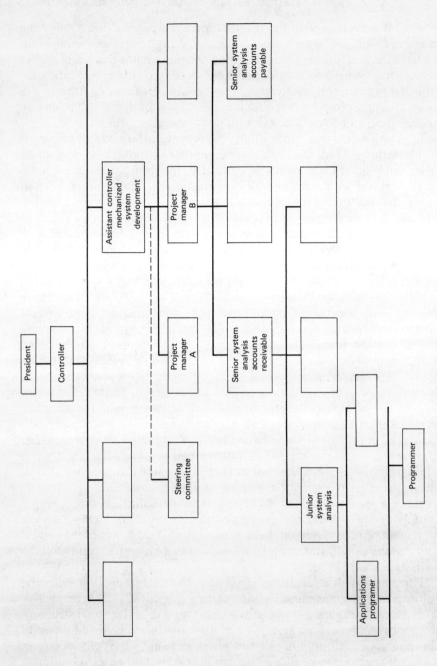

President

Controller

Assistant controller
mechanized
system
development

Steering
committee

Project
manager
A

Project
manager
B

Senior system
analysis
accounts
receivable

Senior system
analysis
accounts
payable

Junior
system
analysis

Applications
programer

Programmer

Figure 2–1 *Traditional systems development organization.*

16

Under this arrangement, project managers reported to the assistant controller, senior systems analysts reported to the project managers, junior analysts, and so on. This chart is not worth detailing. It is presented here only to show the cumbersome inflexibility of communication channels in conventional organization approaches. Note also that, with the responsibility for system development at a departmental assistant level, the steering committee charged with monitoring system projects was also, of necessity, at a comparatively low level. In such circumstances, the steering committee lacked the stature for major commitments of resources. On the other hand, these persons were too high in the organization to be technically competent to evaluate the projects they were charged with supervising.

A later version of the linear approach to organization for systems management is diagrammed in Figure 2–2. In this approach, the infor-

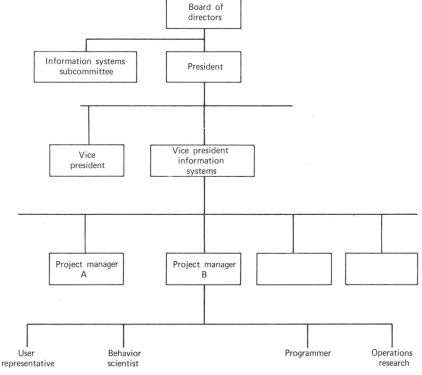

Figure 2–2 *Modern organization for systems development.*

mation systems function is managed by a vice president. As a result the information systems function has direct reporting access to the chief operating officer of the organization. Also, the steering committee function has been made responsive directly to the board of directors because of the extent and magnitude of the commitments involved. Thus the steering committee in such an organization would be composed of vice presidents with the power to allocate resources and also to commit user departments to cooperate actively for system success.

Under the structure diagrammed in Figure 2–2, project managers function at the level of department heads. Each is in charge of multidiscipline team handling system projects relevant to a given area of the business.

This approach represents a marked improvement over the structure outlined in Figure 2–1. By providing for all key members of a system team to be at the same organizational level, a mechanism is established under which team members can communicate through the project manager or members of his staff. Obviously, this is superior to the multilayer structure shown in Figure 2–1, where a programmer who uncovered a problem in a system was three levels of communication away from the project manager who made the decision.

In a later approach, the organizational and communication channels of an individual project are structured according to the working and informational requirements of its specific developmental phases. This approach recognizes the fact that channels of responsibility and communication are different during system development from what they are in the operation of a completed, functional system. Different people and different skills are involved in various phases. Ultimately, for example, the functional system will belong to its user organization or organizations. During development, however, the users serve consulting and quality assurance functions rather than providing direction.

The changing structure of responsibility and communication is similar to the process that takes place in the construction of an office building. During construction, preoccupation is with structures, floors, walls, ceilings, wiring, plumbing, and so on. Coordinating relationships must exist to ensure that wires and pipes are in place before walls and ceilings are finish coated. Thus coordination during construction is highly skill related. Once the building is complete, however, its different segments can be identified as executive offices, departmental offices, mail rooms, file rooms, and so on.

Similarly, studies and experience have shown that a transition takes place in the organizational requirement of a project team during the system development process. During the first few phases of a system project, namely, formation of objectives, definition, and part of preliminary design, communication and reporting channels must be as open ended as possible. Then, after definitions and specifications are established, a more disciplined structure is required to channel efforts toward specified objectives.

Among the earliest users of this type of open-structured approach to project management was the U.S. Air Force Systems Command Headquarters. This agency set up an approach under which it became routine for members of all commands slated to use a system under development to appoint actively participating representatives to the responsible project team. These representatives functioned both as experts on system requirements and as approval authorities on behalf of their own user groups.

Under this approach, individuals are assigned to project teams according to the skills they can contribute. Thus it is not unusual on an air force project to find colonels and lieutenants working side by side on the same level of a project organization. The entire structure is geared toward accomplishment of the job at hand.

Figure 2–3 shows an organizational structure which might be applied during the formation of objectives, definition, and part of the preliminary design phases of a system project. The diagram, which shows a "quasi-linear" approach to the organization of a project team, is characterized frequently as representing the spokes of an umbrella in establishing reporting channels. This dramatizes the fact that all group leaders within the project report directly to the project manager. Furthermore, all have free and open communication with each other.

In examining the diagram in Figure 2–3, it becomes apparent immediately why this approach is suitable for only the first few phases of a system development project. Obviously, if this open-ended communication and reporting approach were applied to routine, productive activities, so much reporting and communication would take place that progress could well be impaired. However, where interaction is mandatory, this is a highly effective way of achieving it.

To round out the organizational picture, Figure 2–4 shows a project structure as it might look from the latter part of the preliminary design phase onward. This structure, obviously, is tailored to a division of responsibilities and workloads into subsystem units for detailed development, testing, conversion, and implementation.

It should be recognized, in reviewing these structural considerations of system projects, that the approach outlined in Figure 2–3 represents a departure from tradition which is not to be considered extreme. This

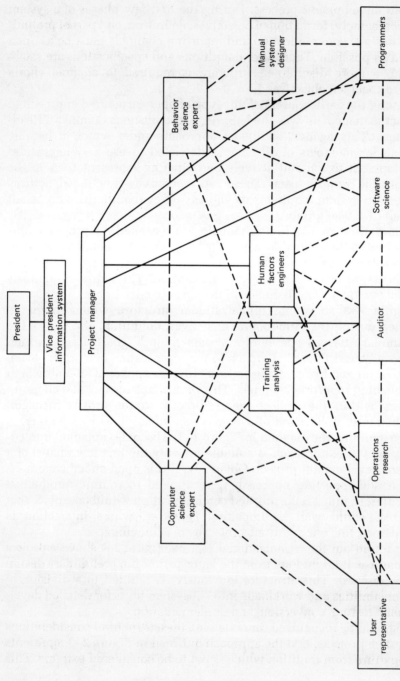

Figure 2-3 Modern systems team organization during formation of objectives, definition, and part of preliminary design. Solid lines represent reporting authority; dotted lines, communications. Level lines depict the possible pay structure.

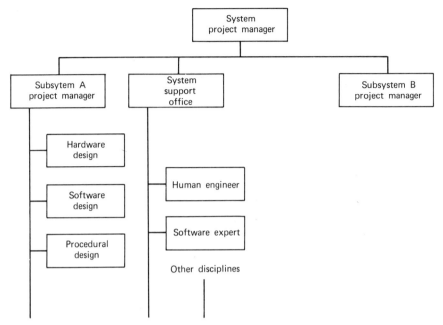

Figure 2–4   *A possible project structure.*

discussion has not intended to imply that systems work cannot take place unless a company is fully reorganized on the basis of the concepts discussed here. Rather, the aim has been to outline the nature and optimum requirements of doing systems work. Furthermore, it is believed that the quasi-linear approach to reporting and communication will become increasingly commonplace among business and governmental organizations during the 1970s. In this connection, it will be noted that Figure 2–3 provides for the retention of organizational and responsibility levels among individuals reporting to the project manager. Thus the net effect has been to open communication and information flow channels at junctures where this free access is critical to project success. This direct communication structure is particularly valuable where creative processes are applied or creative results sought. With direct access throughout an organization, each individual can contribute to the total project to the maximum of his abilities without being restricted, or molded, through conventional, direct linear structures.

Organizationally, it has become an adage of the 1970s that technology has far outstripped management capabilities. By the beginning of the decade, the computers and much of the software necessary for the development and implementation of advanced systems were readily available. The main ingredient missing in putting computers to work productively for management was management itself. Management of the information systems function, therefore, shaped up as the major information system challenge of the 1970s.

THE INFORMATION SYSTEM ENVIRONMENT

If the major information systems challenge is effective management, one of the points requiring management cognizance is the environment within which information systems function. The decade of the 1970s has already been identified as a period of environmental emphasis. From a systems standpoint, the lessons of the 1970s are particularly dramatic since the problems which came to light at the beginning of this decade resulted largely from oversights or neglect in systems management. Companies developed electrical generating systems, for example, without due concern for the smoke pouring out of the power plants and the thermal pollution emanating from atomic reactors. Sewage and industrial disposal systems were developed without regard to the saturation points of rivers, lakes, or even offshore ocean areas. Had disposal of end products been part of the planning for the systems involved, both the environment and the management problems of the 1970s might have been highly different.

The information systems industry sailed into the 1970s in the same sort of craft. Even though the computer did not come on the scene as a major force until the mid-1950s, the last half of the 1960s was marked by extensive suffering from shortsightedness in the planning and implementation of computer-inclusive systems. Developmentally, information systems suffered from designs which were technically dependent on specific hardware or software to a point where systems had to be discarded and all the work redone when computer generations changed.

Furthermore, systems tended to be developed to serve the needs of the computer rather than the people—particularly customers—involved. Extensive publicity (and many lawsuits) resulted from situations in which customers were erroneously charged or hounded by correction notices issued by computer systems which seemed irreversible. This point needs no elaboration; management must insist that computers serve the business which uses them, rather than vice versa.

These early problems resulted, in large part, from the lack of scope which marked many system development efforts. Specifically, a data processing system tended not to be inclusive enough to do the whole job it was supposed to handle. Designers, analysts, and even users did not foresee the problems which could arise. This, in itself, is a major shortcoming in system design—one which must be confronted and overcome if systems are to function as viable management tools.

Moreover, system designers have tended to ignore their own advice. The information processing field has been told for years that its practitioners are in the business of change and that management of change is the name of the game where computer applications are concerned. However, computer-inclusive systems themselves have tended to be designed too rigidly to meet the changes of their own evolving technology. Between systems which were insufficiently inclusive and those which were too rigid to accommodate technological change, a juggernaut effect developed. Computer-using organizations found themselves continually behind, always trying to catch up, but invariably losing ground with each successive management reporting period.

The challenge of the 1970s in terms of system development lies, then, in applying sound investment commitment and depreciation criteria to new information systems. Standards and constraints must be established so that the organization is protected by systems designed with a life span which assures a reasonable return on investment. It is not enough to recognize immediate benefits after implementation of the system. These benefits must be repeatable, for a period at least long enough to return a profit on the total cost of bringing the new system into being.

Environmental factors affecting information systems also call for a resourcefulness and a realistic outlook which will enable management to live with various shortages and shortcomings which threaten to remain with the information systems field as a whole for some time to come. One of these involves perennial shortages of people with the skills necessary to make effective systems happen. Management approaches to these personnel shortages have tended to be panacea oriented. During the so-called second-generation era, heavy emphasis was placed on the training of programmers who could get batch jobs on-the-air in a hurry. Jobs were handled piecemeal, without relationship to each other. Thus programs written for second-generation systems were really not suited for effective implementation on third-generation systems, even though many were switched over through emulation at extreme performance penalties.

Even more damaging was the fact that the assumed solution of manpower problems through massive programmer training never really materialized. Large numbers of persons trained in compiler-level languages to do batch application programming were either professionally unsuited or operationally undertrained to make the transition to third-generation requirements. Hence, major new personnel shortages developed in the systems analysis and software programming areas. These shortages, if anything, are more serious and present greater threats to system development capabilities than the application programming shortage of the late 1950s and early 1960s.

Environmentally, this problem has been compounded almost immeasurably by the failure of educators in universities, colleges, and public school systems to recognize potential opportunities for their graduates. By 1970, for example, colleges throughout the United States, after heavy emphasis on the training of prospective teachers, had graduated a surplus of 28,000 teachers. Engineers and persons with advanced degrees in physical sciences were also suddenly in surplus supply by 1970.

Further complicating the manpower situation was the fact that careers in large business organizations simply became less attractive to the young people who should logically have been prime candidates. In part, the disinterest in business careers in general and data processing careers specifically on the part of young people can be considered a management planning failure. Or, putting the situation conversely, one of the major environmental challenges faced by management in the development of information systems, for the foreseeable future, is to make information systems careers financially and professionally attractive enough to draw qualified people into the field. In particular, these efforts must concentrate on overcoming the objectionable "big brother" image which has grown up around computers in general. Both management and prospective systems people must be made to see the constructive challenges offered by information systems.

Technology itself, in turn, must be oriented more toward the user. From a management standpoint, there are large areas of this problem about which nothing can be done until the technology is ready. For example, it is known that one of the obstacles to more general and effective use of computers is the difficulty of coding information for input. It has been recognized for some time that computers must be made more responsive to the routine language used by people. Input and output must be available more directly. Rather than just waiting for these technical innovations to happen, management can, in fact, design systems which make computers as people responsive as possible at the time they are implemented and which are flexible enough to be ready for expansion when the necessary equipment and technologies are developed.

Here, too, the challenge is not so much to technology as to management foresight and the development of standard, effective management practices.

CHAPTER 3 THE PROJECT TEAM

THE NEED FOR A TEAM APPROACH

Chapter 2 stressed that effective management is the most important ingredient for system success. No place within the spectrum of modern system development is the demand on management more acute than in the selection and establishment of the people who develop and implement new information systems.

The need for people in information systems has been grossly underestimated and misunderstood. Information processing efforts almost invariably require more people to complete a job and make it operational than initial estimates indicate. This is true even for conventional systems development activities involving individual applications to be processed on a batch basis. Both underestimation and requirements seem to expand by multiples—almost on an exponential basis—as on-line and multiple-file processing enter the picture.

Furthermore, there has been an unfortunate (and continuing) tendency on the part of management to regard personnel requirements for information systems on a technical level. Systems work has been considered primarily a technical undertaking. Management has tended to recognize only the need to hire and train junior and senior programmers and junior and senior systems analysts, and these people have been regarded chiefly as computer caretakers. Emphasis has been narrowly focused on the computer, rather than on the problems of an organization as a whole.

Personnel requirements are actually dictated, not by the machines that may be used, but by the problem solving nature of information systems. A system project team must include specialized members who understand the problems to be solved and can provide both guidance and evaluation as to whether proposed solutions will actually work. People of this caliber are just as important (possibly more so) to a

25

system project effort than are programmers, software specialists, or even hardware technicians. In the computer marketplace today, techni-_al skills can be readily acquired from outside sources; expertise on the specific problems of a given department or group within an organization must come from internal sources. This understanding of organizational problems is one of the highly critical skills necessary to a successful system project team.

The history of the data processing and information processing disciplines shows that an understanding of the need for a variety of disciplines in system project work has been achieved at a high cost. Several reliable surveys have established that, almost invariably, systems which fail or fall short of their service objectives do so for non-computer-associated reasons. In other words, there have been many experiences in which computer elements of the system have functioned smoothly but the system has failed or delivered disappointing results because it did not meet the requirements of the operating departments ultimately using the system. After many costly lessons, it has become apparent that the way to satisfy users is to involve them—to get them to incorporate their requirements into the development effort for new systems.

PROJECT TEAM MAKEUP

Chapter 2 touched on the broad scope of disciplines required on project teams assigned to develop information systems. These disciplines are elaborated below. Typical specialists on a project team might include the following types.

Operations researchers are specialists in the quantitative techniques which apply modern mathematical formulas to the analysis, simulation, and projection of results for systems alternatives. Among their contributions, operations researchers can help other members of a project team to understand the requirements for data needed in the design and development of new information systems. By stipulating data requirements early in a project, and by performing analyses and projections as soon as they can feasibly be done, operations researchers make important contributions to directing both the scope and the content of systems efforts.

Within an organization, operations researchers are not limited to quantitative techniques, but this is generally their area on a project team. An operations research department within a large organization will usually have a separate identity and will probably serve broader functions incorporating behavioral, budgetary, mechanical, and other performance factor analysis capabilities.

Auditors must be involved any time there are financial implications for a system under development. These specialists operate at different levels. In some cases, auditors determine the reliability of proposed new financial systems. In others, they must be on hand to validate techniques, approaches, and results. In particular, auditors play a key role in establishing integral controls, which, as already indicated, are among the basic characteristics of modern information systems.

Human factors engineers are necessary to establish optimal relationships between the people, machines, and procedures that a system incorporates. Human factors engineers are specialists in the design of mechanical or control devices requiring human surveillance or operation. Their role is well established in such areas as the design of aircraft or space vehicles and the design of modern industrial production equipment, but their part in information system development is comparatively new. Within a major information system, human factors engineers can play an important role in designing or selecting the most appropriate devices, machines, or work stations for people entering information into a system or deciphering on-line output.

Software specialists are needed any time that a modern computer system enters the picture. Their function involves interfacing job performance programs with the computer equipment to be utilized. They select and/or design such software elements as operating systems, executive programs, and communication control programs.

Data base designers perform several essential tasks. Examples are establishing formats for information records within the system, determining which records are needed, matching data and storage capabilities with file content and magnitude, and determining the structures and interrelationships of data files.

Computer sciences specialists determine equipment, hardware configuration, reliability, maintainability, and other data processing operational criteria. Increasingly, these people have the controlling voice in the selection of the programming languages to be used, particularly since relationships between programming languages and equipment memory size, peripherals, and other specifications are becoming more closely interrelated.

Statisticians must apply their talents because of the sheer magnitude of many modern information systems. Many techniques of statistical analysis are basic tools for gathering data, evaluating information, and establishing criteria for system performance.

Behavioral scientists, particularly *psychologists,* play an important role, because it is vital to predict and, frequently, to alter human behavior so as to enhance system performance or establish compatibility with system requirements.

Facilities engineers must be part of the team, because modern systems present advanced requirements for structures, electrical, communication, installation, maintenance, and other operational facilities.

Programmers need no introduction or elaboration. If computers are to be present, application programs need to be created and/or adapted for the jobs at hand.

Training analysts and instructors are needed to develop curricula and materials as well as to prepare personnel for participation in system development and operation. Training is needed at the outset for people who will be engaged in the system development effort and, as operational status approaches, for those who will be involved in using the system.

Methods and procedures specialists become involved in such areas as the design of clerical functions, the detailing of task and step sequence levels, the design of forms, and the specifications for visual displays.

Administrative personnel, also known as *logistics* personnel, support a system from inception through operation. People in this category range from office managers to purchasing agents and finally to maintenance people.

Users or *customers* are the persons who have been identified with a given problem and who will ultimately use the newly designed system. User and customer personnel must be involved in the system development effort, because their needs represent the yardstick against which the system is measured.

Applications or *requirements specialists* relate closely to user personnel. These specialists have directly applicable experience in industries, operations, or areas where the system will be used. Users of an existing system are not necessarily qualified to judge the value of more advanced techniques, particularly in development phases, since their experience has frequently involved outdated equipment and procedures. Therefore, specialists familiar with the environment within which a system will function and also qualified to understand the advanced implications of new systems are necessary to the development effort.

Systems analysts and *systems designers* possess special skills in data and information processing. Typically, an analyst or designer will block out system functions and processes as specified within stated system objectives and requirements. He will translate basic specifications for system performance into forms and/or terms which programmers and manual methods specialists can use as working guides.

Management sciences professionals are generalists with broad backgrounds. They contribute skills essential to problem solving. Their particular capability lies in developing and guiding interdisciplinary efforts on a prescriptive, rather than a postscriptive, basis.

PROJECT TEAM COMPOSITION

It should be stressed that all of these disciplines are not represented continuously on every project team. Information system projects may be sufficiently straightforward in nature so that some of the specialists described above are not necessary. In other cases, a full range of specialists may be consulted, in passing, for check pointing. On larger projects, direct assistance from a wide range of specialists and disciplines will be required. As a general rule, any increase above the average level, in either the newness or the magnitude of a given system will be reflected in the increased size of the project team and the greater number of disciplines represented.

Furthermore, it should be emphasized that a project team is kaleidoscopic in composition. Actual membership on the team will vary widely with the phase of the project in progress at any given point. Membership will even vary with specific activities within any given phase. For example, operations research people are normally consulted early in a project. Initially, they indicate the types of data needed for quantitative analysis. Until these data have been collected, tested, and verified as to applicability, however, operations research specialists do not participate in system development. As a rule, they do not spend any sizable amount of time on a system project until work has progressed into the design phases.

The same applies to other specialties. Behavioral sciences people, for example, may be expected to be on the scene early. They are also called upon in the final phases of a project to evaluate testing and to assist in conversion procedures. But there is little need for their services during activities concentrating on software design and programming.

Similarly, user members of the project team must be aboard at the outset. They must also be closely involved in preliminary design and, later, in the testing, conversion, and operation of the system. However, user members can reduce their activity to consulting and check-pointing status during programming and technical activities. Conversely, programmers are not needed on a full-time basis until design specifications have been fairly well established.

TEAMWORK IN SYSTEM DEVELOPMENT

Obviously, the most important requirement of a project team is teamwork. Each specialist selected for a team must be acceptable to the specialists from other disciplines and capable of interacting with them.

In the building trades, thousands of years of experience and, more recently, union definitions have clearly established roles and areas of responsibility. There is no doubt where one job stops and another begins. Unfortunately, the information systems field lacks the tradition that serves as a basis for such definite job delineation. Project managers continue to learn about interdisciplinary relationships with each job they supervise.

The interrelationship between people for system projects and the scheduling of their services are particularly critical in the comparatively high proportion of cases where new concepts, techniques, or developments are involved. Obviously, a project manager cannot fall back on experience when his mission deals largely with the new or untried. In much of systems work, there simply is no precedent.

The unique quality of many development projects and the relative newness of the information systems field necessitate assembling a comparatively wide range of talents early in the course of a system project dealing with new developmental areas. In effect, many system projects are untried and can be classified as experimental during their initial phases. It is sometimes difficult, therefore, to convince top management to commit large numbers of skilled people to the early evaluation of project potential. However, experience has shown that thorough early analysis means less likelihood of later failure.

CHAPTER 4 THE SYSTEM LIFE CYCLE

A system project is finite, as distinct from ongoing or continuing. Each system project has a definite beginning and ending. The beginning is marked by identification of a problem or a desire for improvement. The ending comes when the new system is operational. Precisely because its limits are so definite, system development lends itself well to a project approach. Projects, by tradition, are made up of short activity sequences with clearly defined beginnings and endings.

Within the project structure, it has long been customary to divide work increments according to two basic criteria:

1. Projects are subdivided at points where the nature of the work changes. Generally, these changes involve a shifting in the types of activity and skills required.
2. Project subdivisions are based on logical points for management review, approval, and allocation of the resources necessary for continuation.

The project approach to information system development, as might logically be expected, has drawn upon and patterned itself after a number of predecessors. One of the heaviest contributors to information system project methodology has been the classic technique for scientific problem solving. Although there are many individual variations, scientific problem solving is generally subdivided into five stages:

1. Definition of the problem.
2. Analysis of the problem.
3. Selection of alternative solutions.
4. Testing of the selected solution.
5. Implementation.

31

Early efforts at application of project techniques to information system development utilized the classic scientific problem solving methodology. This methodology became inadequate, however, as information systems took on an interdisciplinary nature and demanded resources so great that management check pointing was mandatory.

Furthermore, experience showed that the subdivision points of system projects were not nearly as discrete as those conventionally used in scientific problem solving. By nature, systems work calls for many activities of a cyclical or iterative nature. As will be shown, for example, a good deal of similarity exists between the steps involved in the preliminary and in the detailed design stages of information systems. However, there are major differences in the depth to which activities are carried out and in the expenditures necessary for completion. Therefore, one of the reasons for scheduled check pointing of systems projects is to be sure that progress is, in fact, taking place. Both project and executive-level management people must be alert to avoid situations in which cyclical or iterative activities go over previously covered ground, remaining in the same area rather than moving the project forward.

The cyclical or iterative nature of system projects lends itself better to a control technique utilizing a phased approach than to one which tries to set up discrete, necessarily artificial boundaries. The term "phase" implies the overlapping, natural manner in which a system project moves forward from one area of emphasis to the next. Figure 4–1 illustrates graphically the overlapping nature of a phased project structure. It will be noted that this figure applies specific descriptive names to each of the phases. These names have been selected within the context of this discussion because they describe the major thrust and concentration of the project at the particular juncture represented.

The remainder of this chapter summarizes the eight project phases identified in Figure 4–1. Subsequently, each phase will be the subject of a full chapter.

FORMATION PHASE

This phase formally states objectives and requirements associated with the identified problem to be solved and/or the needs of users of the prospective system. It is the point of project initiation. Formation begins with a request or a suggestion from a user, from management, or from a systems professional that the organization can profitably look into the development of the proposed new system.

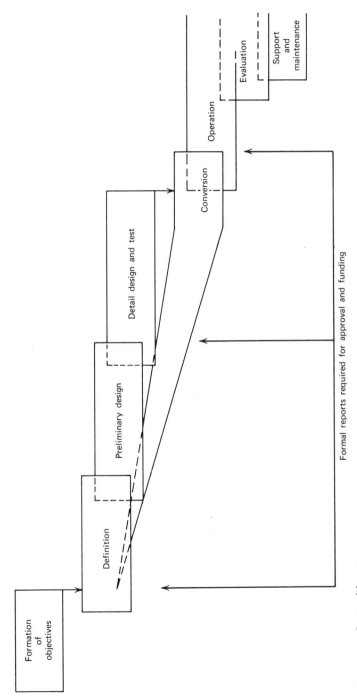

Figure 4-1   System *life* cycle.

33

The formation phase is largely exploratory in nature, with studies covering two separate facets of system potential:

1. The prospective benefits from and feasibility of the proposed new system after it has been developed and brought to operational status must be determined.
2. The resources and investments necessary to develop and implement the proposed system must be identified and quantified.

The amount of exploration justified during a formation phase is directly proportionate to the magnitude of the problem, the size and scope of the proposed system, the prospective benefits identified in the initial request, and (not to be overlooked) management attitudes and economic policies at the time that the suggestion is made. In addition, the current work load within an information systems department will bear on the scheduling of a formation study and the resources committed to it. Specifically, if a department is currently carrying a heavy workload of project commitments, a delay in formation study is likely regardless of the merits of any request.

The chief products of the formation phase are a statement of objectives and a statement of requirements stipulated for the new system, presented as a summary report to high-level management. Although the formation phase report dealing with the feasibility and potential of the proposed system gives only an initial overview, it should be sufficiently complete to justify continuing consideration of the new system into the definition phase.

DEFINITION PHASE

During the second phase of the system project, emphasis is placed on defining the desired results of the system and the information and effort necessary to achieve them. In effect, the definition phase establishes a factual framework upon which the project will build.

Sequentially, work generally begins with the definition of outputs to be delivered to users or customers. Specification then proceeds to identification of input and filed information from which the output can be derived. Also identified are the processes which must take place and the decisions which must be applied in system fulfillment.

As applicable, the definition phase also includes development of descriptions for output, input, processing, decision tables, and files for existing systems which might be directly applicable in the development of the new system. The words "directly applicable" are critical here. Many a past system effort has devoted a good deal of unproductive time and unnecessary effort to detailed studies of existing systems which had no direct bearing on the needs of the system under development. Sound interdisciplinary judgment must be applied during the definition phase to determine the relevance and depth of what is to be studied.

The definition phase should study only *what* is to be accomplished by the system under development. Considerations on *how* the system will operate should be avoided at this point, since this is the main thrust of design phases.

PRELIMINARY DESIGN PHASE

Preliminary design is devoted to the identification, analysis, and selection of the major design options available for development and implementation of the system, as defined during the previous phase. Included in this phase is the use of modeling to identify and project activities which will be required within the completed, operational system. Functional analysis also takes place down to the level at which functions are allocated to men and machines, including identification and determination of requirements in both areas.

Based on the modeling, analysis, and other data gathering activities carried out during the preliminary design phase, three types of feasibility studies are conducted: (a) operational, (b) technical, and (c) economic. These feasibility studies, in turn, become the basis for a preliminary design report to decision-level management. Preliminary design must be closely check pointed and evaluated as to feasibility and payoff potential for a proposed system before authorizing the heavy commitments of resources and expenditures involved in the detailed design phase which follows. Thereafter, since testing is, in itself, a check pointing of detailed design, no further management check pointing takes place until after the testing phase.

DETAIL DESIGN PHASE

The detail design continues the same analysis and development activities of the preliminary design phase, but in greater detail. The functional allocation of operations to men and machines is broken down into the individual operations and tasks necessary for specification of a system to an implementation level. For example, on the machine side, functions are broken down to detail levels so that individual program segments can be specified, functionally diagrammed, coded, tested, and validated. On the manual side (people-performed tasks) of system requirements, analysis activities document the tasks and steps necessary to complete the clerical and other manual functions of the system. Particular attention is paid to the man/machine interface requirements of the system.

During this phase heavy emphasis is placed on system documentation. All of the standards, manuals, training materials, and performance aids which will be needed within the operational system must be completed at this point.

The end product of detailed design is a complete design for an integrated system, including all requirements for the handling and correction of errors and provisions for system failure, recovery, restart, and so on. In other words, at the completion of the detailed design phase, a complete system should be ready for testing.

TESTING PHASE

The identification of a specific testing phase for a system project highlights the transitional nature which led to the use of the word "phase" to describe subdivisions of system projects. Phasing occurs because testing must also take place during the detail design activities, but this early testing is on an individual piece/part system level.

During the testing phase, system elements are assembled for multiple-unit testing. Like building blocks, individually tested modules are combined into subsystems, subsystems into routines, and so on until the complete system has been assembled and exercised. At each of these levels, testing is done under both normal and adverse (degraded) conditions. In other words, everything which can logically go wrong in the implementation of a system is anticipated, and the system and its components are forced to survive testing to determine the ability to cope with these conditions. Ultimately, the entire system is tested as a unit. During these tests, each of the system characteristics identified in Chapter 1 is tested fully against the design requirements developed during the definition phase. Other end products of the definition phase which come into use here are the test data and criteria.

The end product of the testing phase is a fully tested system which can be certified to management as ready for conversion under "live operating conditions."

CONVERSION PHASE

The conversion phase begins when a new system starts replacing the old one in actual operation. It ends when the old system is completely discontinued, with its people reassigned and the equipment either reassigned, modified, or discarded. If a system is completely new to the using organization—as happens, for example, when a company launches a new type of business or service—the conversion process is replaced by a straightforward installation cycle. Installation is similar to conversion, except that there is no old system to phase out.

Conversion activities are planned and timed according to the personnel and equipment schedules stipulated during the detail design phase. Actual conversion techniques can follow either of two alternatives:

1. There can be a straightforward cutover. On a given day the old system ceases to exist and the new one begins, with appropriate balances or transitional functions provided for.
2. Conversion can be segmented, or staged. For example, within a telephone company, conversions for company-wide systems can be scheduled according to individual districts, accumulated on a division level, extended on an area basis, and then applied to cover the organization as a whole. In other organizations, conversions are commonly handled by departments, divisions, geographic areas, and companies as a whole. The formal end of the conversion phase occurs when the system is fully accepted by the user organization as meeting all of the qualitative and quantitative specifications established at the outset of the project and reconfirmed or modified during successive phases.

OPERATIONAL PHASE

The operational phase is not a direct part of the system *development* cycle, but it is an important part of the *life* cycle of the system itself. The operational phase begins with user acceptance of the system after conversion and continues until the system is replaced, modified, or eliminated.

The need for the operational phase stems from the dynamic nature of both systems and their environments. Continuing care and monitoring are necessary for an operational system. Factors to be accounted for in operational continuity include personnel turnover, availability of new equipment or software, new management policies or practices, new maintenance or logistical techniques for keeping the system running smoothly, and outside factors such as new laws, strikes, or emergencies.

An operational system must survive all these conditions, both foreseen and unforeseen. Mechanisms and people must be provided to keep the system operational.

DIVIDING PHASES INTO ACTIVITIES

Up to this point, a proposed project has been divided into phases to ensure logical sequential development and management approval. The phases as outlined above, however, represent project areas too large to be treated as work units. Planning, job assignments, scheduling, and control could not be applied effectively at the phase level of project subdivision. Also, the interaction necessary to system projects could not take place effectively at this level.

System phases are subdivided, therefore, into manageable units, known as activities. Dividing phases into activities makes project development manageable, controllable, bridgeable, and subject to scheduling. Each activity is generally assigned to a group within the project team. Normally, this group is supervised by the person with the skills most appropriate to the major thrust of the activity. There are no firm rules about the size of activity groups; however, the clear intent is to keep the group at a size where communication and coordination can be carried out effectively. The judgment of the project manager must prevail. If activities become large enough to make work achievement cumbersome, they are commonly subdivided, either at a lower task level or through splitting a single activity into two separate activities.

Activities within any given system project should be structured in accordance with two rules:

1. Time durations should be comparatively brief to facilitate the scheduling of interdisciplinary personnel. People are the critical resource in the development of any system project, and an activity which can be accomplished in a short time takes advantage of personnel availabilities and minimizes training and indoctrination.
2. Activities should be sequential to provide a logical work flow pattern. In anything as extensive as a system project, there will be many situations in which one task must be completed, or a given set of data gathered, before another task can be undertaken.

ACTIVITY SCHEDULING AND CONTROL

Since a system project develops through a series of planned activities, each project manager must have a method for continuous planning, scheduling, and control of activities. This control method can utilize any format or technique with which the project manager feels comfortable. There are many methods for scheduling and control of project-type efforts and organizations, including Gantt charts, bar charts, timeline charts, and, of course, PERT-type event networks.

This book will not discuss the various scheduling and control techniques that are available. It is important, however, to mention that many methods exist. Numerous books have been written on the subject, and many others have extensive sections devoted to project and activity scheduling.

For the purposes of convenient illustration and because of general acceptance of the technique in government, business, and data processing circles, this book will use a network-type device for describing, outlining, and keying discussions to specific activities or groups of activities to be considered. Obviously, in compiling the networks it was necessary to devise a set of activity titles and structures as a means of illustrating the principles of system development. These designations and structures were selected entirely for their applicability in illustrating the principles at hand. They should not be construed as rigid or mandatory breakdowns to be applied to all system projects, but rather as frameworks to assist project managers in meeting their specific requirements.

The network format offers a clear device for showing in road map fashion both the time-continuity and the concurrency requirements for activity functions. The networks to be presented in the individual chapters on project phases should, therefore, be considered chiefly as study or discussion guides. They do not adhere to rigid time schedules. No attempt is made to establish start, completion, or duration times for individual activities. As a result, the networks used here do not have the precision necessary for management under PERT (Program Evaluation Review Technique) or CPM (Critical Path Method) techniques. Also, within the networks used in this book, the emphasis is different from that in conventional PERT techniques in four important respects:

1. Emphasis is on *activities* rather than critical events.
2. Emphasis is on *start* sequences for activities as they relate to each other, not on completion times or schedules.
3. Iterations of activities are not shown in the network charts used here.

4.   As a general rule, the networks in this book deal with functional
     activities only. Many standard-type activities, such as planning,
     indoctrination, updating, and communicating, are assumed but
     not included.

CHAPTER 5 THE NEED FOR SYSTEM DEVELOPMENT

OVERVIEW

There are many ways in which a system project can be initiated. Basically, these are individual to the organization itself, since the situation and composition of the systems steering committee will vary from one organization to the next. In general, however, the discussion of the committee in Chapter 2 established that the group is made up of executive- or vice-presidential-level representatives of user groups. As a general rule, the director or vice president in charge of the information systems department will also be a member of the committee. Usually, then, potential projects are brought to the attention of the committee through normal communication and reporting channels leading to its members.

System projects can be recommended for a variety of reasons or for the serving of a number of different purposes. The reasons behind system project requests, it is felt, are actually more important than the mechanisms of communication involved in bringing possibilities to the attention of the committee. The reasons for system project requests include the seven discussed below.

OBSOLESCENCE

An existing system, subsystem, or set of procedures may have fallen into obsolescence. The term "obsolescence," as it applies to system evaluation, simply indicates that the potential for improvement in a particular area is sufficient so that it becomes unprofitable to continue with existing methods, as compared with alternatives which have been opened since the present system was implemented. Commonly, of

41

course, the launching of new projects on the basis of obsolescence involves new computer equipment, new peripherals, new input devices, or other technological products. However, the obsolescence factor can also affect manual methods and procedures, techniques for form design, communication services, and so on.

ECONOMIC ENVIRONMENT

All business and governmental organizations should be responsive, in appropriate areas and ways, to the state of the local, national, and international economy. In particular, a company reacts and is managed differently during a period of economic downturn (or upturn) than during times of stability. For one thing, volumes of business transactions can vary greatly with economic trends. For another, costs of labor, materials, and services will vary markedly. The availability of people will also be vastly different in a rising economy from the labor supply during a falling market. The need for information systems to help management cope with such conditions can become highly critical.

SCIENTIFIC AND TECHNICAL INNOVATION

New devices or methods, in themselves, can be enough to warrant the initiation of information system projects. One dramatic example in this area was the transition between computer generations which took place during the 1960s. The new equipment was so superior in regard to price and performance that it virtually demanded the establishment of new information systems projects.

ORGANIZATIONAL PLANNING

Obviously, system projects, with their magnitude and resource requirements, must be related closely to the plans for the organization as a whole. Planning factors play an important part in determining what systems must be developed. For example, if organizational plans call for growth, systems with expanded capacity will be necessary. If labor contracts call for rising wage scales, the costs of developing and implementing systems will increase. If a company is acquiring a new business or introducing a new product or service, supportive systems may be needed. In any of these cases, and in many more, overall organization plans have a direct bearing on the need for system projects.

COMPETITION

Systems developed and introduced by competitive organizations can be a major factor in new project formation. Competitors, for example, may have systems which give them an edge in regard to manufacturing costs, distribution costs, customer service, or any of a number of other areas. Obviously, when such things happen, great pressure builds to meet or exceed competition.

MARKET DEMAND

Customer buying or usage trends can also be a major factor leading to the need for a system development project. It is an established marketing principle that the more a company is able to meet the demands of its customers, the more sophisticated these demands will become. Therefore, customer services are continually being refined and expanded in virtually every branch of business and government. For the information systems field, this has been a major cause of growth. For example, many small computers were installed in the 1950s for rudimentary customer order processing and billing applications. Ultimately these expanded to include sales analysis reports. Logically, with the advent of random access file devices, inventory control was added to many of these initial installations. Ultimately, manufacturing orders and/or computer-assisted purchasing routines evolved from the same systems.

Another excellent example can be seen in the computer-supported services developed and introduced by banks during the 1960s. The beginning of the decade saw the introduction of computers to relieve overloaded facilities for the processing of checking account transactions. The availability of computers, however, also contributed to the introduction and marketing of such unprecedented (for banks) services as credit card plans, reserve balance checking accounts, guaranteed check cashing services, collection services for business organizations, and savings accounts with interest rates compounded daily. The point in this case is that a balanced cycle was set in motion under which available capacities, spurred by competition, increased customer demands—which in turn led to the development of new systems.

LEGAL CONSIDERATIONS

New laws are another major stimulus for new information systems. This is dramatized particularly by the fact that a law passed in 1936, the Social Security Act, increased the complexity of payroll processing sufficiently to provide a major stimulus for modern data processing growth. Much of the pre-World War II expansion in punched card data processing stemmed directly from laws making employers responsible for computing and processing payroll withholding taxes and other programs. Once the precedent was started, deductions for union dues, savings bonds, credit unions, health insurance plans, and the like became common practice and a further source of complications. Significantly, the first digital computer ordered for commercial use was installed as a specialized payroll processor.

INITIATION OF THE SYSTEM PROJECT REQUEST

Regardless of source, certain basic responsibilities are assumed by the person or department initiating a request for a system project. Implicit in any such request is the requirement that the initiator prepare a formal report to the executive systems steering committee. This must be complete enough to identify the problem, qualify the potential value of the new system, and provide some initial estimate of scope. In particular, the important characteristic of an initiation request for a system project is that it must state problems rather than symptoms. The initiator must think through his presentation sufficiently to be sure that he has identified the basic, root causes of the situation he is calling to the attention of the committee.

Furthermore, each report requesting that a project be initiated should include a statement of expectations for the proposed system. This must cover such areas as projected return on investment for the new system, organizational impact, functional benefits, and increased efficiencies which can be realized.

CONSIDERATION OF INITIATION REQUESTS

In considering reports recommending the start of system projects, the committee reviews each presentation both on its own merits and in comparison with the projected benefits and values for other system projects which have been proposed or are under development. In their evaluation, committee members must satisfy themselves that they have on hand enough data to authorize the exploratory activities which demand the main effort and expenditure during the formation phase. Also bearing upon approvals and/or priorities for new projects are the financial and operating situations of the organization as a whole at the time that requests are made.

The committee, as a group of management people, is charged particularly with the exercise of judgment in the selection, approval, and monitoring of system projects. The application of judgment in a review of formation requests is both appropriate and necessary. It is appropriate because committee members are experienced management people with sufficient background so that their function within the organization lies primarily in the exercising of judgment. It is necessary because sufficient facts will rarely be available within a formation request to justify commitment of resources on a purely quantitative basis. Therefore, the qualitative evaluation which is the special responsibility of high-level, experienced executive personnel must be applied to the authorization of formation studies which initiate system projects.

Actually, the committee makes decisions at two different levels, where project authorization is concerned. The first level deals with the priorities to be assigned to new projects. The priority rating, in turn, will help control the scheduling of project efforts. The second level of decision involves the amount of the available resources that will be committed to the project. Decisions in both areas, of course, are weighed carefully against the nature of the problem, its urgency, and the situation of the organization as a whole.

On the basis of its collective judgment, the committee should reach one of the following decisions:

1. Approve the project and set up priorities and resources for the formation study.
2. Reject the request.
3. Combine the request with other project proposals which may already be pending in some preliminary phase of development.
4. Table the proposal until a time more appropriate for serious consideration.

PROJECT INITIATION

If the committee decides to authorize a project to move into the formation of objectives phase, it issues a formal authorization and policy statement. This includes indications of the areas of the organization to be affected, the functions or systems which may be involved, the people who will be assigned to the work, the time frame within which the formation study is to be completed, and the financial resources to be made available.

Special emphasis should be placed on the limited nature of a formation authorization from the committee. Specifically, the committee should not be asked to approve (and should not act upon) any request which commits a project beyond its formation phase during the initial consideration.

This limited authorization approach is comparatively recent in origin. During the early days of data processing and information system projects, it was common for initiating personnel to come to management with requests for authorization and funding which proposed to commit the sponsors for the full project right from the outset. Such presentations generally undertook to specify the time, staff, and financial requirements needed to carry a project right from inception through completion.

Diligent study of available records has not uncovered a single case in which projects authorized in this way have succeeded in meeting the initially stipulated goals of time, money, and staff. The many disappointing results and cost overruns which marked system projects of the 1950s and 1960s stemmed largely from the tendency of management to write blank checks, making an initial commitment for projects on a blanket basis without recourse to check pointing or progress review. Reasons for failure ran the full gamut of possibilities: hardware was not available as forecast, initial budgets were low to gain acceptance and proved insufficient, staff requirements were grossly understated on the basis of initially available information, conversions and system changeovers proved infinitely more complex than initial forecasts, and, in many cases, promised hardware or software breakthroughs simply did not materialize.

Disappointing experiences with projects handled under such arrangements resulted in a loss of credibility for the data processing or information system function within its organization. By the middle to late 1960s, cynicism was the order of the day.

From the vantage point of clearly focused hindsight, it becomes apparent that in such situations the real problem centered around the authorization of total system projects on the basis of unfounded assumptions and insufficient information. The lesson is clear: A request for project formation demands responsibility on the part of the initiator and responsible consideration by the management committee. Management should not be asked to fund whole projects on the basis of information normally available when the initial request is made. The executive systems steering committee should limit itself to the tentative establishing of priorities and the staffing and funding of a aormation phase only. The formation phase, in turn, is designed to explore and investigate the potential for system development within minimum startup budgets. The idea is to develop the information and perspective necessary to take a more intelligent look at the project as a basis for determination of future, check-pointed, staged commitments.

SETTING UP THE PROJECT TEAM

The decision of the executive systems steering committee authorizes the information systems department to establish a project team which will carry out the formation phase activities and, if the project continues, may carry forward the effort into successive phases. The committee's authorization is acted upon by the information systems manager, who selects the team members, briefs them, and assigns a project manager to this effort.

In a medium- to large-sized organization, a modern information systems department will have a varying number of project managers reporting to the information systems manager. The size of the project manager group depends both on the total project workload authorized by the executive systems steering committee and on the availability of qualified people. Project managers will generally be assigned responsibility for specific areas of the business; that is, an individual project manager, because of his background, training, or professional preference, will tend to interact more naturally with a certain type of user. Project responsibility areas, where possible, should be assigned along these lines.

These flexible assignment criteria serve, in themselves, to introduce the fact that a project manager in a modern information systems organization may come from a variety of backgrounds. This is a fairly recent trend. Traditionally, project managers responsible for computer-inclusive systems have tended to come up through the data processing ranks. Typically, a project manager of the late 1950s or early 1960s had an accounting background educationally and extensive experience in data processing. The chances were good that this person had been a programmer at one time, although he probably had not maintained his technical proficiency during computer generation transitions.

All too frequently, such a background was less than ideal for a project manager functioning in an information systems environment.

For one thing, a traditional accounting and technically oriented data processing background tended to produce a somewhat provincial point of view. A person whose total background had been in accounting and data processing frequently had identification problems in dealing with interdepartmental users and executives with information system requirements. Furthermore, close association with computers did not necessarily fit a person for coping with the complex man/machine requirements of the information systems era.

This is not to say that a person with a data processing background cannot qualify as a project manager. Rather, the point is that a data processing background in itself, no matter how much technical competence is included, is not enough qualification per se. Any data processing professional moving up to project management should have accumulated considerable training and interaction with users and management people.

Just as typically, however, a project manager involved in information systems today may well have come from a behavioral sciences, engineering, production, or business administration background. Truly, the successful project manager is a most unusual man. He combines a blend of skills which include an extensive background in both computer and behavioral sciences. He generally has a particularly strong grasp of quantitative techniques and skills. He has an analytical mind. He is an empathic person who can interact readily with people representing a wide variety of disciplines and skills, both as subordinates on project teams and as customer members of user groups. He is a natural leader and an excellent administrator.

Obviously, no organization is going to find a sufficient supply of individuals who meet all of these criteria. Compromise is inevitable. This is where specialized assignments come in. It is also a factor in determining project team makeup. If an information systems manager realizes that the most logical project leader for a new effort has weaknesses in a given area, subordinates assigned to him on the project team should have strengths to match his weaknesses. For example, if the logical project leader for the job has not worked as a programmer or computer professional, the information systems manager will probably appoint one of his strongest computer technicians to support the team.

In considering the tradeoffs and compromises necessary in the selection and assignment of project managers, it should be pointed out that certain characteristics or traits necessary to a project manager should not be subject to compromise or oversight. Among these are a strong achievement motivation and a high tolerance level for the frustration that is a built-in component of the project manager's job. These are natural skills that he must have.

After the most suitable project manager has been selected for the newly authorized formation phase, the information systems manager works closely with him in picking the staff to do the work. This process, involves, basically, a matching of people, jobs, and schedules on the best-available basis. The needed skills and organizational principles involved have been dealt with previously and will not be discussed here, except to emphasize the fact that special care must be given to the selection of the user representatives on the project team.

The selection of the person (or persons) who will act as user representative is highly critical at this point. The user representative will be the main source of input to the project team on user requirements. Therefore, he must be reliable, he must be articulate, and he must have a first-hand, current knowledge of user operations which will be impacted by the new system.

Moreover, this person must be of a stature which will enable him to undertake the team assignment with the complete support and confidence of user management. He must also have the background and rapport necessary to secure the cooperation of the user organization with the project effort. Both the cooperation of the user group and the support of user management are vital because this person should be able to commit the user group to system principles and evaluations.

As an interactive member of the project team itself, the user representative must also have an appreciation for the concepts of the system and their potential value to his organization. This combination of traits and background should, above all, qualify the person as spokesman for the user group at a level where his commitment will be tantamount to assurance of management backing and cooperation by line members of the user organization.

CHAPTER 6 PURPOSE AND USE OF THE ACTIVITY NETWORK

Figure 6-1 shows an activities network which can be followed in implementing the formation phase of a system project. It should be stressed that this network is not proposed as the only method for carrying out the formation phase. In other words, the activities to be covered in this chapter and subsequent ones, although they have been proved in actual system development situations, are not represented as the only workable approach; alternatives are virtually infinite. Each information system manager and project manager should have the freedom and flexibility to adapt activities and network structures to the requirements of individual projects.

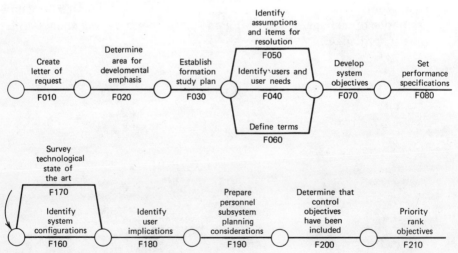

Figure 6–1   Activities network for implementing the formation phase of a system project.

50

The network depicted in Figure 6-1 and others used in this book have been derived, with considerable additional thought and restructuring, from a technique originated some years ago at Bell Telephone Laboratories. The original approach resulted from a study of method and techniques which might be applied to the development of uniform information processing systems throughout the Bell System. The design of the network was a logical extension of extensive efforts by Bell Laboratories to perfect the development of large, complex systems. This organization is generally recognized as the innovator of many techniques now regarded as standard systems engineering practices in government and industry.

The network and its supporting activities are not an end in themselves. The network is a framework, a tool used to indicate when and what kind of support is needed and from whom the support can be expected. It serves as a frame of reference to which all groups key their activities and plans when dealing with one another. A network may also serve as guide for the preparation of PERT or CPM schedules. The network and associated narrative presuppose the presence of skilled system designers and the resources necessary to carry out a complex developmental process.

One purpose of the network is to provide a conceptual diagram of the system development process. Labels for each project phase pave the way for clear communication. There are many ways to partition or break apart a developmental activity into more discrete pieces; many possible sets of terms can be used to refer to these pieces. This particu-

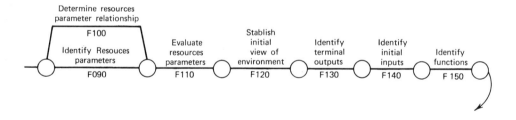

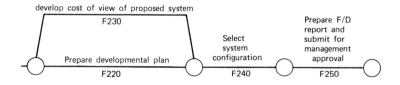

lar partitioning has been demonstrated to be of considerable value.

The second purpose in using this network is to depict the interrelationships of many system development activities and thus foster orderly planning of the developmental efforts of all levels of management. Obviously, all relationships and interdependencies cannot be shown on a generic network such as this one; however, major dependencies and major relationships should be clearly indicated.

The third reason for using this network is to indicate the functional relationships among the various organizational groups that might participate in the development of a complex man/machine information system. This is most desirable since most systems projects today require considerable cooperation from numerous departments. If the functional relationships of these organizational groups are not clearly understood, considerable duplication, even chaos, can result. It seems logical, therefore, to try to identify the group which has the prime responsibility for the accomplishment of a given activity. The supporting or liaison organization should also be identified in activity areas which require specialized support. Using the network in this fashion facilitates a clear understanding of development responsibilities.

A fourth purpose of using this network is to furnish a guide, or road map, through the whole developmental process so that the reader can find himself at any given time in relation to the rest of the subject of development.

Using a pictorial device such as this can be misleading and dangerous, however, unless the user is a trained system development person who accepts this tool as a guide to the kind of activities normally required in designing and developing a typical man/machine computer-based information system. This activity network must not be used as a "cookbook" or a definitive check list, although most of the ingredients for successful system design are incorporated in it. Management must select the appropriate activities from this network and adapt them to the nature of the system under development in order to provide a work plan that suits a particular project.

Although this type of activity network can be used by any level of management to assist in the preparation of a PERT or CPM network, the following limitations should be observed:

1. The network is not a PERT or CPM network. For this reason, is for no other, it should not be slavishly imitated. It lacks the time sequence of a PERT network. It also emphasizes start sequence, not completion sequence.
2. Depending on the complexity of the system development, a single network such as this one may have to be subdivided into

more detailed networks in order to accurately depict the needed activities. Also, the various organizational groups participating in the system development effort may want to subdivide their portions of the network into more specific activities.

3. On a large-scale system development effort, management milestones or check points other than those at the completion of certain phases may be justified.

An activity network may be used in several ways by higher-level management: as a guide in making decisions about resource allocations during the developmental process, as a tool for making organizational changes and assigning responsibility to various groups, and as an aid for making decisions about manpower allocations for various phases in the developmental process and training requirements for the project team. Obviously it serves as a guide to the major check points, or management approval points, in the developmental process; it also indicates the type of documentation and the level of detail which can be expected at each of these points.

Considerable effort has been made to make this network as typical and broadly comprehensive as possible. Yet no single network can possibly reflect each specific developmental activity required for every system, regardless of its nature. In order to make this activity network easily understandable, certain sacrifices or accommodations were necessary. Iterations of activities that start in one phase and complete much later are not shown; that is, if an activity is started in an early phase and then resumed in a subsequent phase, the resumption is not indicated in the latter phase. Also, not all possible system development activities are included in the network. Activities which have been omitted, for instance, are those which are inherent in good system design and therefore would have to be repeated in each phase of development. The following are some examples of these activities:

1. Planning of the actual activities to occur in a given phase is not shown but is assumed to occur early in each system development phase. Planning for staffing, for training requirements, for communications, and the like is assumed to occur outside of the activities depicted in a network.

2. Orientation activities, such as orienting new members of the team, take place at many different levels and at many different times throughout the developmental process. These include briefing sessions and the like.

3. Nearly all the activities shown in this network require formal documentation of some type; however, documentation as an activity is not repeated throughout the network.

4. Performance of many activities necessitates changes in previously prepared documentation, updating and refining it. Documentation must be continuously reviewed and/or approved and placed in the library. This activity is not shown as recurring.
5. Many times throughout the total system development process, there is a need to communicate both within the involved project development organization and with users or other outside organizations. The need for effective organization of the system development team cannot be overstressed. However, for reasons of simplicity the network does not depict all the communication activities necessary to developmental work.

For the sake of simplicity, each activity in the network has been assigned an identifying symbol consisting of one letter and three numerals. The letter portion of the symbol indicates the phase in which the activity originates. Note that the number assignments are spaced by tens. This technique leaves the network open ended. As new activities are added, they can be easily assigned numbers between the existing activities. Obviously, this identifying scheme constitutes a convenient device both for documenting and for machine processing data on a given subject.

In this type of activity network the emphasis is on the activity rather than the event. The activity is indicated by a line; the event, by a circle. This network places emphasis on the earliest start of a given activity and, in order to simplify it, ignores drawing the activity line until the activity is completed; instead the line is tied back into the first activity which is impacted or fed by the preceding one. It follows, then, that any number of predecessor activities may be under way at the time a successor activity is shown to commerce; therefore, this type of activity network can be said to be a start and impact activity network.

CHAPTER 7 FORMATION OF OBJECTIVES PHASE

FORMATION PHASE OVERVIEW

The formation phase is the place where the project takes on its initial form, shape, character. The formation phase begins with authorization from the executive systems steering committee of the organization to examine the potential for and the scope of the implementation effort which will be required for the proposed system. The phase ends with a formal formation of objectives report to the steering committee, recommending future action on the project. On the basis of evidence uncovered, this recommendation can counsel either continuation of the project into its next phase or termination with the formation phase. Should continuation be recommended, the formation report presents and recommends alternative approaches and comparative requirements involved in a decision to continue.

The need for a new system generally stems from the recognition of either a problem or an opportunity. A problem is a trouble area that inhibits progress or causes inefficiencies. An opportunity is a set of circumstances which could enhance progress or increase efficiency. A system development effort is necessary if the problem cannot be readily overcome or if the opportunity cannot be exploited within the existing system. Several kinds of conditions may indicate the need to develop a new system:

- Operational problems with the existing system.
- Economic squeezes or downturns in economy.
- Scientific and/or technological breakthroughs.
- A projection of future business and labor trends.
- New systems developed by competing companies.
- Changing customer demands or expectations.

55

- New services and expanding or changing markets.
- New laws and regulations.

When the need to develop a new system is established, the first formal step is generally to bring the problem or opportunity to the attention of the appropriate levels of management. Figure 7-1, "Activity Network for the Formation of Objectives Phase," demonstrates the process by which management is notified of the need for system development and the objectives of development are determined. The network of activities performed during the formation of objectives phase will be thoroughly detailed below.

F010—CREATE A LETTER OF REQUEST

A letter of request is the first step in communicating to management the need for system development: it may be written at any level, by any department of the organization. It should do three things:

1. State the problem or opportunity and the reasons why a new system is needed. Usually, the reasons will be expressed in terms of service improvement, economic benefit, employee work enhancement, or better management control.
2. State the proposed function of the system, including its anticipated input and output.
3. State the rationale for the proposed project and the determinants

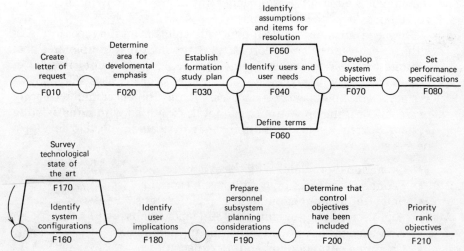

Figure 7–1   Activity network for the formation of objectives phase.

of its priority. The letter should provide enough information for higher management to decide whether to authorize continuing the formation of objectives study, postpone action until a later date, reject the proposal, or rank the priority of this proposal in comparison with others being judged at the same time. If possible, the letter should also provide guidance to higher management concerning the amount of resources that should be dedicated to the study.

F020—DETERMINE AREAS FOR DEVELOPMENTAL EMPHASIS

Management's decision on a proposed new system is usually channeled to the steering committee of the organization or its counterpart. The steering committee ranks projects according to three basic criteria:

1. Identification of need, that is, a demonstration of the way in which present operations fall short of expectations or requirements, or the way in which they will be inadequate to meet further need.
2. Description of how the proposed system would correct or eliminate the problem.
3. Feasibility of the solution within identifiable time and cost restrictions. This information is then weighed against similar data from each of the alternative areas of development.

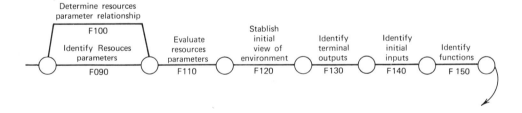

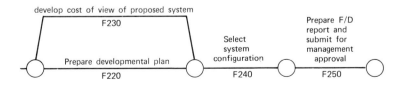

These criteria enable the steering committee to weigh a proposed system in one development area against proposals in other areas. There will be instances in which no clear-cut first priority area evolves, and a "command decision" is required. As a rule, a company is most willing to invest research and development money and time in areas which contribute to long-range company goals. It is equally important not to force implications or to dwell on long-range goals which are inappropriate to the development areas, for the final result in ranking proposed projects must be the selection of the one or ones that the company deems worth pursuing.

F030—DETERMINE STUDY PLAN

Once an area of company operations has been selected for system development, a plan must be developed to provide for direction and control of the study. This study plan should emphasize four elements:

1. Desired results of the study. What results will it produce? When and how will they be measured?
2. A time schedule for the study, specifying target dates for beginning and completion.
3. A cost budget, reflecting the resources to be allocated over the duration of the study.
4. A statement of manpower and skill requirements for the team involved in phase I of the study (formation of objectives phase).

The study plan is necessarily judgmental since the formation stage is primarily a feasibility study. It is impossible to state exactly how much time, money, and manpower will be necessary, or even precisely what the objectives of the study will be. The outer limits of available resources, however, should be considered at the outset.

Management discretion and past experience play a heavy role in the determination of resource allocation, because quantified data are minimal in the early stages. A project manager's part in the development of a study plan, however, is as important as the role of management. Since the project manager heads the development team through the entire formation phase, his participation with management on a study plan is vital to link management intentions and staff implementation. Together with management, the project manager writes a study plan that must receive signatures of approval from the steering committee of the organization.

F040—IDENTIFY USERS AND USER NEEDS

Development emphasis must be derived from a determination of the user activities which are to be supported or enhanced by the system. In this context a user denotes a recipient of output of the fully developed system. The following considerations are essential in determining development emphasis on the basis of prospective users and their needs:

1. Identification of the types of users to be served in some significant way by the system, including unaided personnel, personnel assisted by equipment and other informational needs, and automatic equipment.
2. Determination of user activity over the extended time span to be served by the system. The study team, for example, should not be content to look at the current information requirements of a given user but should attempt to project what he will be doing 5 or 10 years in the future and to derive from this projection an estimate of what his information requirements will be.
3. Identification of locational and functional relationships among users which may suggest a set of total system objectives different from the simple sum of the requirements for the various users.
4. Establishment of boundaries or limits relative to the needs of each type of user. Each possible user must be examined to identify the gross system requirements which will be necessary if that user is to be served. For example, a payroll system must have the capability to store x thousand records. Perhaps it must also have the capability of printing n thousand paychecks per day over a 1 month period. These types of requirements start to structure or to set bounds on the system operation. Consideration of each user will suggest some of these requirements.

After considering the four points above, the study team should conclude activity F040 with a report defining users, potential users, and their needs.

F050—IDENTIFY ASSUMPTIONS AND ITEMS FOR RESOLUTION

As a result of identifying users and their needs, many assumptions and items become apparent that need to be resolved when further information is available. These assumptions or items for resolution should be documented at this time so that they will not be lost or ignored in some later period of design. An example of an assumption might be that all geographic areas of the company will implement the new system. An example of an item for resolution might be that management control reports will be created for local office use. Although this activity begins in phase I, it obviously will continue throughout most of the developmental process. The end product at this time is a document reflecting the assumptions that are not supportable in fact and the items that await resolution.

F060—DEFINE TERMS

Identifying users and user needs creates a unique vocabulary. In order to facilitate communications, all terms which are unique to this developmental effort should be identified and defined as early as practicable. Care should be exercised to avoid conflict between these terms and those in standard usage throughout the company and the related state of the art documentation. When similar things, activities, and techniques are equally applicable to both the man and the machine aspects of the development, it is appropriate to select terms which are sufficiently broad to accommodate both areas. When a specific, unique usage is required, a term must be coined and carefully defined. Considerable care should be exercised, particularly in the area of EDP terminology. This rapidly growing field has developed a new, complex, and undisciplined set of terms and concepts. Different hardware vendors have used different terms to define similar capabilities or concepts. If care is not exercised, serious communications problems can result.

The product of this activity is a glossary of special terms appropriate to the developmental effort at hand. This glossary will expand as the effort progresses.

F070—DEVELOP SYSTEM GOALS

During this activity the needs of the users are translated into objectives to be satisfied by an operational system. These objectives must be identified in sufficient detail so that the study team and subsequent personnel assigned to the definition phase will be able to prescribe a measurable level of performance which a designer will strive to achieve within the system design. Objectives for the system are statements of design intent. They must answer the question, What is the system required to do? Useful system objectives will have the following characteristics:

1. They will communicate unambiguously to the management, users, and members of the development team what the intended goals of the system will be.
2. They will be down to a level of detail which will facilitate measurement of the system's capability.
3. They will be organized in a logical and nonredundant structure. The objectives will specify the goals of system operation in terms of nine parameters:
   a. Output—the information content frequency, physical form, and symbology.
   b. Operating modes—at least for areas which are dictated by resources and constraints.
   c. Personnel skills required.
   d. Operating costs.
   e. Volume of production.
   f. Geographic locations for operation.
   g. Communications requirements within and between systems.
   h. Storage and security of system data.
   i. Backup systems or alternative operating modes.

Obviously, not all of these features can be absolutely characterized at this point. However, this activity has only begun; it will continue much further into the other system design phases. The need for sound system objectives was emphasized in an earlier chapter. Many disappointments with a new system can be traced to the lack of a clear statement of objectives for it.

The end product of this activity is a set of documents providing all the information available at this time about the objectives as derived for user needs.

F080—SET INITIAL PERFORMANCE SPECIFICATIONS

The main purpose of this activity is to establish quantifiable specifications to measure the effectiveness of the new system. Performance specifications are statements of capability and characteristics which enable the system to fulfill an overall purpose and to meet specific operational objectives. For example, system reliability should be in excess of 98% of overall operational time. The major categories of performance specifications would include these ten:

1. Cost of the operation of the ongoing system, as well as the cost for conversion.
2. Time, that is, a response to an input where expressed in terms of access, elapsed turnaround, or process.
3. Accuracy, expressed in terms of frequency of significant errors rather than on the basis of input, process, or output.
4. Availability of the total system, including frequency and duration of degraded performance modes.
5. Flexibility, that is, the type and the number of exception conditions handled by the system.
6. Security, including legal safety and the degree of vulnerability.
7. Capacity, expressed in terms of average and peak loads.
8. Acceptance, expressed in terms of employee, management, customer, and user acceptance.
9. Efficiency or productivity, expressed in a performance ratio.
10. Quality, expressed in terms of tolerance, and appearance.

These specifications should be stated as quantitatively as possible. Initially, they are probably expressed in ranges of acceptability. As development progresses, these ranges will be narrowed. This activity will obviously continue throughout most of the developmental process. The specifications as stated here will serve as main test items during the testing phase.

The final product of this activity is a comprehensive, quantifiable set of performance specifications for each of the ten characteristics of a system discussed in Chapter 1.

F090—IDENTIFY RESOURCE PARAMETERS

It is important during the study phase to establish as accurately as possible the degree of freedom that the design effort will enjoy. In order to accomplish this, a conscientious attempt must be made to identify all the resources and constraints relevant to the development of the particular system. Resources represent capabilities which are available for utilization by the system. These would include such items as hardware, software, personnel, supplies (e.g., cards, tapes, and disks), and facilities, including buildings, desks, and chairs, as well as modes of expression, such as charts, tables, and English codes—and, of course, money. On the other hand, constraints represent the limits on resource capabilities in terms of amount, numbers, or other appropriate units. Constraints also refer to environmental conditions which may impose limits on the system, such as company organization, union contract agreements, laws, and regulations.

For simplicity, we have chosen the term "resource parameter" to indicate the outer limit of a given resource. Beyond this limit the resource no longer exists and would be expressed in terms of constraint.

Some sources of information for data gathering during this activity would include the following:

- Previous systems and their documentation.
- State of the art, vendors, and trade publications.
- Organizational charts and descriptions.
- Long-range plans.
- Financial reports.
- Job descriptions.
- Legal and regulatory documents.
- Union contract agreements.

Resource parameters need not remain constant. Ongoing development may suggest that resources once thought to be adequate will no longer suffice; constraints once thought to be acceptable are intolerable; or contexts once thought to be ideal are only second best. None of these possibilities precludes the desirability of organizing and analyzing resource and constraint information early in the development of a system.

Documentation on operative systems provides resource information, if a new development effort seeks to upgrade an existing system. If, however, the attempt is to develop a new concept addressed to existing problems, resource and constraint information about an existing system can be as misleading as it is helpful. Unless we can make the assumption that the previous system designers did a complete and thorough analysis of the relevant parameters and that nothing about the environment or the system objectives has changed significantly since, a retesting of constraint information is required.

Related feasibility and/or development studies and their documentation (if available and applicable) may also provide sound information, but care must be exercised to determine that the relationship of these studies to the present one is direct and appropriate. Furthermore, it is necessary to be critical to ensure that the study or documentation has been correctly done and the information is acceptable.

The state of the art in relevant areas of development should be assessed for its potential contributions to resource parameter information. It is unrealistic, however, to base the development of systems on resources unproved by state of the art studies or laboratory demonstrations. Considerable grief has been experienced when a development effort has attempted to expand or distort the known state of the art.

Management policy provides guidelines in determining resource parameters. To interpret it literally is prudent; to ignore it is to court disaster. Deriving guidance from policy and attempting to change it when necessary probably constitutes the ideal course of action. Management policy can be interpreted as either a strong set of constraints and deterrents or a sound measure of resources and motivation. The changing trend of management policy and expectations is probably as important a consideration as the "fixed policy" of a company.

Organizational structure is an important source of parameter information, since an information system of any size affects several parts of the structure. If organizational structure interferes with the proposed system, the possibility of change must be carefully assessed.

Traditions, like organizational structures, are difficult to change. Traditions are sometimes as real and as constraining as regulations or contractual obligations. Rarely spelled out, they are elusive and difficult to ascertain. Nevertheless, they should not be ignored; a conscientious effort should be made to assess the system objectives in the light of known or implied traditions. House organs, "old-timers," and advertising all serve as sources of information concerning the traditions of an organization.

The long-range plans of the department and the company should be carefully considered, since they indicate the direction that management reaction is likely to take. If the proposed system complements these plans, little more than pointing to this consistency is necessary. However, if the proposed system development effort runs counter to the long-range plans, reconsideration or change is needed. Also, rarely have all the long-range plans for a company been collected in one logical document. Interviews with the planning department personnel and top corporate managers seem to be the most promising avenue of acquiring long-range planning information.

Financial reports of the company offer a sound source of well-quantified information. The current financial indices, such as return, surplus, and debt ratio, and the trend of all other major measurements offer strong data to support or inhibit the proposed system development effort. If return and capital surpluses have not been consistently high, trend information becomes most important. Rarely is a developmental effort accomplished in a short period of time. Therefore, a trend toward increased rate of return—or at least a high level of stabilized return—is desirable. On the other hand, sometimes the proposed information system has a high money-saving potential. If this can be proved, it may be wise to invest in the development in spite of a decreasing rate of return; the new system may offer potential for halting or reversing the downward trend. In any case, the company's financial report provides a relatively dogmatic "go/no go" indication. Thorough analysis of financial information and its implications for the development and operation costs of the proposed system is mandatory.

Early consideration should be given also to the personnel requirement for operating and managing the new system, even though exact numbers cannot yet be determined. Certain early assumptions, based on the best information available, must be made about what knowledge and skills will be required. Job evaluations and descriptions can provide a status report of available skills and abilities. If it is apparent that the requisite resources are not presently available and cannot be developed before the system is ready to become operational, a serious problem exists. Conversely, if it can be assumed that, through selection, training, or job aids, the knowledge and skill needed to operate, maintain, and manage the system can be developed in the period of time available, a resource rather than a constraint is provided. In any case, early determinations of what is required must be adjusted and quantified as the development effort progresses. It is not enough to analyze only the personnel requirements for operating a new system. Consideration should also be given to the manpower needed for designing and developing the system. Although it is difficult, if not impossible, to define these requirements early, assessment of developmental manpower needs is mandatory. The soundest estimates possible at this time must be made. As the development progresses and the requirements become more precise, these assumptions will be repeatedly re-examined, clarified, and quantified.

Existing facilities of the company are another strong area of resource parameter information. These facilities include such diverse things as an existing data base, existing and unused computer time, buildings, manufacturing gear, other equipment, and unused personnel capabilities. Historically, many system development efforts have been modified by the fact that one or more of these facilities was operating at less than capacity. Making fuller use of these facilities in order to better realize an investment became the motivation for development. On the other hand, limiting the outlook to what is presently available may be unnecessarily restrictive, particularly if the development effort calls for a facility not presently at hand but within the financial capability of the company.

An accurate estimate of the time frame for the development process is needed very early. Information to make a definitive estimate of the time required is usually not available early in the development process, but a reasonable estimate is possible on the basis of such resource information as time studies, feasibility analyses, and past experience with similar developmental efforts. It is most important to consider this estimate as tentative and flexible and to quickly adjust it as new information is assimilated during the development effort. Too many times an early estimate of the completion date has become the fixed date in the mind of management. And too many times this arbitrary date was selected on the basis of very little and too optimistic information.

Another important area of resource constraint is user adjustment. It is reasonable to assume that people can adjust to a given amount of change in a certain amount of time. Therefore, the amount of change which can be successfully introduced and assimilated at any one time by the personnel who will operate and use the system has a constraining influence on the development effort. One should consider how much change is implied, what areas the change will affect, whether or not it is reasonable to expect the personnel involved to accept the change, and by what means the change can be made more acceptable if resistance develops. Multimedia training technology and techniques of system introduction should be planned for in the development effort.

System interface requirements are perhaps the most difficult to assess. Some initial assumptions about the boundaries of the system must first be made, and each boundary must be scrutinized to determine where it fits into or up against the boundaries of other systems. It is important to identify potential as well as real interfaces and to seek out the elusive as well as the obvious ones. Historically, the failure to perform adequate analysis of the interface, interchange, or independent relationships with other systems has contributed to the downfall of many system efforts.

Legal restrictions are a critical area of constraint information, particularly for a utility, monopoly, or governmental organization. This area of information is usually viewed as constraining; however, laws are not wholly restrictive in nature. The law can be regarded from a permissive or even a motivating point of view; this perspective provides resource information as well as constraint information. Rarely does the system developer have sufficient expertise in law to predict the legal ramifications of the system under development. Hence legal counsel should be made a part of the system team and used to determine where and how much the intended system conflicts with or complements existing statutes. Also, labor contracts constitute contractual obligations between a company and its employees, and system efforts should not violate or run counter to these agreements. In the development process, it is difficult to assess the full impact of the proposed system on contractual obligations. For this reason union contracts, employee agreements, and benefit plans should be examined for any implication of constraint.

Personalities can exert a very strong constraint on the development process. Complex systems have been built on the strength and enthusiasm of a single highly motivated individual. Conversely, many a development effort has collapsed because of the negative attitude of one or two influential persons. The design team should appraise themselves of the opinions, intentions, and expectations of corporate and system managers who bear the ultimate responsibility for system effectiveness. It is essential that these persons be kept informed of the development process so that their efforts can be exerted to enhance the effort.

Examining each of the above areas early in system development

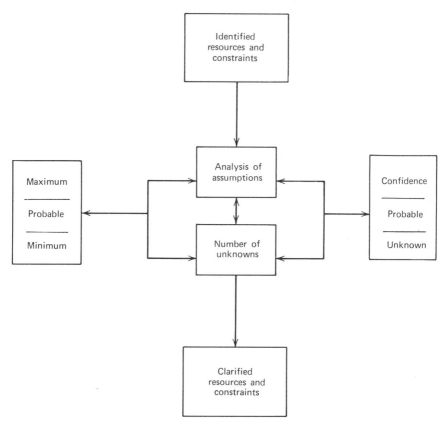

Figure 7–2   Methodology for identifying resource parameters.

should result in a quantified expression of the system results possible within given resource parameters. Admittedly, some of the quantification may be difficult and tentative; yet there are potentially a large number of direct and derivative quantification factors which are very relevant and useful for the discussion that must be made at the conclusion of phase I. The following five seem to be most generally applicable; their interactive efforts are shown in Figure 7–2.

1. The probable maximum that can be obtained even with great effort.
2. The probable minimum that can be expected under the worst circumstances likely to occur.
3. The most probable level the resource is likely to achieve, based on the identified maximum and minimum levels.
4. The degree of confidence in the estimations of most probable levels. This requires analysis of the assumptions used in establishing maximum, minimum, and probable levels.
5. The ease with which resources and constraints can be modified. This requires identification of the criticality of the various resources and the probable levels they will achieve in conjunction with the extremes judged possible. Great discrepancy between maximum and minimum, coupled with a low level of confidence, indicates areas where modification of resources and constraints must be considered.

F100—DETERMINE RESOURCE PARAMETER RELATIONSHIPS

Resources and constraints must be examined together, because they are interdependent. Analysis will indicate which resources must be realigned or optimally aligned to meet the performance specifications of the system more effectively. Each resource and constraint must be examined for its relationship with every other resource and constraint. Resource and constraints are also likely to have some performance effect on the system characteristics. For example, lack of a particular kind of input information may have implications for the level of personnel skills and knowledges.

To identify and depict related resources and constraints, a chart is advisable. This may take the form of a mileage chart, with resources and constraints listed vertically in one column and horizontally in another line. Within this structure, a match point indicates an interrelationship; a no-match point, a lack of interrelationship. Sets of symbols are used to indicate the degree of interrelationship. It is helpful to portray graphically both the type and the extent of interaction.

F110—EVALUATE RESOURCE PARAMETERS

All resource parameters are evaluated to determine whether they should be changed, eliminated, or left alone. For example, a company policy that restricts the impact of a proposed system on certain portions of the organization may be too constraining for the particular system, and it may be desirable to attempt to change this policy. If change is indicated, a plan is prepared to make the change. Identifying parameters, the likely levels they will assume, and their interrelationship makes possible an estimate of the probable impact of these parameters on the system development effort. Comparing the stated requirements and objectives with the resources and constrainsts permits identification of sensitive requirements, critical parameters, imbalances, and potential areas for adjustment.

The exploration of resources and constraints implications for the conversion period and the operational phase can be helpful to almost all of the major design steps which follow. The activities and informa-

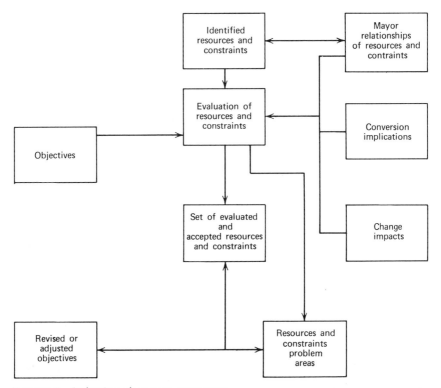

Figure 7–3   *Evaluation of resource parameters.*

tion employed in the evaluation of the resources and constraints are shown in Figure 7–3. As a result of identifying critical and noncritical parameters, the latter become candidates for tradeoff analysis, which allows the designers to blend, mold, and reshape resources and constraints information for optimal use in the new system. Realignment, reshaping, or reconfiguring of these resources and constraints toward optimal alignment with system objectives is a pivotal point of the system development process, an activity that continues throughout the development process.

Each candidate for tradeoff must be translated back into the source type of information, that is, reflected in its original fashion, so that the change can be viewed in that context. This is necessary in order to ensure that the composite analysis has not distorted the parameter to the point where it appears unimportant when it is, in fact, very important. Experience indicates that, if the resource tradeoff analysis has not been done thoroughly and accurately, either the development effort or the operating system will have built-in surprises. Often these surprises have been of a negative type, ranging from distasteful to catastrophic.

The final result of this activity is a list of the resource parameters for the system, with an explanation covering both any plans to change resources and the tradeoff analysis results.

F102—ESTABLISH INITIAL VIEW OF ENVIRONMENT

The environment in which the system will ultimately operate is such an important consideration in the developmental process that the project team must take an early view of environmental capabilities and limitations. Environmental considerations include labor trends, regulatory trends, financial trends, technological developments, changing customer expectations, and changing user needs.

Significant changes in any of these areas, from the time the system is in the early phase of development until it is installed and operating, are crucial to the overall success of the system. It is advisable, therefore, to consider the probable operating environment in the early phase of system development and to project its influence on performance. The environment should be described as it is projected to be both at the time of installation and during the subsequent life of the system.

F130—IDENTIFY TERMINAL OUTPUTS

During the formation of objectives phase, output requirements are derived from the system objectives. Initially the requirements are stated in a general way, except for those which will not change and for which, therefore, specific descriptions can be written. A general statement about an output requirement might be a broad description of the information content needed relative to the company's customers, that is, quantitative and qualitative information and frequency of contact. The expression "terminal output" indicates the end result rather than any intermediate output from one phase to another. It is these end, or terminal, outputs that can be derived logically from the system objectives. Terminal outputs, therefore, are directly related to user needs and induce prescribed user behaviors. Early consideration of terminal output should include the medium of output, such as display, hard copy, or cash; the volume, or number of output items; the frequency of output per day, per week, per month; the quality of output—accuracy, dependability; the destination of output—headquarters, remote location, or many locations. A list of the terminal output requirements completes this activity.

F140—IDENTIFY INITIAL INPUTS

Input requirements are derived from output requirements and provider activities, just as user activities identify output requirements. The same factors which were important for output identification (information content, symbology, medium, volume, frequency, and quality) are also important for input identification; to this list must be added the origin of the input. The term "initial," like the word "terminal," indicates the outer limit, the point at which the input originates. For example, the input for billing a customer for a toll telephone call originates when the customer dials his phone and creates electrical impulses. The identification of initial inputs will not be complete until much later in the system design, but, as is true of all activities in this initial phase, an early, general statement must be made. This statement, a list of the initial input requirements to the system, completes the activity.

F150—IDENTIFY FUNCTIONS

Functions are the procedures by which people and equipment produce results in a system. Functions are derived from the difference between input and output. Determination of the functions that a system requires is termed functional analysis. In this early phase functional analysis can be only definitional; that is to say, functions can be derived logically from existing input/output information. They are factual. No choices, decisions, or designs are prerequisite to their identification.

They are minimally required functions in the light of what is known.

The question, "What must be done to transform input into output?" can be answered in terms of functions. Broadly speaking there are six prime functions that an information system may possess:

1. Receive.
2. Transfer.
3. Record.
4. Store.
5. Process.
6. Present.

Each of these major functions can be broken down into subfunctions (see the Appendix, p. 265). In the oversimplified example of producing a payroll when the output is a monthly paycheck and the input has been simplified to hours worked and rate per hour, the obvious function is compute or, more precisely, multiply the rate times the hours and print. If the same problem were presented in a more realistic fashion, including deductions for benefits and taxes, more functions would be necessary to transfer input into output.

At this point in time, the method of accomplishing a function should not be considered. The selection of a method or of several alternatives should be left to later design phases. Therefore, computer terminology should not be used to define functions. Deriving functions is not a one-time process. Rather, it is a good example of the kind of iterative or cyclical process that occurs in system development work. Although no attempt should be made during the formation phase to analyze functions exhaustively, to the most discrete level of detail, it is necessary to determine the major functions that the system will perform.

F160—SELECT POSSIBLE SYSTEM CONFIGURATIONS

This activity aims at sequencing previously identified functions into logical sets, or configurations, that will achieve the desired system output and satisfy approved performance specifications and system objectives. Even though all necessary functions may not yet be evident, a number of configurations should be hypothesized. Each configuration will later be evaluated in terms of technical demands and operability, and an optimal configuration selected.

Diagrams help to visualize possible sets of system functions and the relationships between them. If pictorial devices are used to represent this hierarchy, they should be supported by narrative descriptions and justifications. These descriptions should include input/output specifications, as developed earlier, with a demonstrable rationale as to why the particular functions shown in the diagrams are required in order to transform the input into output.

System configuration possibilities are chosen at this point without reference to specific hardware, although generic features of hardware can be indicated. For example, the configuration chart may depict a terminal communications medium, a central processing unit, and the like. Unless the system is limited to existing equipment, however, no attempt should be made to identify hardware by brand name or unit number. Actual selection of the hardware occurs much later.

F170—SURVEY TECHNOLOGICAL STATE OF THE ART

Although a development project must never, under any circumstances, recommend procedures which exceed the capabilities of modern technology, it must proceed with a keen awareness of existing technological possibilities and of advances that are probable in the near future. For this reason, the project team should make a brief survey of the current technological state of the art in all areas important to the system. An important consideration would be a survey of current computer hardware and softward capabilities, dealing not with the specific, detailed capabilities of a given machine or software package, but with the general capabilities available in various computers, languages, and software packages. Another area to consider at this time would be hardware devices that are peripheral to the main computer. Peripheral devices run the gamut from keypunching, sorting, and collating to slave computers. They prepare, preprocess, and receive data in relation to the main computer. Communication terminal devices and media should also be explored if the system requires on-line or teleprocessing capabilities.

Human engineering as an area might also be surveyed. Research studies, particularly by aerospace industries and the government, are shedding new light on human capabilities. Reports of these investigations serve as an inexpensive and readily available indication of the state of the art in the design of the human element of the system.

If similar systems are being or have been built, they may provide additional valuable information on the state of the art.

No attempt should be made to design beyond contemporary technology, as a U.S. Defense Department venture showed in the late 1960s and early 1970s. The department set contract specifications well beyond the capabilities of the state of the art; gross financial overruns and bitter disappointments resulted. On the other hand, it is reasonable to project what the state of the technology will be at the time the system is to be implemented. When projections are made with care, design can proceed on a reasonable assumption that the technology will be ready at the time of implementation.

F180—IDENTIFY USER IMPLICATIONS

During this activity, the sum total of system development to this point is translated into its implications for the users of the system. A list of implications derived from this activity will assist in the selection of the most appropriate system configuration. In industry, user implications fall into three main classifications—business, organizational, and customer. Under business implications, consideration should be given to financial, managerial, time, analytical, forcasting, and measurement types of implications. Under organization implications, the number of people affected, the kinds of people affected, the type of effect—whether enriching or degrading, and recruitment, selection, and training implications should be considered. Customer implications include such areas as social, service, error, environmental, and product performance.

This activity requires the formation of objectives teams to hypothesize about the various configurations and the ways in which they will serve the users.

When all of the design and operating implications have been identified and examined, the project team should be able to select an appropriate system configuration. If there is no obvious optimum configuration, the total process of detailing the scope of the developmental area should be reviewed to reassess all of the assumptions and hypotheses upon which it is based. If such a review does not turn up additional information which, when combined with all other known facts, indicates an appropriate system configuration, another look can be taken at the "area" selection process itself.

The formal output of this activity will be an analysis of the user implications in the areas mentioned above.

F190—PREPARE PERSONNEL SUBSYSTEM PLANNING CONSIDERATIONS

Few important areas of information system work have received as little consideration in the past as the personnel subsystem. In the beginning of the computer age, people involved with systems were dehumanized. The needs and requirements of the people who operated a system or were otherwise part of it were completely overlooked, a situation which caused everything from degraded performance of the system to its total collapse.

Human factors engineering began during World War II when the U.S. Army Air Force learned, through dramatic loss of life and aircraft, that designing and engineering aircraft controls and cockpits in relation to human needs were essential to pilot performance. Human engineering is the study of human capabilities and limitations and of the factors that enhance or detract from the exercise of these capabilities. The original thrust of this new discipline was to study the design of knobs, dials, and controls for aircraft. It has subsequently grown to consider ambient lighting, temperature, biomedicine, and life support. The discipline of human engineering gave birth to the concept of a personnel subsystem during the mid-1950s—a concept that was first related to information systems 10 years later, and then only in such areas as console design and form design. By the early 1970s the importance of the human element in the design of a total system could no longer be ignored. A changing labor market, technological skill and knowledge requirements, and urban decay all contributed to realization of the importance of the human side of the system development effort. Without early and careful consideration of the personnel subsystems, the entire fabric of a system is in jeopardy. The design of equipment without regard to its use or control by human beings is hardware engineering, not total system development.

As systems have become more complex, they have created serious economic, political, social, psychological, and even moral problems in addition to technological ones. The most important psychological problem relating to a system arises from the necessity to organize people—to consider them as system components, to select and classify them, to train them, to keep them working for system objectives, and to bring their performances to a peak.

Personnel subsystem design aims at accomplishing optimum man-/machine integration by estimating personnel training requirements and by applying human factors engineering and safety principles. The personnel subsystem is an integral part of the system performance specifications; it should also be considered as a possible constraint, since human factors influence the cost, schedules, and performance parameters of a new system. The personnel subsystem also affects the interface requirements of existing and planned systems.

The personnel subsystem planning document should include three main considerations:

1. Personnel requirements should be stated for the various stages of system development. Any unique problems in personnel planning should be identified. Gross estimates should be made of the numbers of persons and the skills required.

2. Human engineering principles should be applied so that man-/machine interface planning and design considerations will be interpreted in terms of system performance requirements. Equipment design and personnel selection should be structured so that system performance requirements are met within the limitations set by the natural and induced environment, life cycle cost considerations, and human capabilities.

3. The amount and type of training must be stated. Considerable grief and even trauma have resulted from improper training at the time of conversion or initial installation. Sound training, employing modern training technology, inherently has a long lead time. Planning for training, therefore, should start as early as is practicable.

F200—DETERMINE THAT CONTROL OBJECTIVES HAVE BEEN INCLUDED

As stated earlier in Chapter 1 on system characteristics, control is an integral part of any total system. Control does not happen; it is designed. Control objectives must be identified in the areas of (a) system administration, (b) data, (c) error detection, (d) regulatory and company policy requirements, (e) information trail, (f) system reliability, and (g) system maintainability.

Control as applied to system administration (monitoring indications of management and performance) has come to mean diagnostics or on-going performance indicators. Predetermined and built-in control was one of the features most obviously lacking in systems designed during the 1950s and early 1960s. Many designers made the assumption that all input coming to the system would be within acceptable tolerance limits, and hence design was accomplished on the basis of "main line" processing only, without consideration for error conditions. Time and again this method of designing for only pure input and normal conditions was shown to be short sighted. With the advent of "on-line, real-time" communicating systems the whole body of knowledge on audit control and predetermination had to be re-examined. No longer was it possible to reconstruct what had happened in order to find the reasons why something had gone wrong. It became essential to predetermine and build in control features which would audit while in progress. The subject of predetermined control continues to plague us. We have yet to develop a discipline which will effectively predetermine all contingency conditions and the sensitivity or criticality of these conditions and either take corrective action or provide appropriate responses to a control group that will exercise human judgment. Nevertheless, much of the power and importance of modern systems is gained through this prediction and predetermination of control features in the system. During the formation phase no attempt should be made to make these procedures explicit and final. However, consideration for the sensitive and critical areas of processing is important.

Data control and security began to be a major concern of data processing installations in the early 1970s. Fire, theft, and malicious destruction of records combined to prove the importance of data security. Methods of protecting data and ensuring their reconstruction are still being developed. Real-time communicating systems are particularly vulnerable to tampering.

Error detection and control has been considered to be an important part of system development for some time. The most viable source for error detection and control has been found to be control of input at the source. Edits, validations, checks, and justifications for the downstream errors can further compound the problem. The trend has been, therefore, to capture data in as pure a form as possible.

Throughout recent years there has been a trend toward increased government regulations and company policy requirements. Considerable trouble can result if federal, state, and local regulations have not been considered in formulating the design requirements.

The information trail is a relatively new concept in computer systems work. The idea behind this concept is to predetermine any and all paths by which information might flow through the system and to control or check periodically to see that the data are within prescribed bounds. Thus, the auditability of a system is built in as a precondition, rather than reconstructed as in the postaudit situation. Real-time interactive systems require an information trail.

As systems are required to perform increasingly more important functions, their degree of relibility has also become more important. Reliability is not just a hardware feature; it includes the personnel subsystem. It is normally expressed in terms of a percentage of total required performance. Reliability is usually increased through either redundancy or the imposition of stringent controls. The reliability of computer information systems is influenced by such external factors as electrical power requirements, air conditioning requirements, and humidity requirements. Data transmission requirements are affected by impulse noise, random hits, cross talk, cable damage, and so forth. It is unrealistic and uneconomical to attempt to design for 100% reliability on almost any system. Reliability costs money and therefore should be a factor of the nature of the system and the services it is providing.

System maintainability involves the correction of abnormal or undesirable conditions after they have been identified and the routine servicing activities. If the system fails, how long will it be before the appropriate maintenance activities can take place and the system is back in operational order? Some maintenance procedures will automatically be built in; these will be associated with appropriate diagnostic routines. Other maintenance activities, however, require human judgment. All maintenance activities should be considered to decide how much effort to put into prevention or into automation of the maintenance routine. System maintainability and reliability are closely associated, and together they offer a measure of the performance capability of the systems design.

The end result of this activity is a statement of control objectives for each of the system objectives, listing the desired and intended limitations. Some control objectives will be detailed; others, vague. It is important to quantify the control objectives where possible as early as is feasible.

F210—RANK OBJECTIVES

The system objectives should now be examined for their interrelationships and interdependencies in the light of all the information collected, developed, and analyzed thus far. The interrelationships are examined, to the extent possible, to reduce inherent conflicts and to assign a priority to each of the system objectives. The analysis is done at this time to ensure that the objectives can be met in terms of operability, economics, technology, maintainability, and reliability.

This examination will result in the solidification of the system objectives, which serve as the cornerstone of the whole design effort. If later in the system design process it is imperative to change any system objectives, the design effort must be recycled to the formation of objectives phase. Each system objective is weighted according to two main factors:

1.   How important is this objective to the user's needs?

2. How feasible is this objective, with its interrelationships, in terms of economic, technological, and operational considerations?

The end result of this activity is a priority listing of system objectives. The importance of doing this step thoroughly cannot be overemphasized.

F220—PREPARE DEVELOPMENT PLAN

The first part of this activity is to establish a set of development objectives. These objectives are quite different from the ones developed for the operational system in activity F210. The present objectives concern themselves with the money, manpower, and time frame for the *developmental effort* itself. As such, they may be in conflict with the operational objectives of the system. For example, a developmental objective may be to spend a maximum amount of time on development—perhaps 3 years. The operational system may be needed as soon as possible, however, so that careful tradeoff analysis is required between the developmental objectives and the operational objectives established earlier. During this analysis a heavier weighting should be given to the system operational objectives than the development objectives. The latter will form the basis for the development plan. This plan will outline, in both short- and long-range terms, what is expected to take place during the subsequent development effort.

The short-range development plan should cover the time span of the next two development phases, definition and preliminary design. It addresses itself to what specific products will be created during these two phases, what functions will be performed, what schedules will be kept, what costs will be allocated, and what the manpower organization and training needs will be. This plan should be as realistic as possible; it should not just attempt to sell management an undercosted version of the actual facts. Although accurate estimating of what is required in undertaking a development effort for which little is known is difficult, it must be done in order that corporate management can make an educated judgment on the value of continuing a particular undertaking. Furthermore, this short-range plan also establishes and guides the development team in the continued development effort if it is approved; the project manager and the development team will be held accountable for any significant deviations from this plan. The development plan should include such support areas as coordination with users and other involved groups, communications, budget, work space, job aids, special equipment, and manpower requirements in terms of numbers of persons, skills, and knowledge.

The long-range development plan considers the same set of factors, but over the time span of the entire development effort; therefore, it lacks the preciseness and detail of the short-range plan. It considers the general development requirements through the conversion phase. Both short-range and long-range plans are updated as required, but significant changes in the estimates will require explanation. The two end products of this activity, short-range and long-range development plans, will both include a statement of development objectives, a scheduling network, activity time status report forms, perhaps function bar charts, cost milestone report forms, manpower loading reports, financial plans, and status reports.

F230—DEVELOP COST VIEW OF THE PROPOSED SYSTEM

This activity concentrates on cost or economic analysis of the proposed system. The estimates are based on the best judgment that can be made at this time. Cost estimates should be made for all of the proposed system configurations identified in activity F160. The cost study should include two sets of figures: the operational costs of running the system, and the costs required to maintain and support it.

The results of the cost study identify the possible savings or additional costs which would be incurred as a result of adopting and implementing each of the proposed system configurations. The cost figures developed at this time are highly suspect because of the lack of valid, quantifiable data; therefore, costs should be expressed in high-low ranges, with the probable cost indicated. If the development effort continues, the cost figures will be refined as further information becomes available. For a major system the operational cost might be identified as between 2 and 3 million dollars, with a probable figure of 2.5 million dollars. If, on the other hand, the figure were originally identified only as 2.5 million dollars, there would be little chance that the operational cost would ever be precisely as stated; therefore the estimate would have been inaccurate.

The end product of this activity is a cost study for each of the proposed system configurations with supporting analytical data.

F240—SELECT SYSTEM CONFIGURATION

Analysis of all the proposed system configurations and of the relationship of each to system objectives, human factors, and economic considerations leads to selection of the most desirable configuration. The choice may not be too authoritative now, but it is necessary to make a preliminary selection so as to give management some indication of the direction in which the system is going.

F250—PREPARE FORMATION OF OBJECTIVES REPORT AND SUBMIT FOR MANAGEMENT APPROVAL

The formation of objectives report is compiled to provide users and company management with the information necessary to determine whether they will *(a)* approve continuing development, *(b)* request modification and changes, *(c)* discontinue the developmental effort, or *(d)* postpone or reject the effort. If further development is approved, this report will provide the basic set of information for the start of the definition phase.

The amount and type of information needed for management decision making will vary with the nature of the system and the amount of resources made available for the formation of objectives phase. The formation of objectives report does not include all the information developed to date but rather is a summary of the highlights determined thus far.

The format for the report might include twelve parts.

Part 1: An executive summary or abstract of the system, along with signature blocks for the approving authorities.
Part 2: An expanded statement of the problem or opportunity that the system addresses.
Part 3: The objectives of the proposed system.
Part 4: The performance specifications for the system.
Part 5: System resources and constraints.
Part 6: The functions and capabilities of the proposed system.
Part 7: User implications and expressions of how well the proposed system would serve user needs.
Part 8: The economic impact on the company and its status in the market place.
Part 9: The developmental implications, cost, and time schedule.
Part 10: A glossary of the specialized terms used in the report with definitions of these terms.
Part 11: The personnel subsystem planning considerations and thus the effect on the company's current personnel and resulting needs for other personnel.

Part 12: A cross reference to all the detailed documentation developed to date for users or executives who wish further information on certain items in the report.

It is important to note two things at this point: *(a)* continuing the development is based on acceptance of the report; and *(b)* the design effort is currently out of money and resources until this report is accepted and approval is obtained for the next phases of development. When the formation of objectives report is submitted to the users and management, it is usually accompanied by an oral presentation by the development team. As stated earlier, many items examined in the formation of objectives phase will not be described in detail; no apology should be made for the level of detail, since this is in part a function of the resources made available to the formation team. Another point worth mentioning is that not all users will be satisfied with the priorities set for the system objectives, but every effort should be made to state the information honestly rather than merely to sell the system to the users and management.

CHAPTER 8   DEFINITION PHASE

DEFINITION PHASE OVERVIEW

In the formation of objectives phase the general outline of the system was developed. Objectives were stated, user needs were identified, and, in a general way, inputs to and outputs from the system were spelled out. The next step is to specify in more detail what the performance requirements are, and this is done in the definition phase. Another way of describing the definition phase is to say that it establishes the factual basis or framework of the system. For example, if the system has to be built so that the computer can talk to a remote terminal at the regional office and vice versa, this needs to be clearly specified. It is a fact which the system designers must know. Similarly, the definition phase specifies the functions which have to be performed. In a subsequent phase, preliminary design, the system designers will figure out the best way to accomplish the functions that are required. The product of the definition phase is basically the performance specifications which the design must meet; the definer seeks to present as realistic and accurate a picture of the proposed system as possible to the designers.

The formation report and documentation produced during the formation phase give direction to the development effort during definition. In order to determine where to begin the definition effort, the definition team must review what and how much was specified in the formation report. Definition should continue to develop factual information about the system in as great detail as possible. The definer should list any and all available options if they exist and the requirements where there is no choice. Otherwise he is not allowed to choose among alternatives in this phase. Understating and overstating design freedom contribute equally to system failure. Emphasis is on the identification of facts where there is no freedom to choose; later the designers will evaluate and select.

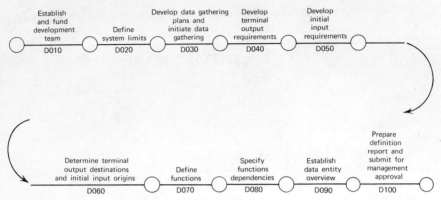

Figure 8-1   *Activity network for the definition phase.*

D010—ESTABLISH AND FUND DEVELOPMENTAL TEAM

The first major activity (see Figure 8–1) in the definition phase is to establish the development team. The formation activity F220 provides an estimate of the manpower and resources required to perform the definition phase. If the formation report is approved for continuing development, the project manager and developmental team must be appointed and organized. The ideas contained in Chapter 2 on the organization of the team and in Chapter 3 on the requirements of the team should be given careful consideration at this point; particular care should be exercised in the appointment of the project manager, since his leadership, guidance, and interpretation of the development effort steer the whole team. The team and funding should match as closely as practicable the plan developed in activity F220.

A company may be required to seek out new employees who have the desired skills and knowledge. It will be difficult in most companies to find the manpower requirements for the developmental team in the existing organization, since people with these desirable characteristics are always in demand. Needless to say, the quality of the overall job of development is a factor of the quality of the people dedicated to the development of the system.

Funds or resources are also needed to provide office space, to pay consultant fees if required, and to pay for a host of administrative or support services to this kind of an organization. Support services such as typing, reproducing, or filing can save considerable time for the team members. Special support services, such as a library service for resource documents and for filing and developmental papers, and a project office for helping to schedule determined manpower requirements, are helpful if the undertaking is very large. These activities are ancillary to the main development team effort and are too often overlooked, with the result that the development team takes time away from the project in order to perform them.

A major portion of this activity is the provision of necessary training to the team members. Even today painfully little formal training exists in the precise skills and knowledge needed for developing systems; however, some does exist in the various special disciplines of system development. Obviously the team members' entering repertoire of such skills and knowledge, the nature of the system under development, and the availability of sound, worth-while training all enter into the derivation of training requirements for the team.

D020—DEFINE SYSTEM LIMITS

One of the most difficult early activities is to determine the precise limits of the system under development. There are many expressions of the limits of the system; for example, they might range from the receipt of a customer's request to the final disposition of his account. Care should be exercised to stretch the limits of the system to their natural boundaries. Considerable grief has been experienced by setting the limits too close to the computer in the past; therefore, the limits of a system might better be expressed in terms of the source or initial inputs and the terminal or final outputs of the system. In most undertakings the limits of the system will either reach into, or interface directly with, those of other systems. In making determinations about how far the tentacles of the system should stretch, one should consider the criticality for and the impact on the system under development as prime indicators of where the boundary should be. Ideally, the total system should be designed in an all-encompassing, comprehensive way. Rarely in actual life, however, do time, resources, or organizational constraints allow this to be done.

It is as important to say what is omitted from the system as to say what is included in the system. This activity will continue to be worked on and refined through the other developmental phases up to conversion; therefore, everything that can be factually set down at this time should be documented. If this is not done well, either much effort will be expended in areas beyond the limits of the system, or several major areas will not be addressed until very late, possibly resulting in a lopsided system.

D030—DEVELOP DATA COLLECTION PLANS AND INITIATE DATA COLLECTION

In a sense we have been gathering data all along; however, we may not have done this as formally and as well as is necessary. There are many methods and techniques which can be used for gathering data. Selection of the most appropriate and viable technique is determined by such factors as money, time, and accuracy requirements. However, it is appropriate here to discuss briefly two techniques on the personnel subsystem side.

An important new methodology which has been developed is called job inventory. Job inventory consists of a written questionnaire or series of questions listing tasks performed, equipment used, and possibly other items such as skills and knowledge. Each person responding to the questionnaire checks the tasks which are part of his job and (usually) indicates the relative importance or frequency of occurrence. Workers' use of particular equipment, the skills and knowledge required for job performance, and other information may be similarly obtained. Because of the large number of data involved, data analysis is generally done by computer. Job inventory results provide a comprehensive picture of the capabilities, experiences, and other characteristics of a pool of employees and the characteristics of different jobs on a task basis. The uses of job inventory data include the following:

- *Skills required.* By comparing the skills available among existing employees with the skills needed in the new system, personnel capabilities which are presently lacking can be identified and provided for before the new system becomes operational.

- *Selection.* By providing more detailed information about each job, more refined tools for selecting personnel can be developed.

- *Matching of jobs and people.* Increased accuracy in personnel assignment becomes possible with the improved data on special skills and experiences needed to perform each job. For example, jobs currently filled by skilled personnel for which less-skilled workers would suffice can be identified.

- *Identification of job families.* Data obtained from job inventories permit the identification of jobs that have different titles but many tasks in common.

- *Training.* Job inventory can be used to identify irrelevant training (i.e., training which is directed toward the performance of specific tasks which are not, in fact, encountered on the job) and training defects. Job inventory data can also provide a more realistic evaluation of training by providing information regarding its adequacy on a task rather than a job basis.

• *Refinement of experience records.* Employees' records can be maintained on a task rather than a job basis through periodic application of job inventory. This enables the development of more refined career ladders and increases the possibility of ensuring that the employee obtains required levels of experience in a broad variety of tasks.

When the job inventory technique has been applied (primarily in the military), it has been found that individuals characterized their jobs honestly and accurately. However, when a new job inventory is developed, the result must be verified. This is generally done through the more tedious technique of observation and interview. The advantages of job inventory are savings in money, time, manpower, training; and ease of large-scale data collection; flexibility to meet changing conditions and requirements; and readily available results, unlike those usually obtained by observation and interview.

A second relatively new means for gathering data is the critical incident technique. This is a method for isolating human characteristics important to a particular job. The method begins with the isolation of critical incidents. These are actual occurrences of human behavior which are considered outstandingly successful or outstandingly unsuccessful. After a large number of such incidents have been collected, they are organized into categories which, when taken together, form an overall view of the essential characteristics for successful job performance. From these categories, check lists of past behaviors may be developed which represent the critical characteristics for effective or ineffective performance.

Since the critical incident technique uses actual occurrences of observed behaviors, it must be done on an existing system if used to isolate the characteristics desirable in the personnel who will be needed for a new system under development. The existing system selected for study must be sufficiently similar to the new one for the results which are obtained to be useful. Behavior characteristics isolated by means of the critical incident technique may be used to characterize jobs in terms of the behaviors required for their successful or unsuccessful performance.

In the critical incident technique employees are asked to provide examples of extremely good or extremely poor on-the-job behavior which they have observed in other workers. Generally those contributing such critical incidents are asked to provide their examples from memory rather than to directly record such incidents as they occur over some period of time. Although direct observations would be preferable, use of the recall of events is frequently necessary, because of the large number of incidents which may have to be collected and the relative rarity of their occurrence. Also, on-site recordings make heavier demands on the time of cooperating personnel than does recalling events from memory.

Many other collection techniques will be covered in later chapters that deal with data collection, reduction, and analysis. The result of this activity will be plans for the collection of data, for storing, reducing, and analyzing them after receipt, and finally for keeping them current.

D040—DEVELOP TERMINAL OUTPUT REQUIREMENTS

This activity is somewhat redundant to activity F130—Identify Terminal Outputs; however, during the definition phase this activity is carried out in much more exacting detail. You will recall that "terminal" means "end product of the system." All outputs from the system which are determined not as a result of design considerations, but rather as a result of definition, should be identified here. These include such requirements as information content, common language code, frequency, accuracy, volumes, and retention. All of these outputs are specified to the extent that they are known or given, but they should not be specified in a way that unnecessarily constrains the design of the system. The outputs are analyzed for peak and average rates, cyclical and periodic properties, trends and patterns reflecting future requirements, and the uses to which these requirements will be put.

Terminal output is a difficult concept for many people to grasp at first. They tend to think of output in terms of reports being printed by the computer or displays on cathode ray tubes. These are indeed output, but they are not terminal output. They are intermediate output inasmuch as they are not the final results of the system. A reports is created for a reason—the reason being that some action can be taken on the information conveyed by the report. This action can range from borrowing money, to increasing productivity, to hiring new employees; this action or behavior constitutes the terminal output. The behavior anticipated or, more precisely, the nature of this behavior governs the requirements for output. Is hard printed copy necessary, or will a diagram or audio signal be just as appropriate? The answer lies, of course, in the nature of the behavior desired as a result of the output.

Perhaps an example would help at this point. Most of us think of checks as being the output from a payroll system. Actually, however, checks are the medium to accomplish the desired output, that is to say, the check transfers funds from the company's account to the employee's account. The effect is a transfer of resources from the company to the employee to reimburse him for his services. The terminal output in this case is putting resources which were the company's into the possession of the employee. In the future we may very probably see more systems designed not to print checks, but simply to alter the company's balance negatively and increase the employee's balance positively, with a record going to the employee which would indicate the amount of federal, state and/or local taxes withheld, union dues, cost of fringe benefits, and so forth.

One further example of terminal output would involve a company's financial report. The terminal output might be the balance sheet and the profit and loss statement if these are used for records purposes only. However, if the officers of the company use the financial report for decision making purposes, then the terminal output can be considered to be the decisions that are prompted by the conditions shown on the report. For example, borrowing money for establishing a new stock offering, reducing product prices, or giving salary increases to employees might be the terminal output in this case.

As was pointed out earlier, terminal output is derived from system objectives after these objectives have been derived from user needs. Careful examination of each terminal output in light of user requirements will reveal any extraneous or perhaps unneeded items.

This activity will not be completed until the end of the preliminary design phase. However, a terminal output requirement list is created during definition and is updated and refined as more information becomes available.

D050—DEVELOP INITIAL INPUT REQUIREMENTS

All system input requirements which are a matter of definition (i.e., are not determined as a result of design considerations) should be identified. As in activity D040, these would include content requirements, common language code requirements, frequency, accuracy, volume, and retention. Like the terminal outputs, these inputs are specified to the extent that they are known or given, but their specification should not needlessly constrain design. They are analyzed for peak and average rates, cyclical and periodic properties, trends and patterns reflecting future requirements, and the uses to which the requirements will be put.

It will be recalled that initial input requirements are derived by examining output requirements. For a payroll system, some content requirements listed would be total amount of wages, taxes, social security number, union dues, deduction for U.S. bonds, employee name, and employee payroll number.

In determining the common language or code requirements, the following.questions would be relevant: Will the checks be printed in English or some other language that employees might use? Will codes for payroll numbers be included? What form (medium) will the output take—cash, currency, check, or money order? Determining the method of payment is necessary since this will involve the inputting of an appropriate medium.

Frequency considerations would probably be governed primarily by the calendar. Will employees be paid monthly, bimonthly, weekly, or at some other interval?

Accuracy for initial input in this case should probably be in the neighborhood of 98% or 99%. However, under special conditions, a much lower accuracy might be acceptable.

Where initial input is coming from would be an important consideration. Is it nation-wide, state-wide, local, or contained within the building? How it is prepared is another important consideration. This list is not exhaustive; it merely illustrates the kinds of questions which must be asked and answered. The term "initial input" implies capturing data as near their source as is practicable. Thus, the initial input point will usually coincide with the system limits that were established earlier. Capturing data as soon as possible has several distinct advantages: system functions can be maximized, the data are less contaminated by uncontrolled processing and hence more error free, and the movement, flow, and timing of the data are more subject to control.

From the questions given above it is easy to see how the definer continues to develop the factual framework of the system. It is possible that many of the answers to these questions are not fixed at this time. If they are not, the options and degrees of freedom are indicated, leaving the answers to be decided during design.

Again, this activity will not be completed until the preliminary design phase is finished. It is important, however, for the designers to capture and document the nature of all initial system inputs as early as practicable.

D060—DETERMINE TERMINAL OUTPUT DESTINATIONS AND INITIAL INPUT ORIGINS

This activity is concerned with determining the destinations of system outputs and the origins of system inputs. These may be expressed in the following ways: user activities which provide input, user activities which receive output, media parameters (e.g., magnetic tape, cathode ray tube), physical and/or geographical locations of the providers and users if known or given, and the organizational area (or group) if given.

Where input data appear to be currently unavailable, possible sources are specified. Selection of alternatives is not done during the definition phase. The destinations of output and the origins of input are important in determining how to capture or how to depict the information requirements. Furthermore, this information is vital in determining the appropriate media to bring the information in or take the output out in a timely manner.

The end result of this activity is a requirements list for each initial input origin and each terminal output destination. This activity will not be complete until the detail design phase.

D070—DEFINE FUNCTIONS

The input/output requirements dictate the nature and types of functions required to transform inputs into outputs. The process of determining functions is called function analysis; the object is to determine the functions (or processes) which must be performed regardless of how they will be done. They are definitional and factual; that is, they can be logically derived from existing output and input requirements. No choices, decisions, or designs are prerequisite to their identification. They are minimally required functions in the light of what is known.

The key question is, What must be done to transform the input into output? The answer to this question will describe the functions. For example, to use the payroll system again, if wages are computed on the basis of the amount of time worked at a certain rate of pay, one can deduce that a wage computation function is necessary (more specifically, multiplication). Function analysis is performed from the gross to the specific level.

One of the mistakes typically made in the past was trying to decide what functions in a company's operation should be computerized. Functions which involve simple clerical skills were deemed appropriate for mechanization. Studies performed during the late 1960s indicated, however, that this was not a money making way to approach system development work. As stated earlier, functions are derived from the difference between the input and the output, inputs are derived from output, output is derived from the objectives of the system, and the objectives are derived from user needs. The result is a system which does indeed achieve corporate goals. Later during preliminary design these functions will be defined further so that they may be allocated to either the manual side of the system or the hardware/software side.

The end result of this activity is a document in which each function is defined and the interrelationships between functions are spelled out.

D080—SPECIFY FUNCTION DEPENDENCIES

This activity is concerned with identifying function dependencies, which are implied when functions are broken down from gross to more specific levels. If different functions are dependent on common input or common output, they are functionally dependent and related. Also, if functions must be performed in the same discrete time frame, they may be said to be dependent. A function dependency chart is created which indicates the hierarchical relationship of functions and depicts their time sequence. This is more easily said than done. Various arrangements of functions will have to be tried out before the definer can settle on the factual set that is required.

Functions may be at mixed levels of grossness during preliminary design. They will be assigned to the level where they can be allocated in their entirety to either the machine or the manual side of the system. Again this analysis should also help to determine whether the inputs and outputs are realistic with respect to the state of the art.

D090—ESTABLISH THE DATA ENTITY OVERVIEW

The data entity overview is a representation of all the data entities required by the system. The relationships between these entities are depicted in a data entity diagram with supporting descriptions and narratives.

The data entity overview developed at this point is the first step toward data base design and must be at a gross level. The overview will continue to serve as a common reference point until a logical data base structure is developed. The data entity overview depicts the information requirements of the total system and should not be limited to the data base.

From these data entities and their relationships, certain objectives for the data base can be derived. In doing this, consideration should be given to the nature of the demands on the data base, such as frequency of access, required accuracy, response times, and expansion needs; the broad classes of information which might be included (e.g., customer identification number, geographic location code); and the opportunity to meet the data base objectives of the new system by using, expanding, or transforming an existing data base.

This activity will result in four documented products. One is a data base description which identifies the information and the activities of the data base. The data entity overview diagram depicts pictorially the data entities and their relationships. A third document is a data entity overview narrative, which supports the data entity diagram. Finally, a data entity properties description work sheet describes the characteristics and requirements for each data entity. This activity will not be completed until the detail design phase.

D100—PREPARE DEFINITION REPORT AND SUBMIT FOR MANAGEMENT APPROVAL

The definition report reflects the factual framework within which subsequent design and development must take place. It is compiled to provide corporate management with information necessary for the following:

1. Approve continued development as described.
2. Request modifications and/or changes.
3. Discontinue, postpone, or redirect the effort.

This activity also provides the basis for the preliminary design phase work.

The level of detail in the report should reflect as realistic a picture as possible of the system, specifying requirements when there is no freedom of choice. It also identifies options but leaves the selection of alternatives to the designers when the factual framework does not dictate a specific course of action.

The following types of information should be included and should be as precise, factual, specific, and clear as possible:

Executive approval summary.
System objectives.
System description, including performance specifications.
Output functions, process functions, input functions.
Required operational resources and constraints.
Required developmental resources and constraints.
Control, security, and audit requirements.
Economic, operational, and technological feasibility information.

Scheduling information.
Glossary of terms.
Recommendations.

Before this report is finalized and submitted for approval, it should be checked by all disciplines and organizations represented on the development team, so that detailed backup information for the report is available. There are three end products of this activity: the definition report, the updated developmental plan for the preliminary design phase, and the updated cost study of the system.

It is important to keep in mind that many activities started during the formation of objectives phase are also worked on during the definition phase, even though they have not been shown on the network diagram. Hence, for all activities which were not completed in the formation phase, additional information will be developed during the definition phase, and the documentation for these activities should reflect the most current information available.

CHAPTER 9   PRELIMINARY DESIGN PHASE

PRELIMINARY DESIGN PHASE OVERVIEW

Ideally all fact finding that can be done without selecting alternatives has been completed in the definition phase. During preliminary design, major alternatives are analyzed and selected, and the design of the system begins to take shape. The design process is broken into two phases, preliminary and detail, because of the amount of work and resources required. Preliminary design ends when all functions of the system can be allocated in their entirety to either the man (manual) or the equipment side of the system. At that point a formal managerial review will determine whether the effort is promising enough to continue. The nature of system development work changes rather dramatically from pure fact finding and data gathering in the definition phase to making judgments and selecting among alternatives during the design phase.

P010—PREPARE GENERALIZED MODEL OF SYSTEM

The first major activity of preliminary design (see Figure 9–1) is to develop a generalized model of the system. Modeling permits the constituent parts of the system to be studied and quantified. A model (a facsimile or representation of the real-life system) makes it possible to examine probable consequences without the risk of real-life experimentation. Through effective use of the model, the validity of the basic premises of the system can be examined before making any physical commitment of labor, material, or capital.

    In the preparation of the model, specific attention should be given to building flexibility into it, using the most appropriate tools and

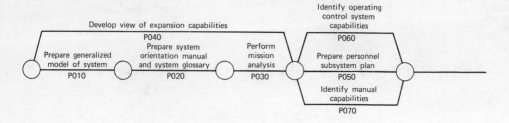

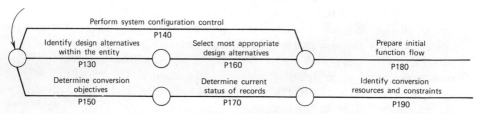

Figure 9-1   *Activity network for the preliminary design phase.*

techniques available, and ensuring that the model represents the system as closely as possible. The model should be refined and updated throughout the subsequent design development process. The built-in flexibility of the model should allow it to grow as system design progresses.

P020—PREPARE SYSTEM ORIENTATION MANUAL AND SYSTEM GLOSSARY

The manual prepared in this activity is an introductory document summarizing advance information about the proposed information system. It provides an overview for senior-level managers and includes a brief description of the new system's purpose, capability, and advantages, including expected savings in both money and manpower. It also provides an estimate of personnel requirements, training implications, necessary facilities, and cross references to additional documentation

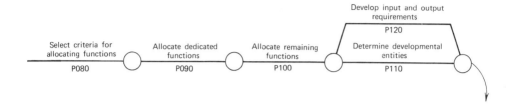

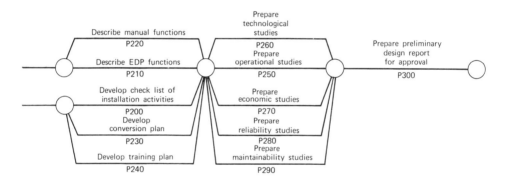

for more detailed backup information. If the areas of the operation that will be the first to get the new system are known, it lists them.

This manual is written for users and higher-level management as a preview of the new system. As such, it should contain a system glossary of special terms and their definitions, so that a common understanding of the language of the new system is possible. This manual, if properly written for users, can do a great deal to reduce or minimize resistance to change on their part. Hence, it should be written not from a designer's point of view, but from a user's. It should be factual and realistic, rather than an employee information "snow job."

One can expect reactions from both users and management after reading such an orientation manual. Possibly subsequent communication between the design team and the readers of the manual will be required to clear up any misunderstandings at this time. Although the manual will not be completed until after detail design has started, at this point it will provide management and users with information regarding needed changes and sufficient time to plan for accommodating them.

P030—PERFORM MISSION ANALYSIS

Mission analysis is the analyzing of how various elements of a system interact during the completion of one or more of the missions required of the system. To perform this activity, several representative mission cycles are selected and subdivided into segments. The segments can then be sequenced into mission profiles. By deriving and grouping mission segments, the analyst can show the effect of one segment on the system's ability to meet other operational objectives. Selection of representative mission cycles must take the following into account:

1. Routine modes of system operation.
2. Nonroutine but important modes of operation.
3. Any contingencies of operations with which the system must be able to cope.

"Mission analysis" is a relatively new term in the world of system development. As an analytical tool it was relatively unimportant during the era of batch and sequential processing. Each batch sequence or program might have been considered a particular mission. These programs did not interact, except sequentually, in receiving input from or giving help to one another. However, with the third generation, on-line, real-time computers used today, systems can be built which perform many missions simultaneously. A mission is defined as a major system objective or a cohesive set of objectives. Therefore, if we visualize a system covering not only payroll but also various other disbursement operations associated with different revenue operations, and in addition covering certain inventory operations, then the main missions of the system are inventory, revenue, and disbursements.

A mission cycle is the time span over which a given mission is in operation. In the business world this is usually daily, weekly, monthly, quarterly, or annually. In the case of a monthly payroll, the mission cycle is monthly. In the case of a daily inventory, the mission cycle is daily. Therefore, the cycle is dependent on the nature of the mission.

A mission segment is a discrete part of a mission cycle. For the payroll example, the monthly cycle might be segmented into update activities, computational activities, and finalization checking activities. The segments can then be sequenced into a graphic portrayal of a mission profile with time on the abscissa. By superimposing one graphic representation of a mission profile onto another mission profile, one can readily determine whether system capabilities are exceeded during certain times of the cycle. This should be done not only for routine operating modes of the system but also for nonroutine, contingency or degraded modes. Further consideration should be given to any major contingencies which the system should be able to handle.

Results of this activity are not completed until the detail design phase. Analysis will produce graphic representations of the mission modes at various times and under varying conditions to ensure that the composite load can still be met by the system.

P040—DEVELOP VIEW OF EXPANSION CAPABILITIES

As a result of modeling and performing mission analysis, plans can now be made for the expansion capabilities of the system. Accommodating additional requirements may necessitate reconfiguration for expansion of the system. The kinds and numbers of additional requirements that may occur during the projected lifetime of the system will determine the extent of the expansion capability to be designed into it. Examples of built-in expansion capabilities are the following:

- A system designed to serve 500,000 customers initially, but able to accommodate a 15% growth rate over the first 2 years and to double the number of customers served over the projected life of the system.
- A system designed to serve billing or revenue activities initially and disbursements later.
- A system designed to accommodate one region of a company operation initially and all regions later.

The important consideration here is a design a system with enough built-in growth and flexibility to accommodate for normal projected growth patterns over its lifetime. This cannot always be done easily, and the high cost of providing for unusual growth should cause one to design only for needed expansion capabilities.

The end result of this activity is a list of expansion capabilities required by the system in order to meet planned and predicted growth.

P050—PREPARE PERSONNEL SUBSYSTEM PLAN

During this activity a plan (sequence of activities) is formulated and periodically updated to meet personnel subsystem (PSS) development objectives and requirements. The plan outlines what is expected to take place in personnel subsystem matters during subsequent system development efforts, in both short- and long-range terms. In short, it serves as a basic planning document for all personnel subsystem activities in the new information system. It lists all of the necessary personnel subsystem design activities and provides the essential who, what, and when information for each. It includes references to other documents which can be used for development of the personnel subsystem and lists any items that are not being developed for the system with an explanation as to why they have been omitted.

In short-range terms the plan considers all personnel system design activities through the next approval point (end of preliminary design) and expresses them in detail. In long-range terms the plan considers personnel subsystem activities beyond the next approval point and indicates their start and completion dates.

The end result of this activity is a plan for addressing the required personnel subsystem development activities. The activities needed for full personnel subsystem development will be indicated as we progress down the activity network.

P060—IDENTIFY OPERATING CONTROL SYSTEM CAPABILITIES

During this activity all current and planned vendor and manufacturer operating control system software packages are reviewed to determine the capabilities that are or will be available to support the system under development. Some capabilities which should be considered are the following: communications—the number and type of terminals that can be supported; data base (files)—shared data requirements, sequential update, random retrieval; processing mode—batch and/or on-line conversational; and processing time frame—real-time response in seconds, daily processing, etc.

These operating control system capabilities are then evaluated according to the corresponding needs of the system under development. This comparison will lead to decisions to provide essential capabilities that are lacking by additional software development or, where this is not feasible, to change system objectives or requirements. In the latter case, recycling to the formation of objectives phase will be necessary.

The end result of this activity is a document reflecting the capabilities of existing operating control systems and the requirements for an operating control system to meet the needs of the system under development, indicating where any deficiencies may exist.

P070—IDENTIFY MANUAL CAPABILITIES

During this activity, a view of the anticipated manual environment at the time when the system becomes operational is developed. This view will enable system developers to understand the range of human capabilities for which the system can and must be designed. The people to be considered include not only operators and support forces, but also such system users as all levels of company management, technicians such as installers, vendor-supplied personnel, supervisors, secretaries, and clerk-typists. The description of the manual environment will include at least the following:

1. Relevant skills, knowledge, and experience expected to be available over the life span of the system.
2. Anticipated labor market conditions and employee turnover for major categories of personnel over the life span of the system.
3. Required plans and policies for ensuring an adequate manual environment over the life span of the system.

In most instances, an elaborate data gathering effort is not required at this point. Rather, the description of the manual environment takes the form of reasonable assumptions based on existing information. The manual capabilities required for the system under development are compared with the capabilities currently available. Again, this comparison will lead to a decision to provide capabilities where they are lacking (by training, hiring, etc.) or, where this is not feasible, to change the system objectives, in which case it will be necessary to recycle to the formation of objectives phase.

P080—SELECT CRITERIA FOR ALLOCATING FUNCTIONS

The functions of the system may be allocated between the equipment and the human side on the basis of a wide variety of criteria. In this activity, the different criteria are considered and a strategy for allocating functions is selected. Some of the considerations in establishing criteria are the following:

• Proposed system performance requirements, such as processing

time, frequency and reliability of input/output, and response time.
- Development constraints and resources, such as targeted installation dates and manpower availability.
- Control and security requirements.
- Operating cost and maintainability.
- Company organizational requirements.

General strategies for allocating functions to either side of the system might include the following:

- Use of the generalized model to simulate different allocations of functions.
- Simulation of the different functions to determine the appropriateness of allocation.
- Designer selection, based on good judgment and experience.
- Designer analysis of how the function can be best performed.

The object of this activity is to establish criteria and strategies that make possible an unambiguous allocation to manual, EAM, or EDP processing. Therefore, the result of this activity is a documented strategy which allows for the consistant and logical allocation of all the functions in the system deemed necessary to convert inputs to outputs.

P090—ALLOCATE DEDICATED FUNCTIONS

The next activity is concerned with allocating functions that clearly belong to either equipment or people. Basically, functions will be dedicated according to the following criteria:

1. System requirements, for example:
   a. An explicit output requirement, such as machine printout.
   b. An explicit input requirement, such as mark-sense data.
2. The availability of only one choice, for example:
   a. A requirement for 12,000 computations per hour.
   b. A requirement for compilation of 15,000 digitized random data elements into 25 classified and serial sets of digital data.
   c. A requirement for reading a check endorsement.
3. Stated system objectives, for example:
   a. Present personnel tasks must be preserved.
   b. Present equipment facilities must be used.

No definite statement can be made as to the relative effectiveness of men and machines. In specific situations, however, the following relationships indicate tendencies of strength or weakness for the typical or average case. The lists are based on that given by Harold Van Cott and James Altman.

Man Superior to Machine

1. Ability to handle unexpected events without previous experiences or programming.
2. Ability to recognize objects and places despite varying conditions for recognition.
3. Ability to profit from experience.
4. Sensitivity to a wide range of stimulus patterns.
5. Originality in putting to use information required incidental to the operation of the system.
6. Ability to detect signals despite interference.
7. Ability for improvising and adapting to flexible procedures.
8. Capability for tracking through clutter in a wide variety of stimulations.
9. Ability to perform under some degree of overload.
10. Ability to select own inputs.
11. Ability to make inductive generalizations from specific observations.

Machine Superior to Man

1. Monitoring men or other machines.
2. Exerting large amount of force, smoothing, and precision.
3. Performing routine repetitive tasks and computations.
4. Computing and handling large amounts of stored information.
5. Using logical rules for processing information.
6. Responding quickly to control signals.

Although the term "man/machine capabilities" may appear to imply an all-or-none approach to capabilities, this is not intended. Frequently the best solution for meeting a system requirement is to assign a combination of activities to men and machines, so that the strengths of each can be maximized and the weaknesses minimized. In summary, men are more adaptable since they have the ability to apply originality to varied and unexpected conditions. Machines have speed, accuracy, and the capacity to handle routine, repetitive, and large-volume tasks.

The end result of this activity will be an allocation statement for all dedicated functions of the system.

P100—ALLOCATE REMAINING FUNCTIONS

Where a clear advantage is not apparent for EDP, EAM, or manual allocation, a detailed analysis should be made of all feasible ways of allocating the functions, and each alternative configuration should be evaluated through an appropriate rating process. In some instances, this will entail a partial task analysis of the manual procedures. If no capability for accomplishing the function within the allowable resources can be identified, a redetermination of either system requirements and objectives or resources and constraints will be needed.

The overall allocation should be verified to ensure compatibility with the system performance specifications and the development objectives. In making any modification, care should be exercised that the changes do not exceed the limits, that is, infringe on critical objectives or exceed resources.

The allocation of functions which involve decision making is a major consideration in this activity and may require the application of decision analysis. This analysis is stopped, however, as soon as an allocation of the decision making function can be made to man or machine.

Some factors which should be taken into consideration in the final allocation of functions are the following:

1. Cost
   a. How does the cost of one computer compare with that of another in the light of relative capabilities?
   b. How do the costs of higher versus lower-job-grade personnel compare in the light of the task's complexity?
   c. What are the relative advantages, in terms of costs, of people versus machines—will additional people cost less than a larger computer!
2. Availability
   a. Designer may have the freedom to select particular machines, but can they be supplied when and where they are wanted?
   b. What are the constraints of the labor market if more people are approved?
3. Expandability
   a. Can there be increases in volume or customer services with minimal reprogramming?
   b. Can people absorb the increased volumes of the future ?
4. Flexibility
   a. What are the relative capabilities of the different computers?
   b. What storage and input/output devices are available and

compatible with the computers? Scanners? Tape drives? Disc? Drum?

   c. Is greater flexibility needed than machines can provide?

5. Speed, language, and software
   a. What are the relative speeds of the computer?
   b. What are the access times?
   c. What language is required by a particular machine? Is it easily learned and used by programmers?
   d. What software packages are available for particular computers?

6. Experience with manufacturers
   a. Do they service the equipment promptly and effectively?
   b. Do they meet delivery dates well?
   c. What is the reliability of their equipment?
   d. Do they provide programmer training and support?

In order to complete this allocation it may be necessary to use not only decision analysis but also contingency analysis, job inventory, and input output analysis.

The result of this activity is that all functions are broken down until they can be allocated in their entirety to hardware, software, or people, with a supporting rationale for the allocation of each function.

P110—DETERMINE DEVELOPMENT ENTITIES

This is the first time in the development process that the system can be divided into its constituent parts. This segmentation is done in order to reduce the development effort into manageable parts, herein called development entities. How the system is divided or segmented will be a function of the following factors:

- Nature of the system to be developed.
- Resources and constraints present.
- Functions that must be performed during the development effort.
- Existing organizational arrangement.
- Specific knowledge and skills required for the development effort.

The development team must be examined to determine that its organization meets three criteria:

1. It is operationally sound; for example, it provides adequate framework for communications, delegation, and control of work.
2. It is technically sound; for example, it furnishes the requisite

skill and knowledge to achieve the stated development objectives.

3. It is economically sound; for example, it maximizes available resources while minimizing constraints.

Traditionally, developmental efforts have been broken into segments based on functions of the operational system. This criterion for segmenting the development effort is highly suspect. An apparently more viable method involves segmenting along the functions of development rather than the functions of the operation of the system.

Any methodology used to break the system apart carries with it some inherent disadvantages, but these can be minimized through the use of well-designed communication procedures. Many system development efforts have failed because of organizational difficulties arising from the way in which the system was cut into segments, or from lack of effective communication between the groups working on the various parts of the system. When the system is segmented, responsibility and authority must be delegated to an extent commensurate with the segmentation.

The end result of this activity is a development entity description which depicts the segments of the total development effort and shows their logical relationships.

P120—DEVELOP INPUT AND OUTPUT REQUIREMENTS

After segmenting the development effort into its manageable parts, the interfaces and interdependencies between the segments must be determined. This determination is made by analyzing the many functions making up each development entity to identify the input/output requirements for that entity. Initially, this should be accomplished without negotiations with the other development entities. Working individually should ensure that each development entity will have an understanding of its own input and output requirements when the negotiations begin. Since output from one segment of the system often becomes input to another, a firm understanding of these requirements is mandatory.

As these data entity input/output requirements become firm, they should be negotiated between the development entities to ensure a common understanding. Eventually, all input/output requirements should be specified in detail for all interfaces between the development entities.

The four products result from this activity:

- An interface record description of each external output from each segment.
- An interface record description of all external outputs from each development entity.
- A manual interface record to cover all requirements between manual tasks in the system.
- A machine interface record to ensure machine compatibility.

P130—IDENTIFY DESIGN ALTERNATIVES WITHIN THE ENTITY

During this activity the degree of freedom or design alternatives within an entity are developed and documented in a flow diagram or decision table. Initially, these alternatives will be at a very broad level. As the design of the system becomes more detailed, however, the development of the alternatives also becomes increasingly detailed. The activity may be considered to be complete with the conclusion of the detail design phase.

The provision of design alternatives within the entity should not adversely effect the agreement for input/output requirements for that entity without an appropriate agreement from any other development entities that may be affected.

P140—PERFORM SYSTEM CONFIGURATION CONTROL

Once the system development effort is segmented into parts, it is organizationally advisable to create a system configuration group to ensure that the sum of the parts will equal the whole. In other words, configuration management will make certain that the fragmentation of the development effort is not detrimental to the effort as a whole.

The configuration control group applies the concept known as base line design. "Base line design" means, in simple terms, that the design of the system is frozen at the end of definition, and that any changes in the performance specifications after that phase must pass through the configuration control group. These people have the responsibility for determining the ramifications and implications on all the system characteristics before any change can be approved. Later in the development process, the design will be frozen at both the end of preliminary design and at the end of implementation and test. At these points in the development process, the base line is drawn; designers cannot deviate from it without requesting permission from the configuration control group.

The product of this group is the base line documentation for each point. Each request for a deviation from the base line is carefully evaluated to determine its full effect before permission is granted to change the design.

P150—DETERMINE CONVERSION OBJECTIVES

The overall objectives which must be satisfied during the subsequent conversion phase are addressed during this activity. The conversion objectives should take into account not only the data base and EDP equipment conversion needs, but also the personnel conversion requirements, such as training, job aids selection, and conversion practices.

It helps to think of conversion as a separate subsequent development effort. Conversion, in this sense, means all the activities necessary to get the new system set up and going, and to do away with all the replaced methods, procedures, and processes of the old system. Therefore, the objectives of conversion are different from the development and system objectives of the new operational system. Sometimes the terms "conversion" and "installation" are used interchangeably. Actually, however, conversion involves phasing out an old system and phasing in a new one; installation implies putting in a system where none existed before. In both cases, careful planning, design, and organization are necessary.

The conversion subsystem will merge the old and the new systems together in such a way that the old one is eliminated, the new one remains, and the company continues to operate without a major setback. The analytical techniques employed in building the conversion subsystem are the same as those used for the development of any system. It is important to consider conversion objectives early so that their effects on the design can be determined. System objectives may have to be altered or modified because of conversion problems; it may be impossible to convert from the present system to what is considered the optimum new design. This does not mean that the system should be designed for easy conversion but rather that these possibilities should be considered so that sound decisions can be made.

The end result of this activity is a narrative describing the conversion objectives for the new system.

P160—SELECT MOST APPROPRIATE DESIGN ALTERNATIVES

During this activity, various techniques are used by the design groups to select the most appropriate design alternatives within their development entity. In some cases, a decision among alternatives will not be possible until a greater amount of detail has been developed. In this case, further development will be necessary for all the alternatives until a choice (or judgment) can be made. It is imperative that documentation be written for all the alternatives considered, including careful explanations of why some alternatives were rejected and others selected. This will prevent needless recycling through the same decision later on in design.

This activity will continue throughout the design process, and the level of detail will increase as the design proceeds.

P170—SURVEY CURRENT STATUS OF RECORDS

This activity is also a part of the conversion subsystem development. The records of information which will be converted for use in the new system are reviewed and appraised for their current condition. Major emphasis should be placed on identifying the degree of difficulty that will be encountered during conversion. If available, experience and comparable conversions will serve as viable indicators of the degree of difficulty.

If the records are currently in a manual form but will be processed by a machine, procedures must be designed for transformation to a machine-readable form. If records are currently in a machine-readable form, but the language format or structure is different from the one anticipated, special procedures will be needed to accommodate the transformation. Information that is needed for the new system, but is not captured in some form currently, will also have to be accommodated.

The end result of this activity is a documented report on the status of the records that exist at this time. It is used by the designers in planning their conversion activities.

P180—PREPARE INITIAL FUNCTION FLOW

A function flow chart shows the work flow throughout the new system from a functional point of view. This flow chart clarifies the functional relationships, dependencies, boundaries, and sequences. It also shows the allocation of functions to men or equipment.

The function flow chart should be at a level of detail sufficient enough to portray the full allocation among manual, EDP, and EAM functions. Further analysis of any of the allocated functions should lead only to subfunctions of the same allocated type.

The end product of this activity is a function flow chart depicting the sequence and the relationships of the system functions included in all development entities (see Figure 9–2).

P190—IDENTIFY CONVERSION RESOURCES AND CONSTRAINTS

This is another conversion subsystem activity. During the activity, the

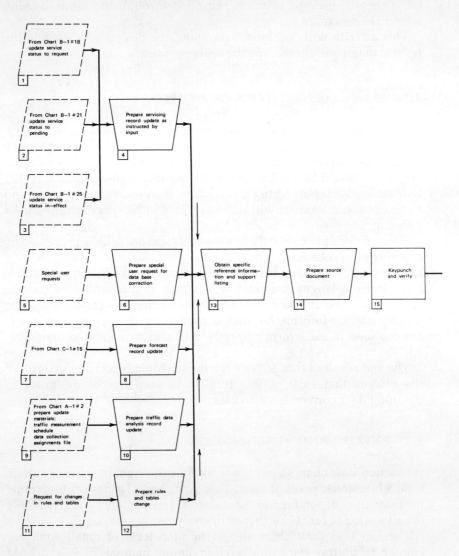

Figure 9-2   *Example of function flow chart.*

designers identify the resources and constraints directly related to conversion. This activity can probably be performed most effectively by the conversion team. Resources and constraints would be such items as manpower available for the conversion, time frame for the conversion, equipment available for the conversion, or company policies and directions.

See activities F090 and F100 for a discussion of the resource parameters and relationships which are applicable during this activity.

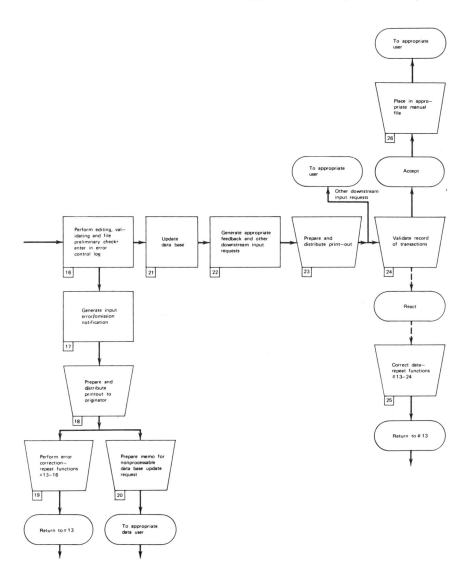

P200—DEVELOP CHECK LIST OF CONVERSION OR
INSTALLATION ACTIVITIES

A very large number of activities have to take place in order to ensure
both a successful system conversion and harmonious functioning thereafter. Because of the long lead time required to accommodate many of
them, they should be identified as early as possible. The majority of
these installation/conversion activities fall into the following categories:

1. Site preparation and maintenance.
2. Hardware and communication requirements.
3. Work force procurement and personnel policy.
4. Work force projection and job definition.
5. Supervisory and managerial preparation.
6. Organizational and procedural alignment.
7. Productivity measurement.
8. Labor relations.
9. Public relations.
10. Safety and morale provisions.
11. Printing and related (production or manufacturing) operations.
12. Conversion team selection.

At this time, all significant preparation activities for the installation
and/or conversion of the new system should be entered on the check
list. The twelve categories above are not to be considered all inclusive,
nor are they at the level of detail that is required. They are merely
suggestive of the kinds of considerations which should appear on the
installation activities check list.

P210—DESCRIBE EDP FUNCTIONS

Although EDP functions were identified during function allocation, no
attempt was made to prepare a detailed description of each function.
During this activity, however, each EDP function should be described
to a level of detail that will make it possible for functional analysis to be
performed later.

The description of the EDP function should cover each of its characteristics: input, output, process, dynamics, control, interaction, and so
forth. The descriptions should not be at the program level at this time,
but rather at the requirement level for each EDP function regardless of
whether it is allocated to hardware, software, or peripheral devices.

P220—DESCRIBE MANUAL FUNCTIONS

Like the EDP functions, each manual function should be described in considerable detail. The description should cover the following points: inputs (and sources), outputs (and destinations), and subfunctions.

When further analysis of any function has been pursued, either during allocation of functions or evaluation of alternatives, all information developed thus far should now be captured. The information may include such things as the following:

- Tasks, subtasks, steps.
- Processing frequencies, volumes, and so forth.
- Tasks, characteristics (e.g., criticality, performance time).

Any information still missing on human functions should be developed and recorded as a part of this activity.

P230—DEVELOP CONVERSION OR INSTALLATION PLAN

In this activity a conversion plan is developed. All activities which must take place in order to convert to or install the system under development are included. Items for consideration would include the following:

1. Training to be accomplished.
2. Nature of the conversion, that is, flash or progressive, region by region, district by district, and so forth.
3. Conversion of the existing data, that is, records purification requirements, input format changes, data base formation, and the like.
4. Interface with existing systems.
5. Schedule for conversion-oriented activities.
6. Personnel requirements for conversion activities.
7. Estimated budget for conversion activities.

This plan for conversion activities corresponds to the developmental plan for the new system and should be updated as required.

P240—DEVELOP TRAINING PLAN

The training development plan is devised to provide for all personnel affected by the system, that is, supervisory, managerial, staff, maintenance and support, users, trainers, installation and application, conversion, and system operations employees. The plan should recognize both short- and long-range training requirements. In particular, the plan includes provisions for indoctrination and orientation of all personnel. It may also cover non-project-oriented training, such as courses in job design and training development for managers, supervisors, and analysts.

A training program will be designed for the personnel selected and assigned to the conversion team. This program will seek to upgrade the skills and knowledge of persons necessary for the transformation of records, practices, and environment into the forms (format, media) necessary for successful operation of the new system.

In the process of developing a training plan, recruiting and selection plans and job performance aids are examined as alternatives or complements to training. Hiring the skills and knowledge needed, building in performance through job performance aids, and the development of training programs are all examined in order to optimize design.

This plan will not be fully developed until the end of the implementation and test phase.

P250—PREPARE OPERATIONAL STUDIES

During this activity, various types of operational studies are required to answer two questions: (a) If the system is successfully developed, will it be successfully used? (b) Will the managers adapt to the system, or will they resist or ignore it?

Achieving the full potential of the system may require substantial operational changes, such as changes in corporate policies, staff and line reorganizations, or the construction of new facilities. It will certainly require the support of operating managers and their staffs, and it may also depend on the cooperation of dealers, suppliers, and even customers.

Enough information has been developed at this point in time so that sound operational studies can be conducted. These studies may use the models of the system discussed earlier. In addition, certain forms of simulation or quantitative techniques may prove necessary in order to answer critical questions about the operatability of the new system. It is important to find out early whether there are operational problems with the design of the system.

The results of these operational studies will be included in the preliminary design report.

P260—PREPARE TECHNOLOGICAL STUDIES

All system design decisions on projections based on expectations regarding the state of the art should be carefully examined and evaluated. System design should be based not on unrealized technological breakthroughs, but rather on what is possible within the limits of current working technology. In no case should system design be premised on technology beyond laboratory-proved techniques.

The feasibility of questionable technology should be tested in one of the following ways:

1. Has this technology been proved anywhere in the business world?
2. Has this technology been proved by a laboratory method?
3. Can this technology be proved by some other testing method?

Dramatic examples, familiar to all of us, of the consequences of designing beyond the state of the art exist in the world of the military. The TFX and C5A aircraft both experienced problems caused by designing beyond the current technology. More recently, the Lockheed 1–11, using the Rolls Royce engine for power, ran into great difficulty because its design was based on anticipated technological breakthroughs that did not materialize. The reason for citing military problems is that we know more about them than those that have occurred in the industrial world of information systems design. Perhaps three examples involving computer-based information systems will illustrate this point. The Burroughs/TWA management information system, the General Electric-Massachusetts Institute of Technology and the General Electric retailers' system all were victims of technological problems caused by designing beyond the state of the art. Although all of these systems were conceived as very large and complex, they either did not meet user expectations or were abandoned during development.

P270—PREPARE ECONOMIC STUDIES

Based on what is known of the system at this time, figures are developed to project the cost or the savings anticipated for the new system. The range of cost or savings projected earlier in the formation of objectives phase is narrowed considerably at this time. It is expected highly reliable cost data can be produced during this activity. This information is vital to the preliminary design report to management.

The model of the system developed earlier should now be of considerable help in the costing of the proposed system. There is no one
acceptable way to cost every system regardless of its nature. Many
worth-while books on economic and cost studies exist, and anyone
interested in performing such studies should refer to the book of his
choice.

P280—PREPARE RELIABILITY STUDIES

Enough quantitative information should now be available to study the
reliability of the proposed system. This study should include such
considerations as control, security, availability, maintainability, data
flow, throughput, uptime, and accuracy or quality. This study should
reveal exposed, weak, or vulnerable areas of the design—in short, any
neglected areas that are likely to cause failure, downtime fallback, or
degraded performance.

Quantification of the study results should be expressed in ranges of
probable, maximum, and minimum performance. Consideration
should be given to building in techniques which will increase reliability to acceptable levels. These techniques might include redundancy,
various edits and verification, fallback or backup procedures, emergency procedures, and preventative maintenance routines.

The studies resulting from this activity should indicate that the
design of the system has sufficient reliability designed into it to meet
user needs and system objectives.

P290—PREPARE MAINTAINABILITY STUDIES

Again, this study takes the information developed thus far and projects
it to the operational system to determine the difficulty or ease with
which the system can be maintained in its intended environment.
Particularly in the world of computer-based systems, there have been
many instances where the total cost of maintaining a system was
greater than the cost of developing it. The ease with which a system can
be supported and maintained is a design feature and not happenstance.

These studies should indicate the amount of effort and resources
required for the system to meet its performance requirements in its
intended operational environment over its intended life. This information will be included in the preliminary design report.

P300—PREPARE PRELIMINARY DESIGN REPORT FOR APPROVAL

The preliminary design report should follow the basic format suggested earlier for the formation of objectives report (see activity F250). The report should include all the highlights and pertinent information developed thus far with references to the detailed documentation as needed. The fact that this is a major milestone and that the project will not continue without additional funding and approval by management should be kept constantly in mind.

The design process is halted between preliminary and detail design, so that management can take a good look at the prospects for the new system before all the resources needed for programming and further development are expended. This seems to be the earliest point in the development process where a quantified and reasonable judgment can and should be made as to the worth of the system before expending the resources required to perform the activities in detail design. Therefore, before development continues, corporate management and the users of the system must agree to the performance specifications and the measurements provided by the economic, technological, and operational studies included in the preliminary design report.

On the basis of this report corporate management can request four different actions:

1. Continue development of the system.
2. Modify the system.
3. Discontinue the development effort.
4. Postpone or redirect the effort.

If the choice is to continue the development effort, the appropriate funding and resource allocations for the detail design and test phases will follow. The preliminary design report also serves as the base line for subsequent development.

CHAPTER 10   DETAIL DESIGN PHASE

OVERVIEW OF THE DETAIL DESIGN PHASE

During the detail design phase, two major development efforts take place concurrently. The nature and simultaneity of the work suggest the appropriate way to organize the development team for this phase: into two separate but related design groups both working to complete the detail system structure.

The first group, possibly called equipment designers, develop the logic of the machine functions in order to produce program specifications. The second group, perhaps termed manual designers, develop the logic of the manual side of the system. Both of these design groups are dependent on specific systems information from the preliminary design phase in order to do their work. The initial function flow chart and the equipment functions and manual functions reports developed during preliminary design serve as the prime input documents to these groups.

The development of the manual side of the system has been slightly overemphasized in this book in order to get its relative importance back into perspective. Historically, in computer-based information systems, the personnel subsystem side of development has suffered from too little, too late. Too little attention has been given to design of the manual procedures. When resulting problems can no longer be ignored, it has generally been too late to eliminate them through design; therefore, it remains up to the system users to devise a way of living with the difficulties or trying to train people to avoid them. It is a credit to man's ingenuity that many a near disaster has been averted, largely as a result of instinctive self-preservation. Nevertheless, the price paid for failure to design the manual subsystem (the personnel subsystem) adequately has been alarming in terms of management disillusionment, customer dissatisfaction, and worker frustration.

118

The main reason for the lack of consideration for the personnel subsystem seems to be that many people fail to recognize the connection between the design of this subsystem (or the lack of design) and the subsequent problems and disappointing results. For example, excessive overtime by system workers, massive retraining, temporary reassignment of computer programmers to field offices to clear work flow bottlenecks, high turnover rate, and low employee morale are indications of faulty personnel subsystem design.

The analytical techniques, approaches, and disciplines used to design the system have a great deal of commonality between personnel subsystem design and equipment design. Yet almost every system is inherently short-shifted on the personnel subsystem side. Perhaps this occurs because the costs of the computer, its associated gear, and its subsequent downtime are so apparent and dramatic that the tendency is to allocate most of the development resources to avoid easily pinpointed defects in equipment design. However, this is a short-sighted viewpoint since errors, contingencies, and personnel sabotage have caused untold grief in the computer room.

DD010—IDENTIFY POSITIONS

This activity (see Figure 10–1) involves using the initial function flow chart and the descriptions of activities in supporting documents to analyze the manual functions of the developmental entity. Special criteria related to job performance and training requirements are then applied to these functions in order to synthesize them into tentative positions. "Positions," in this usage, designates manual modules of work; they may be made up of one or more tasks, and they may be job size or less than job size. Use of the term "position" to express this manual module of work is an important concept because it allows the designer to design and document manual work without consideration for an individual's characteristics and motivations, as would be the case if he had to design jobs instead of positions. Positions are roughly analogous to programs for the computer. They are integral and related pieces of work. By designing them at job size or less, positions can be grouped in different ways to locally structure jobs on the basis of volumes, individual motivations, or skill levels.

This technique of job design and documentation was developed by American Telephone and Telegraph Company and American Institutes for Research on a joint research project in the early 1960s. It has been used in a wide variety of applications throughout the Bell System and the aerospace industry.

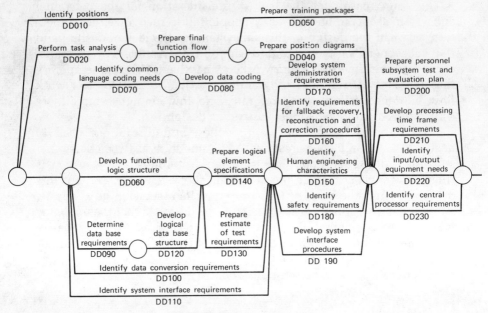

Figure 10-1   *Activity network for detail design and test phases.*

DD020—PERFORM TASK ANALYSIS

The manual functions within positions are analyzed to the task level, each task being characterized, as far as possible with the existing information, in terms of input/output, performance time, frequency of occurrence, criticality, skill and knowledge requirements, and other relevant factors. A preliminary breakdown is made of each task into steps, and alternative ways of performing the task are identified. To avoid duplication of effort, the analysis should be closely coordinated with other, similar analyses conducted for the purposes of human engineering, forms design, and work space layout.

"Tasks," as used herein, denote major functions within a position. Two major analytical techniques are used to derive tasks within a position. The first of these is decision analysis. This technique involves examining the functions which have been derived by function analysis to identify those which require the making of decisions. There are three important questions which the designers should ask about the system functions they are analyzing:

1.   Does the function require that a decision be made?
2.   What information is required to make the decision?

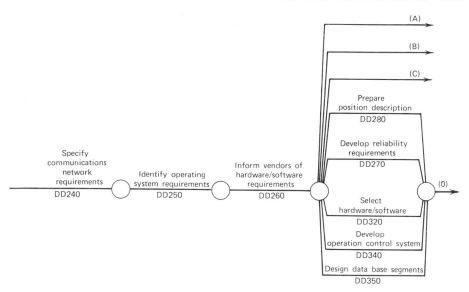

3. What functions, machine or manual, are required to execute the decision?

Having developed answers to these questions about manual functions within a position, the designers have a three-fold responsibility:

1. To make sure that the information required for the decision making process is available.
2. To decide how to organize the information so that it is readily accessible.
3. To design the function necessary to make the right decisions by:
   a. Providing the most efficient order for accomplishing the decisions.

   b. Providing the means for eliminating wrong possibilities.

Decision tables are a viable tool in designing and sometimes in documenting these analyses.

The second analytical technique for deriving tasks is contingency analysis. Like decision analysis, contingency analysis is aimed toward a particular kind of design problem. It focuses on designs that will eliminate or accommodate expected contingencies.

In performing a contingency analysis, the designer asks, "What can go wrong with this process, its inputs and/or its outputs?" This technique may be performed at different points in the development effort. It is particularly useful at the detail level as a means for validating and checking the completeness of the design. One of the great lacks in the past has been the absence of procedures for making corrections when things go wrong.

In contingency analysis, after potential trouble spots are identified, they are evaluated to determine their probable occurrence. With this information, the designers then determine the direction of their efforts. There are two kinds of provisions that can be made for contingencies, preventive and corrective.

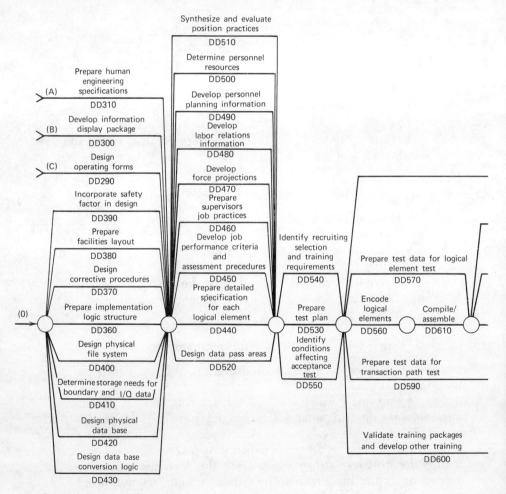

Figure 10-1   (continued).

- *Preventive:* The design effort tries to eliminate or minimize the possibility of the error or contingency taking place.
- *Corrective:* After careful study of the potential problems, it is decided that the possibility of errors cannot be completely eliminated. Therefore, the designer creates procedures for correcting errors after they occur.

It is important for designers to carry out contingency analysis so that many of the so-called "surprises" encountered in the conversion of a new system can be eliminated.

The end result of this activity is a task analysis diagram which depicts the sequence and relationships of the tasks within a position and has all relevant quantified data attached.

DD030—PREPARE FINAL FUNCTION FLOW CHART

The final function flow chart is drawn to reflect the refined structure of manual functions. A refinement of the flow chart drawn earlier in activity P180, it depicts the full information flow for the whole

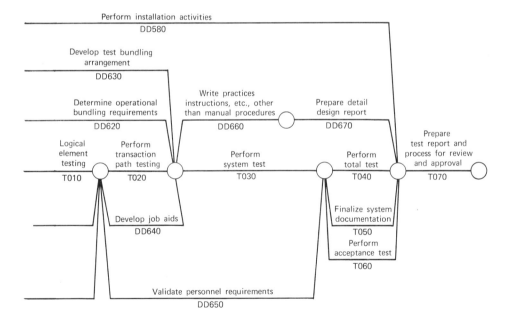

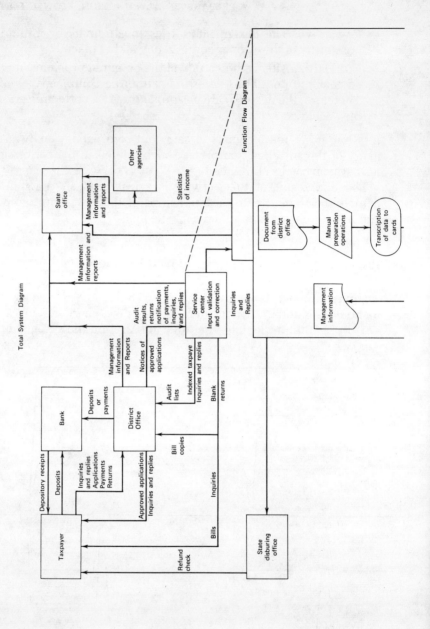

Total System Diagram

Function Flow Diagram

124

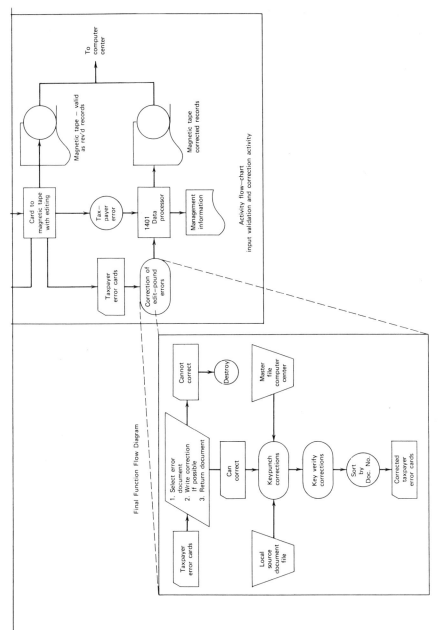

Figure 10-2   *Example of the derivation of the final function flow diagram.*

125

development entity in terms of positions, EAM activities, and EDP functions. Later, the final function flow chart will serve as a training aid for the trainee and a job aid for the worker. Also, it will provide a diagrammatic guide to the relative positions of functions within the

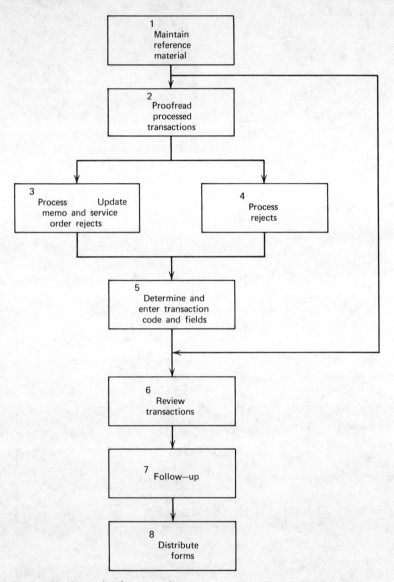

Figure 10-3   *Example of position diagram.*

total system. Thus, in addition to being part of the development documentation, the final function flow chart becomes part of the operating documentation.

The end result of this activity should be a flow chart which indicates diagramatically how the information flows, what is happening, and who is doing it in a manual, EAM, and EDP sense. As such, it should conform with existing standards of symbology for representing these activities or functions (see Figure 10–2).

DD040—PREPARE POSITION DIAGRAMS

During this activity a diagrammatic representation of the normal work tasks and steps within a position is drawn. This diagram indicates the sequence and relationships of tasks and steps within the position, as well as the major decision points. This diagram will be used later both as an instruction tool and as operating documentation (see Figure 10–3).

DD050—PREPARE TRAINING PACKAGES

The position diagram and task analysis documentation are analyzed for their training implications. At this time, further materials are identified which will have to be developed for training purposes. Usually these training materials will consist of (but are not necessary limited to) the following:

1. Position practices.
2. Set of training objectives.
3. Complete set of course materials (including training aids).
4. Performance examination.
5. Instructor's guide.

This activity results in a planning and control document outlining the instructional guidance and training objectives needed to assist in the following:

1. Providing for the human performance required by the designs and objectives of the new system.
2. Providing for the required number of qualified employees in time for the conversion and operation of the new system. It also fixes responsibility for execution and support of the plan.

This informational and guidance document will be used to develop programs and courses needed to meet the training requirements of the new system. It should also serve as a reference in the process of selecting and scheduling individuals to receive the training.

After the development of the plan, or in conjunction with it, a training program will be designed for the personnel selected and assigned to the conversion team. Training needs should also be addressed to upgrade the skills and knowledge of the persons required for the transformation of the records, practices, and work environment necessary for the operation of the new system.

In developing the training plan, consideration should be given to the alternatives of the recruitment of new employees and/or the provision of job aids.

DD060—DEVELOP FUNCTIONAL LOGIC STRUCTURE

The functional logic structure is a modular organization of the required equipment logic without consideration for the particular hardware, vendor software, or statistics associated with specific implementation. By using the techniques of function analysis and input/output analysis, each function is divided into its major components. This division continues until the lowest level of process within a function has been defined. After a major function has been modularized in this fashion, the technique of design synthesis is used to identify any modules having common logic, data requirements, and/or occurrence within the same time frame; these modules are then analyzed to determine whether their common characteristics warrant their being synthesized. If they do, modules possessing the common characteristics are combined at the functional level most appropriate for accessibility.

The combined techniques of function analysis and design synthesis allow one to optimize the modularization of the logic of the system. There are many ways—for example, in logic structures, decision tables, or flow charts—of depicting this graphically.

DD070—IDENTIFY COMMON LANGUAGE CODING NEEDS

The need for coding and common language within a system will grow like Topsy unless carefully controlled. During this activity, all coding needs and common language needs should be identified and brought together to minimize the number of codes and special languages contained within the system.

A considerable body of knowledge which has been built up in the last few years indicates what kind of coding structures to avoid, as well as those to strive for, for qualitative and quantitative reasons. Generally speaking, people work well with codes that approximate the English language, whereas machines work well with numeric codes. Compromises and tradeoffs are required. Generally speaking, machines can also code and decode faster than human beings can. Therefore, designers should seek, whenever necessary, to accommodate the personnel subsystem side of the system.

DD080—DEVELOP DATA CODING

Sometimes codes developed to satisfy manual operations cannot easily be manipulated within the computer. During this activity, the need for these special codes is identified. Then machine codes and translator tables are developed to conform with the limitations of the computer.

This activity may result in a matrix which specifies a machine-oriented code and relates each of these items to the manually-oriented code item. This documentation should also include the requirements for tables, matrices, and lookups within the computer file for translation.

DD090—DETERMINE DATA BASE REQUIREMENTS

The objective of this activity is to determine the data base requirement of each function to be served by the computerized data base. These requirements are expressed as the properties of the information elements or data entities which were previously defined. When all data requirements have been defined, it must be decided which items are candidates for the data base. Candidates for this kind of mechanized data base usually have certain characteristics: they are semipermanent, fairly frequently accessed, and capable of being arrayed in a logical structure.

In this fashion, input is transformed into the computerized data base rather than being reintroduced each time that it is needed for processing. It is held resident in the structure of the data base and is ready upon call.

DD100—IDENTIFY DATA CONVERSION REQUIREMENTS

All data which are currently being used by the system and are to be replaced are evaluated against the data requirements of the new system. Data which are not currently in the format, language, or structure to be used by the new system are identified at this time and evaluated in terms of the amount of effort needed for reconciliation and transformation so that they will meet the requirements of the new system. These data are further analyzed for their quality and accuracy to determine the amount of purification required.

A listing is made for all data and data conversion requirements which identifies what must be generated, converted, purified, and/or reconstructed. This listing indicates the source of the data and the actions which must be performed on them. The examination of data also includes requirements for the manual subsystem for input to the system or for formation of the data base.

DD110—IDENTIFY SYSTEM INTERFACE REQUIREMENTS

Other current systems in use, either manual or machine, may either produce needed input for the new system or require output from it. During this activity these needs are identified. Data which another system will receive are evaluated to determine whether there are differing format codes or structure requirements, and the actions proposed to reconcile the differences are identified. Other systems which will supply data to the new system are listed, along with the actions proposed to efficiently and effectively provide data to the new system while still maintaining the integrity of the current systems.

Another area covered during this activity is the specifying of routines or procedures currently being performed by other systems that will be replaced by the new system. This is necessary so that plans for the "phasing out" of the older systems can be made.

In most of the information processing world today, this is a somewhat tedious and complex activity. It must be done well, however, in order to keep from adversely affecting either the design of the new system or the performance of existing systems with which it will interface.

DD120—DEVELOP LOGICAL DATA BASE STRUCTURE

The logical data base structure for the new system is developed through the analysis of data entity and property requirements and descriptions. The logical data base structure and the functional logic structure are largely dependent on each other. Therefore, the two development efforts must be closely coordinated and controlled;

changes or refinements to either structure may be required in order to optimize their interaction.

If the specified data requirements are to be added to an existing logical data base structure, the designer must do three things:

1. Extend it to encompass the new entries.
2. Update the logical data base entity/property description list.
3. Verify that the new names and descriptions are not in conflict with existing ones.

DD130—PREPARE ESTIMATE OF TEST REQUIREMENTS

All testing requirements must be identified and estimated as early as practicable. Besides specifying data test requirements, the estimate should include such factors as probable time required for testing on the central processing unit and ancillary equipment and the personnel required. Obviously, this is an iterative process which should be reviewed and updated to ensure that there is adequate lead time to fulfill the test requirements.

Test requirements should be derived not only for main line processing, but for all contingency conditions. Preparations should also be made for interface testing between manual and machine, machine and machine, and manual and manual functions.

DD140—PREPARE LOGICAL ELEMENT SPECIFICATIONS

A detailed description of each logical element should be prepared. The description specifies the conditions under which each element is inputted, as well as the processing to be accomplished by the element. Algorithms should be described when known, and flow charts, decision tables, and matrices should be used as appropriate to support or clarify the narratives and requirements. This is particularly true for higher-level elements when they can serve to reflect sequence and relationship.

A list of input fields, indicating the source for each, and output fields, indicating the destination and use of each, is prepared for each logical element.

DD150—IDENTIFY HUMAN ENGINEERING CHARACTERISTICS

This activity involves identifying all of the areas of the system in which human engineering effort is required in order to optimize the effectiveness, comfort, and safety of personnel. These areas will include the work space layout, controls and displays, and ambient conditions (e.g., lighting, temperature) which are required to bring human performance needs and system objectives into optimal alignment.

This activity will usually involve using tradeoff analysis, which may be supported by many other analytical techniques, including modeling, simulation, laboratory experimentation, and field observation. The human engineering characteristics identified here will subsequently be refined and incorporated into procurement and design specifications of the input/output equipment, communications networks, work facilities, job aids, and other items related to the personnel subsystem.

Few areas of information system development work have been so thoroughly neglected and yet hold such great potential for optimizing the system as human engineering. The lack of appropriate human engineering in a system is not painfully apparent unless one must work within the system. A major developmental objective for every system involving manual processing should be to optimize the use of the personnel resources required to operate, maintain, and support the system.

DD160—IDENTIFY REQUIREMENTS FOR FALLBACK, RECOVERY, RECONSTRUCTION, AND CORRECTIVE PROCEDURES

During this activity the designers should review the operational aspects of the system to identify potential failures or errors, and to determine the probable frequency and impact of each upon the system. Failures may occur in such areas as manual positions, files, computers, schedules, air conditioning, logic, terminals, and communication network facilities, or because of the disability of a large number of people (e.g., work stoppage, strike, and/or civil disobedience). The results of these findings are required for the following purposes:

Failure identification.
Failure isolation.
Remedial procedures.
Reconstruction of obliterated data.
System recovery procedures.
Decision to fall back to alternative operations if necessary.

After the potential failures are determined, they must be analyzed for their criticality. For example, if a processing delay of one day is tolerable, then any failure that can be corrected in less than one day will not require alternative modes of operation of fallback procedures.

The basic plan for corrective procedures developed during this activity will become a design constraint later in the development process. This activity will continue through subsequent detailed levels of design so that the requirements can be refined. The final plan will accommodate the equipment, software, backup files, and personnel subsystem.

DD170—DEVELOP SYSTEM ADMINISTRATION REQUIREMENTS

It is most important to identify the information requirements for administration of the system. In order to accomplish this, a thorough analysis of legal, operational, and auditing considerations is required. In general, it will be necessary to accumulate information to monitor the performance of three subsystems: hardware, software, and personnel.

Careful consideration should be given to the requirements for assessment of human performance in the system in both quantitative and qualitative terms. Special routines may be needed for accumulating and classifying the errors in input arising from manual sources. The accumulated information will later be analyzed and translated into specific procedures for the measurement of job performance.

Tradeoff analysis will be required to determine where automated diagnostic routines for system administration are merited. Diagnostic routines should be built in where functions or outputs are critical to achieving system performance. Furthermore, the medium and the timeliness of the results of these diagnostic routines require careful consideration. Where automated diagnostic routines are not merited, procedures for managerial diagnostics should be determined.

DD180—IDENTIFY SAFETY REQUIREMENTS

A detailed analysis of all manual equipment interfaces of the system involving potential hazards should be made. This analysis should involve not only operational personnel but also custodial employees, testers, and supervisors. During this activity requirements for safety procedures, precautions, and training are identified and plans for implementing them are developed.

Most information systems do not have a high potential for hazard or bodily harm to employees; certainly one could not compare the amount of exposure here to that in systems in coal mines or steel mills. Nevertheless, high voltage, heavy equipment, and work space layouts merit safety consideration.

DD190—DEVELOP SYSTEM INTERFACE PROCEDURES

This activity is a logical extension of activity DD110 (Identify System Interface Requirements). All the procedures necessary for the new system to interface with existing systems are completely designed. The system interface requirements are translated into functions, with input and output specifications. Control procedures must be included in the development of the functions. For each function a decision must be made to either modify an existing manual or machine system or to create a new procedure to handle the interface requirements. Functions must be allocated to man or machine.

Position practices must be written or modified. Training must be developed for manual functions, and logic structured and described for machine functions.

Testing requirements, as well as personnel, hardware, and software requirements for implementing the system interface procedure, must be estimated.

DD200—PREPARE PERSONNEL SUBSYSTEM TEST AND EVALUATION PLAN

During this activity a basic plan is developed to test whether the personnel subsystem effort will produce the human performance necessary to satisfy the system requirements. The system objectives should be used to determine which personnel subsystem products are emphasized during testing. Also, knowledge of the system objectives and requirements should be used to establish the criteria for determining the criticality of the tasks to be tested.

This planning document provides for the systematic and comprehensive testing of all personnel subsystem products in the new information system. It should help to test the following:

- The interactive efforts of human performance with other system performance.
- The ability of selected personnel to operate, maintain, and support the system.
- The adequacy of the personnel subsystem products developed for the system.

DD210—DEVELOP PROCESSING TIME FRAME REQUIREMENTS

During this activity the time frame in which a project will be operating is specified. There are two types of time frame:

1. A period of time during the hour, day, week, and so forth when a project will or will not be available.
2. A required response time for a group of projects to be completed.

An example of the first type is a specification similar to the following: projects a, b, and c will be on line between 9 A.M. and 5 P.M. Monday through Friday. The second type of time frame is illustrated by the following conditions: projects x, y, and z must provide a combined turn-around time of less than 3.4 seconds for an inventory inquiry.

The modeling started in activity P010 and the mission analysis begun in activity P030 will provide valuable data for accomplishing this activity.

DD220—IDENTIFY INPUT/OUTPUT EQUIPMENT NEEDS

This is a preliminary identification of the characteristics needed in the input and output equipment to satisfy the system or a part of the system. Specific identification of hardware devices is not necessary at this time. A typical device indicator may be a cathode ray tube or printer. The size, volume, and/or speed to be accommodated by the device must be defined in order to make the proper identification.

The considerations for input/output equipment should include all relevant human engineering characteristics, such as type font requirements, control display relationships, video display resolution, hard copy requirements, the number of copies required at a location, the way in which the terminals will be used, and their locations. After these needs are identified, they should be refined, combined, and adjusted to establish a comprehensive group of requirements which must be satisfied.

Data base storage requirements are also determined during this activity. Identification of the requirements is based on such factors as volume, size, speed, frequency of access, and structure. Activity F170—Survey Technological State of the Art, will provide an important input to assist in completion of this activity.

DD230—IDENTIFY CENTRAL PROCESSOR REQUIREMENTS

All requirements developed earlier for the central processing unit are combined, reviewed, and synthesized during this activity. Factors which must be considered include speed, volume, capacity, and ability to work with input/output device requirements.

Much has been written concerning the selection process involved in determining the correct central processing unit; therefore this subject will not be developed in detail here. It is important to point out, however, that the system objectives and requirements should play a very strong role in the selection of the central processing equipment. Cost, speed, and sophistication are secondary to the primary purpose of meeting these requirements and objectives. Considerable mischief has been caused in the systems world by predetermining which central processor is required and then trying to determine what it should do. It is interesting to note that this is the earliest point in time when the characteristics and requirements for the central processing unit can validly be determined.

If one is not selecting a computer to power the new system, but rather is using existing power on a central processing unit, then during this activity he would determine whether he has a fit or a modification is required.

DD240—SPECIFY COMMUNICATION NETWORK REQUIREMENTS

All communications media and equipment needs to reach the system objective and meet the requirements of the parts of the system should be identified now. These needs are analyzed and refined, combined, and adjusted to develop a comprehensive group of communication network requirements. The requirements must be reviewed to insure consistency with the current state of the art before they are finalized. Also, the size and volume of data to be handled by the equipment must be defined in order to adequately determine the requirements. Band width, channel capacity, and speed are factors critical to meeting the performance specifications.

This activity concerns itself not only with communications over phone lines, microwaves, and coaxial cable, but also with communications within the personnel subsystem. Therefore, such items as intracompany mail, U.S. Post Office mail, telephone communications, and memoranda may be included in communications network design.

Again, many books deal with communications network design, and the reader should refer to other texts for a more detailed treatment of this subject.

DD250—IDENTIFY OPERATING SYSTEM REQUIREMENTS

The requirements for software control of the hardware and the project programs are determined during this activity. These requirements should be expressed in terms of the capabilities required of the master or control software, frequently called the data management systems. Included would be consideration of error and recovering needs and the type of processing required (e.g., multiprogramming, batch sequential, or communicating on-line).

This activity is an extension of the one started in F160—Identify System Configurations. It will obviously draw very heavily on the earlier set of activities in this phase dealing with central processing unit requirements, input/output needs, and time frame requirements.

DD260—INFORM VENDORS OF HARDWARE/SOFTWARE REQUIREMENTS

At this point, all the information needed by vendors to make proposals is summarized to form a request for a proposal. The request for a proposal should include five items:

1. System description—outline of functions and description of system input/output, with data sizes and volumes specified.
2. Hardware requirements—central processing unit peripheral equipment, input/output devices, and communication requirements.
3. Software requirements—operating systems, software control programs, data management services.
4. Administrative information—system restrictions such as facility size, maximum and minimum cost of system, intent to purchase, rent, or lease equipment, and deadline for submitting proposals.
5. A request for information concerning any special training that vendors will provide.

This activity again breaks with past practice of involving vendors very early in the design of the system and thus having the system designed for their equipment or software. Instead, this strategy asks the vendor to design and build to meet the system specifications, rather than adapting the system to meet off-the-shelf hardware requirements. A variation of this is for the vendor to modify his off-the-shelf hardware to meet the system performance specifications. Sometimes this requires only software modifications or enhancements; at other times it means actual engineering redesign. Of course the economics of the various alternatives must be carefully considered.

DD270—DEVELOP RELIABILITY REQUIREMENTS

This activity is a further refinement of the work carried on in activity P280—Prepare Reliability Studies, and relates directly to activity

F080—Set Initial Performance Specifications. During this activity the detailed specifications are developed for system reliability. These quantified specifications include the areas of control, security, availability, throughput, and maintainability. Components of the system, such as hardware, software, and people, are examined to establish the specifications for the degree of reliability needed to meet system objectives and user needs. Included also are procedures for fallback, recovery and reconstruction, emergencies, and operation during degraded mode. Times and methods for and related to preventative maintenance must be established.

These reliability figures will be used as standards for testing and also for later evaluation. They should not be established arbitrarily but derived from user needs and performance specifications. Reliability figures also dictate certain design considerations, particularly in the area of maintainability. Maintainability does not just happen; it is the result of deliberate design effort. Maintainability design concentrates not only on fixing things after a failure, but also on preventing breakdowns.

DD280—PREPARE POSITION DESCRIPTION

This activity gets most of its information from three earlier activities: DD010—Identify Positions, DD020—Perform Task Analysis, and DD040—Prepare Position Diagrams. Each task within a position is broken down into detailed steps. A particular group of tasks and steps is selected from a number of alternatives. Each step is then described as clearly and directly as possible to serve as a guide for the operating personnel who will be performing the task and steps. These descriptions are detailed enough to help the personnel involved make a smooth transition to the new system. Each step is augmented by appropriate supporting information, such as warnings or cautions and references to the corrective procedures and exhibits designed in activity DD370.

Each position description should be written for the person who will be performing the position. Therefore, the language level, amount of detail, sequence, and relationships are governed by the user, that is, the person who will carry out these tasks and steps. Short imperative sentences usually have proved most effective.

DD290—DESIGN OPERATING FORMS

All forms to be used in the operation of the new system should receive careful design consideration. Traditionally, forms have been designed for machine utilization, to the detriment of their use by people. This has caused errors, frustrations, and low production. Various designs of each form will probably need to be tried out in order to achieve an optimum design. Persons skilled in human engineering are particularly knowledgeable about the do's and don'ts of form design.

The acceptance of forms design is particularly critical to system success. It is important, therefore, that users have a voice in the design of new forms and in the selection of optimum forms.

Forms, as used in this context, should include displays of cathode ray tubes as well as hard copy.

DD300—DEVELOP INFORMATION DISPLAY PACKAGE

All forms, manual and machine, as well as format specifications for display devices, are collected and assembled into a single package. Forms or formats developed for input or output media, temporary display, and multipurpose use in the operation system are included. Additional identifying information in the display package indicates the inventory of forms that should be on hand, the reordering cycle, printing specifications, and distribution information.

This display package will have several uses, among them the following:

1. An aid in familarizing local managers and supervisors with the new procedures and routines and also the total span of the new system.
2. A reference manual for the use of personnel responsible for corrective procedures.
3. A means of identifying measurable workload data in terms of the number of forms that are routed, processed, stored, translated, or transposed into other formats (during a given workload cycle) these, in turn, may be used as consumption data for the procurement of forms.
4. A means of validating machine output in accordance with the format specifications.

This package is organized so that it can be broken down into the appropriate operating or supervisory units of the system.

DD310—PREPARE HUMAN ENGINEERING SPECIFICATIONS

This activity "flushes out" plans which were developed earlier in P050—Prepare Personnel Subsystem Plan. During this activity, detailed human engineering specifications are prepared for all operations in the system, including both people and equipment. In general, these specifications will cover the following matters:

1. Construction and arrangement of the facilities to maximize the efficiency and well being of employees.
2. Specific types and makes of equipment that meet human engineering specifications.
3. Environmental controls (for lighting, temperature, humidity, and so forth).
4. Job performance aids.

The specifications are prepared in a form suitable for direct implementation (i.e., check list, blueprint, and measurements).

DD320—SELECT HARDWARE/SOFTWARE

By this time vendor proposals as requested in activity DD260—Inform Vendors of Hardware/Software Requirements, are available for evaluation. These proposals are analyzed and evaluated in terms of the system performance requirements. Negotiation may occur with the vendors to modify proposals so as to fit the systems requirements more closely. In addition, equipment delivery, installation, and other dates may require further negotiations. Economic analysis of the relative merits of renting and purchasing should be updated.

The purchasing and legal departments should offer their considered criticisms of vendor proposals. Performance demonstrations and tests may be required to ascertain the validity of the proposals. Capabilities which are not proved by test or demonstration should not be considered as valid parts of the proposal.

DD340—DEVELOP OPERATING CONTROL SYSTEM

The operating control system software and hardware configurations and the program logic must be all woven together into a cohesive resource which meets system performance parameters. During this activity all modifications and rearrangements in vendor-supplied operating control systems software are performed. Tables, subroutines, and utilities are interfaced; this is accomplished by elaborate input/output relationship analysis.

This activity will not be finalized at this time but will continue through the implementation and test stage.

DD350—DESIGN DATA BASE SEGMENTS

The objective of this design activity is to establish data sets and segments for the data base which will satisfy the implementation needs. The field, volume, sizes, activity, and distribution data are analyzed to determine the optimum arrangement for serving the system functions within the constraints of the operating control system. They are the management system and system performance requirements. The data sets are determined, labeled, and structured; the segments are determined, labeled, and detailed as to field contents. This design is based on the properties and entities and is developed for the logical data base structure.

DD360—PREPARE IMPLEMENTATION LOGIC STRUCTURE

During this activity the logic structure suited to the implementation is developed. This involves synthesizing and relating the logic structure and its supporting documentation to such things as the implementation data segment design, implementation aspects of common modules, vendor software, utilities, operating control system, data management system, and hardware configuration. All of the logical elements at all levels should be included. This structure should be complete enough to plan coding and testing.

This activity produces implementation logic structures in the form of decision tables, programs, flow charts, and various other types. Included as a part of the documentation are data set descriptions and statistics, logical element structures, and descriptive narratives.

DD370—DESIGN CORRECTIVE PROCEDURES

The objective of this activity is to design procedures for the correction of any fallacious or emergency condition likely to exist. These procedures will apply to such things as software, manual operations, equipment, and site. They will be developed at different levels—that is, procedures affecting all developmental entities will be developed at the system level; those unique to a particular developmental entity, at the entity level.

Several factors enter into the development of corrective procedures, such as the criticality of a particular failure, its effect on completion time, its expected frequency, and the additional cost of developing the corrective procedure itself. On the basis of these factors, estimates are made of support and maintenance requirements, which specify the requisite skill and knowledge levels of maintenance personnel, facilities needed, types of maintenance (central versus local), and the like. Finally, procedures are designed for the positions of support and maintenance.

The primary technique used during corrective procedure design is contingency analysis, which basically asks the question, "What happens if . . . ?" Corrective procedures to handle "if" conditions are documented for the personnel subsystem and built into programs on the software equipment side, where these error conditions are critical enough to merit built-in corrective procedures.

The corrective procedures will include procedures for failure identification, fault isolation, reconstruction, fallback, and recovery.

DD380—PREPARE FACILITIES LAYOUT

In this activity all of the physical requirements for site location and workload that have been previously identified are reviewed. Care should be taken to ensure that the requirements are comprehensive and satisfy all of the system needs. After thorough analysis and evaluation, a design for the physical layout is created.

This design takes the form of a graphic, pictorial view of the physical facilities. It depicts the relationship of machines, people, and communications equipment. Space requirements for supplies, retention of files, and supporting activities are considered. One form of physical facilities design is a common blueprint, showing the location of each desk and other piece of equipment, room sizes, and so forth. Further development of this design will indicate each manual interface on the facilities layout. These interfaces will be checked to ensure that they comply with the human engineering characteristics identified and specified earlier. As more information becomes available, the facilities design and documentation will be updated to reflect such things as specific hardware components by manufacturer and model.

If the company is large enough to have a building and engineering department, this group should be both consulted and involved in the design of the facilities layout. If such a group is not available to the design team, acquiring the services of a consultant group is suggested. This activity is closely related to earlier activity P200—Develop Check List of Conversion or Installation Activities.

DD390—INCORPORATE SAFETY FACTORS IN DESIGN

During this activity design will concentrate on safety assurance throughout the system. By using the techniques and body of knowledge set forth in the discipline of safety engineering, the design and facilities layout should be revised, modified, or accepted by safety engineering people. Also, safety devices (i.e., fire extinguishers, smoke sensors, a sprinkler system, machine guards, etc.) should be built into each of the system components.

DD400—DESIGN PHYSICAL FILE SYSTEM

The objective of this activity is to complete the physical design of the file system (structure, transit, and other data). From vendors' specifications, data statistics, and system simulation results, details for the remaining hardware required for the complete file system are selected. Required data are obtained, and the implementation specifications prepared for the file system aspects of fallback, reconstruction, and recovery. Hardware recommendations provided in earlier phases should be reviewed, and updated information provided. This activity includes gathering all remaining requirements, such as those for the system library, to complete the listing of all secondary storage hardware needs.

DD410—DETERMINE STORAGE NEEDS FOR BOUNDARY AND INPUT/OUTPUT DATA

The objective of this activity is to develop the requirements, layouts, and statistics for data storage needs, such as input, output, and boundary. Data-pass-area data (in-core) are identified. Specifications of all data records and interim data storage designs are completed. Data communications, administration control, and operating control system requirements for the installation are obtained. These data storage needs are summarized for the file system, and associated volume and use statistics are prepared. Data simulation, as required to obtain the optimum secondary storage design for the system to be installed, should be determined and prepared. In addition, storage needs for the operation assurance test file are obtained at this time.

DD420—DESIGN PHYSICAL DATA BASE

The design activity here is to develop optimum allocation and arrangement of the data segment design on the secondary storage devices and to prepare load and control information. The specific techniques will be guided largely by a particular vendor's utility and software specifications if these are chosen. Considerations include the analysis of statistics provided for the data segment design and model simulation results.

The physical design of an optimum data base is still such a new subject that few rules and regulations which are likely to stand the test of time exist at this writing. Therefore, this subject is purposely left open.

DD430—DESIGN DATA BASE CONVERSION LOGIC

During this activity, the record format selected for the conversion subsystem is evaluated against the record format prescribed for the new system data base. This results in the design of the subsystem required to transfer the machine-readable format to the new data base. Utility software may be modified to accomplish the format translation. The logical elements which have been designed to insert control information and construct data call records must be coded and the overall logic assembled into an operational set of machine instructions. During this phase, agreement on testing procedures and control of conversion must be reached between system designers, the configuration control group, user representatives, and appropriate support groups. The logic developed can be tested through the process of constructing a data base, thus concluding this activity.

DD440—PREPARE DETAILED SPECIFICATIONS
FOR EACH LOGICAL ELEMENT

During this activity the detailed specifications are pulled together or developed for each logical element. These specifications will serve as a base for the development of coding and may include the following:

- The data used and their source; the details of calls to the data base will be included.
- The data changed or created and their disposition.
- The layout of the data records and work areas.
- Interface records, internal input and output exhibits.
- Narrative descriptions.
- List of routines used, calls for, to which control is passed.
- Detailed logic documentation.

The decision table is the primary technique for documentation of this type of detailed logic. Decision tables can be used either as units or in small groups.

It is recognized that not all logical processes can be described distinctly in decision table notations, and that on occasion it will be necessary to use one of the following to supplement them:

- Procedural narrative with the statements written in either English or a high-order form of programming language.
- Look-up tables or matrices, exhibits, reference materials.
- Flow chart.

DD450—DEVELOP JOB PERFORMANCE CRITERIA AND ASSESSMENT PROCEDURES

During this activity, a minimum objectively measurable level of job performance is established for each manual position in the new system. As an integral part of this activity, procedures are developed for measuring human performance against the established criteria in terms of quality and quantity of work produced. For both the establishment of the criteria and the assessment procedures developed, position practices and all other related job, task, and work flow information previously assembled in the system should be considered.

DD460—PREPARE SUPERVISORY JOB PRACTICES

During this activity a document is created which delineates the responsibilities and authority in each supervisory job in the new system. The supervisory job practice includes a statement of the resources allocated for accomplishing the objectives of that portion of the system. A section of this practice should provide guidance for accommodating various kinds of contingencies; another section should deal with administrative measurements for the supervisory group.

The supervisory job practice is probably not organized in a task/step fashion, since this format would be inappropriate for supervisory jobs. The supervisory job practice may contain the forms and the display package, including the forms and displays over which the supervisor exercises some control.

DD470—DEVELOP FORCE PROJECTIONS

The objective of this activity is to produce projections of the various types of personnel required, the turnover rates, the replacement actions that will be required on a long-range basis, and the availability of personnel with the appropriate skills in the labor market.

When developed, the major output of this activity is a series of data compilations in formats which may be used for personnel planning. They also represent a complete picture of the actions to be taken regarding the manpower requirements of the new system. Included is a contingency plan, which is a fallback position in the event that the manpower resources are not available in the labor market. The force projection should be comprehensive enough to indicate the planned disposition of displaced personnel as a result of installing the new system.

DD480—DEVELOP LABOR RELATIONS INFORMATION

During this activity all information relating to (a) New positions of the system being implemented, (b) Positions in the current system being revised, and (c) Positions in the current system which will be eliminated must be collected and analyzed to permit timely planning of the company's bargaining position on matters subject to negotiation with labor unions. Mental, educational, and physical prerequisites, human factor constraints such as any mental stress associated with an automated environment, including isolation, and other matters which fall within the scope of collective bargaining (i.e., wages, working hours, working conditions) are included.

This document will be used by the company group responsible for negotiating with the labor union on matters subject to collective bargaining and will serve three purposes:

1. To advise management on all matters pertaining to present contract items which will require new negotiations with the labor union.
2. To provide the labor relations group with advanced planning information for conducting wide surveys in preparation of the company's position on negotiable matters.
3. To provide the operating managers with pertinent information regarding the job requirements of the new information system.

DD490—DEVELOP PERSONNEL PLANNING INFORMATION

In this activity, estimates are made of the kinds and numbers of personnel required. The estimate of the numbers will be considerably more tentative at this stage than the corresponding estimates of skill, knowledge, and aptitude requirements. The former estimate depends on accurate operating statistics, such as volumes, frequencies, and "peaks," whereas the latter can be developed in large measure through reference to the position practices.

Requirements should be listed by functional unit identity; total requirements should be broken down into numbers of employees required for the total test, conversion, and cutover portions of development, as well as those needed for the operational system. New positions in the system should be identified. Exhibits should be included which contain skill and knowledge prerequisites for new positions, as well as any personnel problems encountered during analysis.

Optional groupings of positions into jobs in supervisory structures should be developed. A recommended organizational structure should be developed after considering such factors as the flow of data, operational effectiveness, interfacing with other systems, groupings of functions into a manageable organizational entity, and sphere of control.

The documentation developed will be a tangible product which can be used to assess the capacity to support personnel requirements from existing resources, to develop plans for procurement and training of additional personnel if necessary, and to commence labor negotiations.

DD500—DETERMINE PERSONNEL RESOURCES

The purpose of this activity is to identify and describe the current company and manpower base from which user personnel will be drawn. Important considerations include the following:

Laws and regulations affecting employees.
Labor relations agreements.
Characteristics of local labor market.
Local personnel policies.
Skills and knowledge of current personnel.
Local training practices.

This information will be used to establish training requirements, plan personnel procurement, validate personnel practices, tailor elements of the training package, and perform many other activities in personnel subsystem development.

DD510—SYNTHESIZE AND EVALUATE POSITION PRACTICES

The objective of this activity is to synthesize the five parts of each position practice into a cohesive whole and to evaluate its relationship with other positions practices. The five parts of a position practice are as follows:

Function flow chart, which portrays all the positions and machine functions making up the system. It shows the flow of work among them and the interactions. This document begins, it will be recalled, as the initial function flow chart from the preliminary design phase, and at the end of the detail design phase will be in completed form.

Position diagram, which depicts the tasks and the order of their accomplishment, plus the major decision points within the position. This is a graphic illustration of the work flow in the position.

Position description, which presents the steps to be performed in each task, using direct, instruction-like statements. It also includes appropriate supporting information, such as warnings or cautions and references to the corrective procedures and exhibits.

Corrective procedures, which outline steps to be followed in dealing with contingencies that are expected on the job. These procedures are separated from the normal procedures so that they are readily available when needed but otherwise are not in the way.

Exhibits, which provide graphic support for the narrative sections. These may include samples of media, pictures of hardware, schematic representations of procedures, and the like. Exhibits are located in the practice in such a way as to best support the work or activities. After the positions are synthesized into whole positions, they are evaluated for consistency, completeness, and understability and are revised and re-edited as needed.

The evaluation of position practices cannot be thorough and exhaustive until worker performance using these practices can be assessed. This means that a training program must be developed and representative workers trained before the practices can be fully validated. However, a "walk through" evaluation of each position design and documentation is essential as early as practicable in the development effort. This type of evaluation will help to reveal inconsistencies and incompleteness in areas where more information is required to finalize the design work. Particular attention should be given to interface requirements between positions in order to ensure an optimally designed work flow.

DD520—DESIGN DATA PASS AREAS

During this activity, the most advantageous means by which records or fields can be passed among or between projects by way of the computer memory core are determined. The requirement can be satisfied by either a common or an individual data pass area. A common data pass area is an area within core that can be shared by many sequentially processed projects for temporary storage of information coming from or going to the outside world, other projects, or the data base. An individual data pass area is an area within core that is shared with two projects or by a project and a data base and is used to pass information only between those two entities.

The result of this activity will be a completed layout document with appropriate references to the projects or logical elements; they include identification of the common or individual data pass areas. This activity will continue throughout the detail design phase, particularly during the period when the operational bundling is being developed.

DD530—PREPARE TEST PLAN

A test plan must be prepared in accordance with established procedures for each level of design to satisfy the specifications established during definition or design activities. This should include the items:

- Desired schedule of results.
- How to evaluate results, that is, criteria to be used.
- Configuration required (core, disk, tape drives, communication facilities, terminals, etc.).
- Volume of test data.
- Duration variable requirements, for example, start with light load and slowly build to saturation point.
- When and how simulation can be used, for example, simulate 50 terminals competing for the same resources.
- Personnel required if unique.
- Training required if unique.

Testing, to be successful, must be planned and scheduled in such a manner that each successive test is meaningful and adds to the information accumulated in prior events. This can be illustrated by saying that testing of the recovery procedures should not receive an intentional disruption but, if one occurs, should follow the disruption to see whether the recovery procedures are workable.

DD540—IDENTIFY RECRUITING, SELECTION,
AND TRAINING REQUIREMENTS

During this activity determinations are made, in collaboration with user groups, as to how the personnel requirements for the project are to be mapped, both in short and in long-range terms. The alternatives to choose from are recruitment, selection from available personnel, provision of training and job aids, or any combination of these three alternatives.

A major output of these determinations is a comprehensive set of training requirements for the system. These are stated as objectives in terms of the number of courses needed, skills and knowledge to be taught in each course, and evaluation techniques to be used.

Training needs are based on an inventory of personnel skills and knowledge. Also, objectives for recruiting and selection must be considered as a part of the overall design for providing the required personnel inventory. It may be that it is cheaper to recruit than to train, or to provide job aids than to train; these alternatives should be carefully considered and tradeoff studies performed as indicated.

DD550—IDENTIFY CONDITIONS AFFECTING ACCEPTANCE TEST

During this activity, the system design group and the users or their representatives meet and agree on all conditions affecting the acceptance test. Analysis of such things as the test plan (DD530) and the other materials developed thus far should result in a plan for an acceptance test agreed to by both parties. The vital conditions affecting this plan are detailed in the acceptance test package, which covers the test schedule, evaluation criteria, and a list of responsibilities associated with the acceptance test. Usually, some independent group such as an internal auditing organization should be involved in the acceptance test and the tests that will precede acceptance. The internal audit group will certify test results to management. All aspects of the conversion should be explored with the users to make certain that the system will operate as specified.

DD560—ENCODE LOGICAL ELEMENTS

This activity involves programming in the traditional sense. Since many good books and articles treat the subject of programming in detail, it will not be treated here. The interested reader should refer to current literature on this subject. It suffices to say here that the encoding is done primarily from the results of activity DD440—Prepare Detailed Specifications for Each Logical Element.

DD570—PREPARE TEST DATA FOR LOGICAL ELEMENT TESTING

As logical elements are encoded, test data should be developed and documented concurrently to ensure that each logical element will receive complete testing. Test data input, whether manually prepared or available in the form of input to a test data generator, should be retained for future use in checking the results of modification to the logical element. Once again activity DD440—Prepare Detail Specification for Each Logical Element, is the primary data source for this activity.

DD580—PERFORM INSTALLATION ACTIVITIES

Implementation of the many activities necessary to ensure successful installation of the system can begin at this time. The primary input for this activity is P200, performed during preliminary design and entitled, Develop Check List of Conversion or Installation activities. Such activities are the following:

- Site preparation and maintenance.
- Hardware and communication requirements and checkout.
- Work force procurement and personnel policy.
- Work force preparation and job definition.
- Supervisory and managerial preparation.
- Organizational and procedural alignment.
- Productivity measurement.
- Labor relations
- Public relations.
- Safety provisions.
- Printing and related (manufacturing) operations.

As one can imagine, user groups in various special organizations, such as engineering and building services, are likely to be involved in this activity. Also, should this activity require the building of a new computer site, considerable lead time will be required.

DD590—PREPARE TEST DATA FOR TRANSACTION PATH TEST

All data required to test every condition processed by the system logic is developed and documented here. Each transaction that can be introduced into the system must be tested from the point of origin to the final termination point or, in other words, from the outer boundary in the input side to the outer boundary on the user or terminal output side.

DD600—VALIDATE TRAINING PACKAGES AND DEVELOP OTHER TRAINING

During this activity, each of the elements of each training package should be validated against the tested and corrected position practice. In general, this validation should ensure compatibility, understanding, consistency, and completeness. The previously designed training programs are developed by formulating training objectives and evaluation procedures. All materials will already have been tried out on groups of subjects in a simulated training environment and revised as necessary.

In addition to the training courses associated directly with the position practices, usually there will be training outlines and instructor materials for the following:

- Courses for instructor personnel.
- Orientation courses for system users.
- Courses for system administration for supervisors and managers.
- Courses for system maintenance and support personnel.

Primary input for this activity will come from activity P240—Develop Training Plan.

DD610—COMPILE/ASSEMBLE

All logical elements are compiled/assembled on the particular machine that will be used for testing. If object code programming is to be used during the testing, corresponding store statements must be added to the source program at the time patches are made so that the program is kept up to date. Recompilation/reassemblies should be performed as often as warranted.

This procedural step would not be necessary if the program were written in actual machine language. However, since this practice is rare today, it is assumed that a high-order language will be used.

DD620—DETERMINE OPERATIONAL BUNDLING REQUIREMENTS

During this activity, the best operational bundling arrangements of programmed modules are developed to meet the requirements of the

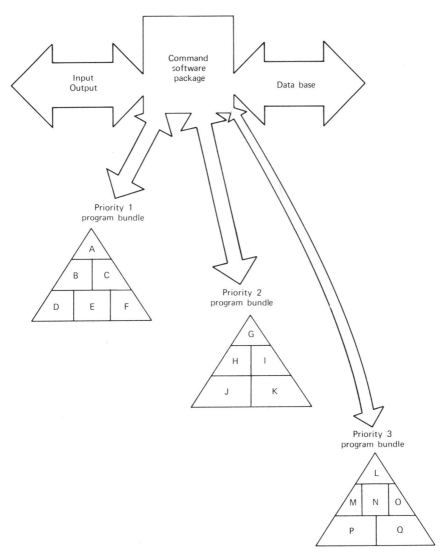

Figure 10-4 *Graphic example of operational bundling of program modules.*

system. If the system is to be implemented on more than one hardware configuration, the bundling arrangements will be the result of analyzing all the information about the various hardware configurations, such as internal timings, transfer times, results of transaction past testing, data base organization, operating schedules, and frequency of access.

Bundling in the program modules was not necessary when most systems were operated on a batch basis; however, on-line, real-time systems require bundled programs. These bundled programs are spatial relationships developed between the bundles and usually accessed by some type of high-order command software.

Considerable inefficiency can result if the bundling is not arranged in an optimal way. Optimizing is primarily controlled by three factors: type of usage of the system, hardware configuration, and the software command language that is used. Mathematical modeling of the system is particularly helpful in selecting the optimal bundling arrangements, (See Figure 10-4).

DD630—DEVELOP TEST BUNDLING ARRANGEMENT

Programmed modules are combined into load modules so that they can be tested. This bundling arrangement may be quite different from that used for the operational system because different objectives are involved. One is testing the individual requirements of the system, whereas the other is performing in the operational environment. Therefore, the requirements for testing the modules may cause quite different bundling arrangements.

Test bundling should allow for testing of the individual components of the system for not only software for programming problems, but also software for command and control language problems, hardware problems, and/or manual preparation problems. The bundling situation that will work best is the one that identifies clearly where a problem occurred and, if possible, what caused it.

DD640—DEVELOP PERFORMANCE AIDS

During this activity, the requirements for performance or job aids are developed. Job performance aids are the materials essential to the efficient functioning of the personnel subsystem. These might include such things as position practices and exhibits of material. Some examples are the following:

• Wall signs indicating safety precautions.
• Placards containing operational instructions for peripheral equipment.
• Lists of input codes attached to remote terminals.

During position and task analysis, various requirements will have been identified for job performance aids over and above the exhibits incorporated into the position practices. Also, some aids may have been prepared during the process of developing training materials. Job performance aids that are properly designed and used can serve the following purposes:

- Assist man by in by indicating what action should be taken.
- Reduce required decisions to a minimum.
- Reduce training time.
- Increase the probability of successful performance.
- Reduce replacement and selection cost.
- Permit the employment and utilization of personnel with lower aptitudes and at lower salaries.

Job performance aids requirements for the system can best be determined if the following steps of logic are followed:

- Determine the need or the desirability of performance aids for the various positions and/or tasks assigned to an employee.
- Determine what the performance aid should do to fill the need of each task for which an aid is identified.
- Create an aid to perform the functions just identified.
- Evaluate the effectiveness of the aid created.
- Coordinate changes in the aid with changes that occur in the system and/or position for which the aid was created. (This is particularly important during the testing phase, for if the aid is not current it may contribute to an error by specifying an incorrect action.)

Performance aids are usually much cheaper and more effective than training, and they reduce training time. Therefore, care and consideration should be exercised in the identification and development of effective job aids.

DD650—VALIDATE PERSONNEL REQUIREMENT

This validation is performed in terms of the required skills and knowledge, aptitudes, and other personnel characteristics that are important for effective work performance. The requirements are based on a review of the position practices, job performance aids, and training materials. This validation should include consideration of workload data, such as input/output volume ranges and anticipated frequency per work week and work month, which were used in determining the number of required positions, and man-hours of nonavailability for the absence rate, which was employed as an add-on factor to cover vacations, sick leaves, and so forth.

Having established the workload data considerations, the incremental requirements for short term (system test) as well as long term (conversion) and the fully operated system should be determined. Also, stresses encountered in the new positions, which are peculiar to the system being implemented, should be compared with those in similar positions which already exist in current systems. This validation is usually accomplished by some form of testing simulation.

DD660—WRITE PRACTICES, INSTRUCTIONS OTHER THAN MANUAL PROCEDURES

During this activity all operational documentation required to maintain and support the system is developed. The resulting products should be validated during the system total tests. The products include facsimiles of the operational formats required for the new information system. These facsimiles should provide sufficient detail to permit the initial ordering of forms as well as reserve quantities.

Each format package will achieve the following:

- Provide a ready reference manual of all forms which are unique to and which interface with the new system.
- Update the training of personnel in manual and support positions.
- Allow the control of forms, thus avoiding duplications of efforts.
- Help to familiarize local managers and supervisors with revised processing or display formats of new information.
- Serve as a guide for supervisors, stressing overall job responsibility and the job performance of personnel under their supervision as a means of defining measurable workload data (i.e., forms which are handled, routed, processed, translated into other formats).

Another important instructional piece of material is a supervisory practice. The status of a supervisor is important and is often misunderstood, especially by the first-line supervisor. To the workers, the supervisor represents management, and it is his business to see that management is represented fairly and that its many, seemingly odd demands on the employees are understood and accepted. His directions must be motivated by wisdom and judgment, rather than by the authority of his job alone. To management, the supervisor represents the worker; only through the supervisor can management perceive the needs and the many problems of the individual employee. Only through him can management learn the good and bad effects of its actions.

The supervisor's job practice should reflect the responsibilities, authority, and activities involved during the supervision of employees assigned to his part of the new system. The practice should also include guidance data for planning and coordinating the programs, projects, and goals of the unit supervisor, as well as an organizational chart depicting his supervisory unit responsibility as related to other parts of the organization. Statement of the unit mission, goals, and/or objectives is mandatory. A mission, it will be recalled, is the end result that an organization is responsible for achieving or producing.

A section on personnel requirements information, indicating the experience, education, training, and like qualifications for individuals within the unit is helpful. Also included would be the policy statements used for selection of employees, discipline, scheduling, overtime, temporary employment, excused absences, individual recognition, reassignment, grievances, safety and health, union relations, and any other unique-to-the-job policies that need specification. It is also necessary to include in the supervisory practice a statement of the authority invested in this job to commit, obligate, and/or expend funds, the amount of limitations, the account categories (capital, expense, etc.), if any, and the limitations on the purposes for which money can be spent. The routine for obtaining approval of expenditures beyond the supervisor's responsibilty should be indicated.

Usually it is worth while to include a section on the use of the company's materials; this will include a narrative statement of the company's maintenance and replacement policies in regard to items of major equipment. Included are procedures concerning acquisitions and maintenance sources. Also, routines to be followed in ordering various materials used by the unit are specified.

All performance of measurements by the unit should be clearly indicated, with explanations as to how they are accumulated, calculated, and depicted.

DD670—PREPARE DETAIL DESIGN REPORT

After all the detail design activities have nearly been completed, and the system design has been agreed upon with the design group and with users, a detail design report can be prepared. In addition to describing the design of the system as it currently stands, the report should highlight any changes introduced during the detail design phase that will have an impact on the planned performance of the system. The detail design report should be reviewed and approved by all organizations involved in the development effort and then submitted to the appropriate levels of management for approval. It is helpful to know that several decisions can still be made: approval for continued development, request for modifications and changes, postponement, or cancellation. Probably the most important audience, in regard to accepting the detail design report, is the user organizations. If they are not fully satisfied at this point, they will surely work against the successful conversion or installation of the system. The detail design report, therefore, is a formal document which requires acknowledgement and approval of the design at this point in time.

The complete detail design spells out the design specifications of the system, the "thing" that will be built and tested.

CHAPTER 11   TESTING PHASE

TESTING PHASE OVERVIEW

Testing the system has always been a rather traumatic process. One of the principal reasons for this trauma is a lack of thorough definition and specification of the system requirements before the testing phase. Therefore, it used to be that one of the first steps in testing was to determine what the test criteria should be. Under the methodology put forth in this book, however, the process of developing test criteria starts in the definition phase and is elaborated on in the preliminary design phase; finally, the detailed quantifications are made in the detail design phase. Therefore, all the tests to requirements are already determined and documented at the time that the test phase is started.

The test phase is not as isolated as each of the other phases. It can be seen, from the activity diagram of the detail design and test phases, (Figure 10-1), that they overlap considerably; testing actually starts halfway through the detail design phase or sooner. The test plan for the sequence of testing and the allocation of resources for the testing was, it will be recalled, developed much earlier.

In order for testing to be accomplished successfully, it has been found that it must proceed from each specific design entity, manual or machine, to successively larger design entities, until one builds up to the system test level. On the program side, this has been known for years as debugging the program. In the days of batch processing this was a relatively straightforward procedure. However, in the multi-processing environment of today, debugging, or testing, has become exponentially difficult. A given program module may work perfectly in isolation, but when interfaced with other programs in a real-time environment it may not work. Because of this exponential difficulty, our methodology for testing must be incremental. To analogize, the initial

159

testing is on a piece/part basis. After each part is proved, subassemblies such as transmissions and differentials are tested. As the subassemblies are proved, subsystems such as the power, braking, and electrical subsystems are tested, finally arriving at system testing.

Throughout this process, a varied diet of valid and invalid data is sent to the entity in test. Therefore, testing is done not only for main line processing, but also for all kinds of error or contingency conditions. It is this part of testing that will "flush out" any interface problems before such large modules have been built that the error condition is difficult to identify.

Test generators will most probably be employed on the EDP side; simulation and modeling, on the personnel subsystem side. The test results, in all cases, are documented; furthermore, the internal audit group or like organization should certify each test result.

T010—LOGICAL ELEMENT TESTING

During this activity, each logical element developed in activity DD440 is tested to see whether it meets design specifications. This testing is usually done first in the form of a desk check; that is, the programmer or encoder checks through the logic of his particular logical element to assure himself it is complete. During compilation and assembly, gross errors may be identified and corrected. This is sometimes called unit testing because it is concerned only with a program unit, which is any functional sequence of source coding that can be compiled and executed as a logical entity. Although the unit need not be a single object module, all units should be as small as possible. After the units are tested and debugged, related units are chained together to verify the logical interfaces between them in preparation for transaction testing. The test data should contain enough variation to exercise all of the logic in each unit. As each program entity is successfully proved, it is so certified and documented.

T020—PERFORM TRANSACTION PATH TESTING

Transaction path testing, the second level of testing performed during the testing phase, begins when the program entities within the transaction path have successfully completed logical element or unit testing. Essentially, a transaction path is a group of program units that constitute a logical processing path for any given transaction. The procedure is for the transactions to enter the system one at a time so that a detailed analysis of each path can be made. Initially, each transaction is allowed to complete before a subsequent transaction is entered. Later, however, as testing progresses, the transaction will be queued, providing a gradual transition to the next level of subsystem testing. Subsystem testing exercises the whole EDP system from the time that the input is encoded into machine-readable form until the hardware is completely done with its portion of the system. The other side of subsystem testing involves all the manual procedures within the system (personnel subsystem testing). Whenever possible, position practices and other manual procedures should be utilized to further satisfy the primary objective of cross checking the manual and EDP interfaces of the system being developed.

Transaction path testing is complete when the following conditions are satisfied:

- All transaction types have been processed successfully.
- Any transactions developed using the position practices produce acceptable results.
- All outputs produced by the system are complete, accurate, and properly interfaced with position practices and meet design specifications.
- All logic and procedural problems have been corrected and are operating according to the design or defined criteria.
- The designers are satisfied that the system is ready for advanced testing.

T030—PERFORM SYSTEM TEST

As is the case with many other developmental activities, the system test is deceptively simple to talk about and very complex to carry out. As the word "system" indicates, this is the test of the whole system, with manual and EDP subsystems integrated for testing purposes. Each system characteristic discussed earlier is tested to its designed limits. System testing starts at the most straightforward, simplistic level and progresses to a bombardment of the system with overloads and bad data. All requirements that have been quantified are now proved. Testing is required because it is a foregone fact that certain things will have been overlooked, and the system test is designed to identify and correct these areas. Procedures for fallback, recovery, and reconstruction are also tested.

Unless system testing is done in a methodical way, one will end up with an awareness of error conditions but with very little knowledge of what caused them or how to correct them. Therefore, it is suggested that the system test should begin with known valid data, processed in a light-load situation. When the problems of handling these data are cleared, more valid data can be introduced for a heavier demand on the system. The testing should be carried out to the extreme number of transactions for which the system was planned. When known valid data are handled correctly in all cases, certain types of known errors are introduced. As each type of error is introduced, an examination is made to see that the system is handling these errors in the designed fashion. When the system can handle all its intended input, whether valid or faulty, as it is designed to, and can accomplish this in the volume for which it was designed, then the major contingencies that can befall the system, such as loss of power, scrambled or lost data, and other types of major malfunctions, must be introduced. If under these conditions the system can perform to its fallback requirements, the system test has been successful.

What is most important is that the successful system test be certified by an independent group, such as the internal audit group, so that the company's resources are protected, users are guaranteed results, and the system design group has officially accomplished its task. Also, the documented test data will be used when the system is in a maintenance mode. System testing is conducted with the same configuration, EDP, EAM, and manual procedures that will be used for the operational system. This testing is usually done in a simulation or modeling environment so that the test results can easily be isolated and the real operations of the company are not affected.

A successful system test will prove three things:

- That the system meets defined and designed performance measures, using the same test data as in transaction path testing, supplemented by new test data if the results of transaction path testing indicate the need.
- That the best bundling arrangement for maximum performance under ideal and controlled conditions to be used in the total test and the operational system has been accomplished.
- That all interfaces (e.g., project to project, man to machine, man to man) are procedurally sound.

T040—PERFORM TOTAL TEST

When system testing is complete, the system should be virtually free of all logic and procedural errors. Therefore, the total test can begin. The objective of the total test is to test for weaknesses not found in lower levels of testing, and to ensure that the system will function as required under conditions as close as possible to those that will be encountered in the operational environment.

The total test may be divided into two parts. The first part, volume testing, should begin with low volumes of group transactions with data from real life. This will be followed by using the same transactions but mixed as each test is successfully completed; the volume should be increased until the saturation level is reached for the different transaction types. The second part is the testing of fallback, recovery, and reconstruction procedures, which must be tested to ensure that they are complete and that no data are lost while they are in effect.

Throughout the total test phase, the system must be evaluated to ensure that reliability, maintainability, control, and security requirements are met. The total test should employ data from the real world; in many cases these are duplicates of the media passing through the old system. The system should not be hurried through the total test phase. The full amount of time required by the thoroughness or completeness of the design should be allowed so that the system can successfully handle all that it was designed to handle. Once again, documentation and certification of the test results are most important to all concerned, and are particularly valuable when the system reaches the support and maintenance phase.

T050—FINALIZE SYSTEM DOCUMENTATION

During this activity, all system design documentation to be included in the permanent system library is updated and entered into the library. Permanent documentation of conversion-oriented activities is also entered into the library. Care should be exercised that all documentation entered into this library has the proper approval and concurrence of all of the design organizations involved. This library will serve as the reference blueprints for the maintenance designers throughout the operational life of the system. The documentation should meet all requirements in regard to symbology, language, qualification, form and indexing.

T060—PERFORM ACCEPTANCE TEST

During this activity, the system is established in a portion of the live environment in which it will operate. The acceptance test must verify four things for the user:

- The procedures operate in the live environment at their designed performance criteria.
- The procedures are performed according to the objectives.
- The integrity of all data is maintained and controlled.
- The personnel operating in the live environment are sufficiently trained.

Performance of an acceptance test with the user groups involved is an activity that has too often been overlooked in the past. It is important not only to user acceptance, motivation, and understanding, but also as a final live environmental test of the validity of the system. There will probably be disagreements between the design organization and the using organizations as to what constitutes the meeting of requirements. These disagreements should be arbitrated by an independent organization, such as the internal audit group. Review of the acceptance test performance figures should involve the higher levels of management in both groups.

Usually, the acceptance test is not performed on the total scope in which the system will operate, but rather on a more limited basis, such as a particular district or geographic area which is representative of the whole. Care must be exercised that the representative area selected has all known conditions associated with it. This will be a matter of negotiation between the design organization and the using organizations.

As a result of a successful acceptance test, responsibility for system success is transferred from the design organization to the using organizations. Therefore, budgeted funds, manpower, and performance measurements of the system will become the responsibility of the using organization. Hence the user's voice, as to what constitutes acceptance of the system, should have more weight than that of the design organization.

T070—PREPARE TEST REPORT AND PROGRESS FOR REVIEW AND APPROVAL

Up to this point, the new system has not affected the company's profit and loss statement except for the developmental funds associated with the project. It has not affected the live operations of the company or customers in any significant way. If the system goes into the conversion phase, however, it will affect both profit and customer service. Therefore, before conversion can start, approval by upper management must be sought. In order for management to make this decision a comprehensive test report must be prepared.

This report indicates in detail how the system meets its designed and defined specifications. It indicates what tolerances are built into the system and gives maximum and minimum performance levels. Included are such subjects as accuracy, quantity, time frame, volume frequencies, and error rates. When the report is prepared, it will be concurred on by the system design organization and the using organizations. Again, it will be certified by some independent organization, such as the internal audit group.

The implementation plan for how the system is to be converted will, of course, be a part of the test report. This plan, it will be recalled, was developed earlier. With management acceptance of the test report, the responsibility for operation of the system passes from the system design group to the using organization, and conversion can start.

CHAPTER 12   CONVERSION PHASE

CONVERSION PHASE OVERVIEW

Anyone who has been associated with development of computer-based systems for the last several years will recognize that the conversion phase is probably the most traumatic. Traditionally, it requires a kind of weekend-and-nighttime dedication in order to be accomplished. Unforeseen difficulties crop up at an increasing rate as the computer hangs up, files are damaged, tempers become short, and the hours seem endless. Frequently, large clerical groups of people are required to correct and re-enter data during the conversion phase. Records purification and conversion to mechanized form exceed all estimates of time and money required. The training package is usually not complete, and people are guessing what procedures they should use for the new system.

If one has followed the discipline outlined in this text, most of these problems will have been anticipated and designed for. The conversion phase is concerned with putting the fully tested system into operation. It usually involves the creation of new machine-readable records, the training of operating personnel, the installation of new hardware, and the implementation of new procedures. Conversion ends when the design becomes a real system which can be observed in operation. As mentioned earlier, "conversion" and "installation" are sometimes used interchangeably, but they are not synonomous terms. "Conversion," as used here, means to change from one system to another. "Installation" denotes setting up a system for the first time. Conversion involves phasing out the old system and phasing in a new one. Installation implies the installation of a system where none existed before. In both cases, careful planning, design, and organization are necessary.

The conversion subsystem, it will be recalled, started in the preliminary design phase (actually, there was a look at the conversion implications in the formation of objectives phase). Conversion must be done in such a way that the company continues to operate without a serious business setback.

The techniques employed in the development of the conversion subsystem are the same as those used for the development of any system. The close relationship between the conversion subsystem and the total system and the effects that one has on the other must always be taken into consideration. It is possible that system objectives may have to be changed because of conversion problems.

RESPONSIBILITY FOR CONVERSION

The development of a conversion subsystem is the responsibility of the systems development group. Because of the nature of the effort, however, the using organization which will assume responsibility for the operation of the new system must be consulted early and often during the development of the conversion plan.

The conversion itself is the joint responsibility of the using organizations and the systems design organization. The system design group will be working toward achievement of the development objectives of the subsystem and will provide guidance and counseling to the using organizations. Because of its intimate knowledge of both the system and the developmental objectives, the system development group will assume the dominant role, especially during the early part of the conversion phase.

The principal activities conducted by the system development group during the conversion phase are heavily oriented toward training both managers and workers in the using organizations. Often, however, more than training will be required. The members of the using organizations will be called upon to change their work habits and, in some cases, their whole approach to the job. The conversion process can be a period of fear, anxiety, and frustration for these people. Relieving these fears, anxieties, and frustrations by anticipating them and taking necessary action whenever symptoms occur is important to successful conversion. A significant contribution can be made by keeping the user organization's management well informed of what it can expect from the very beginning of the conversion.

A direct responsibility for the development of the conversion processes will often lie with a group that is not directly responsible for the design of the total system. This has several advantages; the conversion design subsystem group will have to study the existing systems to much greater depth of detail than will the total system group. More importantly, separation of responsibility in this way will reduce the possibility that unwarranted tradeoffs may be made in the interest of conversion.

CONVERSION CONSIDERATIONS

There are many things which must be considered and designed in developing and executing the conversion subsystem. It is helpful to keep in mind that this subsystem has the same characteristics as the total system, that is, there are certain inputs, processes, outputs, control procedures, dynamics, and so forth. The processes which are unique to conversion deal mostly with changing records, content, form symbology, data base, input, and output. Figure 12–1 graphically depicts the major conversion activities. Training certainly will be a part of the conversion activity. Training and machine programs for the processes involved in the conversion of records are specifically designed for and used only during the conversion phase. The manpower required for

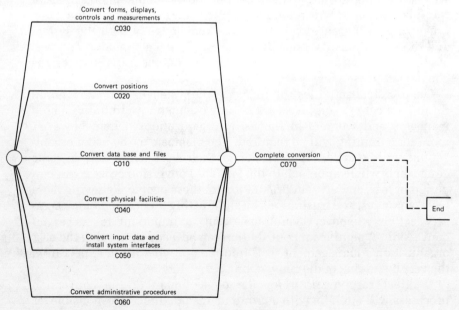

Figure 12-1   *Activity network for the conversion phase.*

each part of the conversion process will, of course, be considered by the conversion subsystem development manager. However, the conversion subsystem development group must also give attention to personnel demands that will be placed on the line organization during the conversion process, so that the proper people can be identified, recruited, and trained.

The conversion subsystem development group is responsible for the scheduling of the whole conversion process. This is done in conjunction with the using organization when the system is a large one and involves several interdepartmental interfaces. This situation can be especially difficult, since the requirements of all departments must be considered to ensure a smooth, harmonious workload. Certain techniques such as PERT and critical path scheduling are very useful in controlling this process.

Records purification, which was addressed earlier, is often one of the main problems associated with conversion. Whenever practicable, machines should be used to accomplish the records purification. Machines are more precise then people on repetitive functions, and they will not introduce many new errors. When people are used for records purification, double verification should be employed to reduce human error.

SUCCESSFUL CONVERSION

A successful conversion recognizes and prepares for situations that will exist when the last vestiges of the old system have been eliminated and the new system is fully operational. Some of the considerations to ensure a smooth conversion and successful operation early in the life of the system include the following:

- The using organization must be involved early, and the ideas generated therein should be carefully considered.
- The using organization should be kept informed of the direction of the design; new concepts should be introduced to its people as they are generated.
- Well-designed and thoroughly documented manual procedures must be provided.
- Training must be provided early enough to ensure readiness by the conversion date.
- Conversion subsystem routines must be planned well in advance of the actual conversion date.

Preparation and involvement on the part of the using organization are essential to successful conversion.

C010—CONVERT PHYSICAL FACILITIES

During this activity, the physical facilities are constructed or transformed according to the design requirements for the new system. Included are not only the traditional site preparation type of activities, but also such factors as the following:

- Hardware and communications procurement and checkout.
- Work force procurement and personnel policy.
- Work force preparation and job definition.
- Supervisory and managerial preparation.
- Organizational and procedural realignment.
- Productivity measurement.
- Labor relations.
- Public relations.
- Safety and morale provisions.
- Printing and related manufacturing operations.

All of these activities were started during the preliminary design phase, as activities P150, P170, P190, P200, P230, and P240. It will be recalled that the facilities layout was prepared during detail design in activity DD380.

C020—CONVERT DATA BASE AND FILES

This activity also was started during the preliminary design phase. Activity P170 was further amplified during the detail design and test phases (see activities DD100 and DD430). During this activity, the control type of information required by the data base design and data management techniques being employed must be inserted into the transformed records as the conversion procedures and logic are performed. The live records are placed in the data base as prescribed. Once the data base has been established, and the files purified and converted, this activity concludes with the updating of the data base and files with transactions that have accumulated to date. The importance of this data base cannot be overstressed; enough data must be used to create the anticipated operational conditions.

C030—CONVERT FORMS, DISPLAYS, CONTROLS, AND MEASUREMENTS

During this activity, all forms and displays are instituted. Care should be exercised to see that old forms are withdrawn from the system flow. Also, during this activity, the new controls and various types of measurements are put into use. These controls and measurements relate primarily to the parameters required to ensure system reliability, maintainability, and security. They will provide the using organization with the tools necessary to manage the system and to determine where and when something is outside design tolerences. Again, the activities which are implemented here started much earlier in the system design process.

C040—CONVERT INPUT DATA AND INSTALL SYSTEM INTERFACES

In this activity, the procedures previously developed to prepare current data for the new system, and to interface the system with the existing systems, are put into the operation. These procedures must be functional before the time when the new system is finally converted.

These procedures relate primarily to the boundaries of the system, both on the initial input side and on the terminal output side. They ensure that information is captured near the source and is, if designed that way, in machine-readable form; also they ensure that the terminal output of the system arrives at its destination in usable form with the prescribed quality and timeliness specified.

The term "system interfaces" also refers to the boundaries of the new system, and its interaction with other systems, in receiving information from or passing information to other systems. This procedure of converting input data and system interfaces is another of the problem areas that has not received sufficient attention in the past. Therefore, systems have experienced considerable difficulty during conversion because of faulty or improperly prepared input or ill-defined system interfaces.

C050—CONVERT ADMINISTRATIVE PROCEDURES

During this activity, all procedures to control the operational system, such as scheduling, setting priorities, and implementing personnel policies, are started. These administrative procedures are instituted under the jurisdiction of the using, line organization. The supervisory job practices developed earlier serve as the primary vehicle for communicating these responsibilities to first- and second-level management people. Administrators will be trained in all of the control and measurement functions of the system. They will be provided with routines for various kinds of contingencies, including procedures for degraded system performance during fallback or recovery mode. All deficiencies which are recognized during conversion will be reported through the administrative procedures back to the responsible system design organization. The purpose here is not to fix blame, but rather to see that deficiencies are recognized early and that corrective actions are taken.

In any well-designed system there would be training for persons on the management level regarding their functions, their spans of control, their organizational assignments, delegation of authority, and unity of supervision. Furthermore, they would receive training and documentation concerning personnel policies for selection, discipline, scheduling, overtime, temporary employment, leaves of absence, excused absences, individual recognition, reassignment, grievance procedures, safety and health, union relations, and any other unique policies for the new systems.

Most importantly, supervisors would be trained to understand the performance measurements for which they will be held accountable. They should be taught how this information is gathered, manipulated, and depicted to their management. They should be given a clear understanding of the relative importance of each of these measurements, and, finally, they should recognize what their contributions mean to the success of the overall system.

C060—CONVERT POSITIONS

During this activity, all personnel who will be operating the new system during its initial installation or in full operation are trained. All affected personnel must be given a clear understanding of not only the new positions, but also the old positions which will remain in effect during the conversion phase. As a result of this activity, the involved personnel must be able to operate the system in both the conversion and live operational environments.

Personnel will be trained to a predetermined performance level for their positions in the new system. The training will most probably be done by incremental training programs. The employees will be given an overview of what the system accomplishes, and how it accomplishes its objectives. They will receive specific training in the media functions and performance criteria of their particular tasks. The training will be done from materials which are prepared and based primarily on the position practices. This training may be in the form of classroom work, programmed instruction, computer-assisted training, or multimedia training. Hopefully, the training materials will recognize the entering repertoires of skills and knowledge possessed by the people to be trained.

Qualitative and quantitative criteria pertaining to the results of the task being performed (e.g., how accurate, how much output per hour, what quantity) are established as performance requirements. For example, it may be decided that an error clerk must be able to process an average of 235 rejects per day.

The conversion of the positions is generally accomplished by means of a training package which consists of five elements. The first is a position practice, which describes how to perform a manual position or function within the system. Each practice normally has the five sections described under Activity DD510.

The second element of the training package is the training objectives—a set of course objectives that describe in behavioral terms what the student will be able to do after the course is completed. These are stated in terms of the nature and quantity of performance expected. They are used to familiarize the student with what he is to learn to do in the course.

The third element of the training package is the course materials. These materials include training aids to be used in the actual instruction of the employees. They also give the sequence in which the training materials should be presented for most effective learning.

The fourth element of the training package is a performance examination. This is a mastery test to be used in determining whether the student can successfully perform on the position and the tasks for which he has been trained. In some cases, this may be a written test; in others, practical exercises or case work problems are provided.

The fifth element of the training package is an instructor's guide to be used by the instructor in order that the training may be effective. This will contain test answers, training strategy, and recommendations on the training environment and the use of the training materials. The elements of the training package should be developed with the specific training strategy for the position concerned in mind, and with a view toward providing an appropriate learning experience, one that will enable the employee to meet the training objectives for his position.

This strategy is reflected in detail in the instructor's guide for each training package. It is important that the training specified should be followed in each case so that the student is taught job action and acquires a knowledge of the subject in the context of a realistic environment. The instructor's guide should also contain information on recommended class size (maximum), the use of audiovisual devices, recommended training methods, methods of testing, and other guidance information which will assist the instructor in qualifying the employee to perform on the position in question.

C070—COMPLETE CONVERSION

Usually a conversion of a large system is accomplished in incremental stages, rather than as a flash cutover. This activity, then, recognizes the need for an incremental type of approach to conversion. After the first area of company operation has been successfully converted, the schedule for subsequent conversion can begin. This, of course, will be a repetition of all the activities cited earlier for the conversion of the initial site. Therefore, there will be more data base conversions, more sites to prepare, more training, and, perhaps, more system interfaces. This activity will probably continue until all the intended operations of the company are converted to the new system. Any enhancements or changes to the system found to be necessary due to subsequent conversions should be carefully evaluated and then documented in the formal reference library.

CHAPTER **13**   OPERATION PHASE

OPERATION PHASE OVERVIEW

The operation phase is not a part of the development process per se. However, it must be recognized that the operation phase exists, because during this phase there is considerable wear and tear on the system. The system dynamics are put into play; there will be personnel turnover, additional requirements placed on the system, changes in the environment in which the system operates, alterations in the system interfaces with other systems, and other types of performance stresses. Unless these conditions are recognized and accommodated, the system performance will be seriously degraded. It is for these reasons that there needs to be an evaluation and support phase and a maintenance phase in the system life cycle.

OPERATION PHASE DISCUSSION

No activity network description of what happens during an operation phase is given here because it would be artificial and of questionable value to create one. Furthermore, this book is more interested in the development of a system. The operation of an ongoing system is a traditional management kind of responsibility. How to manage successfully has been treated very well in many other books; therefore, the techniques and procedures for managing the on-going operation of the system will not be discussed in detail here. It is important that procedures have been established, along with the control and administrative measurements of the system, to feed back to the design maintenance group any implications of problems with the system. Problems arise for all the reasons mentioned above and must be clearly identified and accommodated or the continued success of the system is in jeopardy.

175

One of the major operational problems of computer-based information systems has been a continual demand to change and upgrade the hardware EDP configuration. This has resulted from the fact that computer manufacturers were able throughout the 1960s to introduce newer, faster, and, in some cases, less expensive equipment to the market. Generally speaking, management was anxious to take advantage of these possible savings. Changing hardware and software every few years caused a considerable amount of upheaval in EDP operations throughout industry.

By the late 1960s computer manufacturers had advanced the state of the art in regard to the hardware for computer-based systems to the point where more power and versatility were available than industry could use. In spite of the advances in hardware and software, few honest real-time interactive systems were in existence at the end of the 1960s. Also, few corporate computer-based models were then in existence. It can truthfully be said that most systems were overpowered in the hardware sense at that point in time. Most of the systems used in industry were still actually linear or batch systems which had had their files and programs converted to run in an emulation mode on the new equipment. This was wasteful but perhaps inevitable, as the skill and knowledge to take full advantage of the new hardware and software packages did not yet exist in the design area. Probably the most sophisticated application using the full capabilities of the hardware and software then available was the space program.

In industry, management's problem was one of a technological catch-up. This was a serious problem for many reasons, including the following:

- Colleges and universities were not in a position to teach the required skills and knowledge.
- Computer manufacturers, while having skill and knowledge to build these sophisticated hardware systems, did not possess the corresponding know-how to build the type of systems which were required by industry; therefore their educational groups tended to teach the portion of the subject they knew best, and this did not fill the bill.
- People who had learned the computer trade during the first and second generation of hardware became obsolete. They found it increasingly difficult to make the transition to the more complex world of multiprocessing and real-time design. Many of these older designers had moved into areas of responsibility and authority for the design of new systems, and unfortunately they served as deterrents to the advancement of the technology.

- The methodology for the development of a complex computer-based system was, in the late 1960s, still a somewhat ill-defined art form. Little industrial research had been done on how the process should take place.
- The cost of the new high-powered equipment was such that few companies were willing to use it for experimentation in trial-and-error type of design.

For these reasons, the problem of design know-how became the most critical one to be solved by industry as it moved forward into the 1970s. Nor is this problem likely to be solved completely in the immediate future. Because developing complex systems is an interdisciplinary effort, requiring a new style of management and a blend of various skills, it will probably be some time before this part of the management process has been mastered.

This brief discussion of design problems is appropriate during the operation phase because they can cause untold grief and trauma in making a system operational or even in trying to keep it operational. The operations side of system work has shown several marked trends. Some of these are as follows:

- There has been a centralization of computer facilities in order to use larger and more complex computers. This was made possible and, in some cases, practical by the use of telecommunications gear from remote sites in order to take advantage of personnel who had acquired some on-the-job knowledge of how to run the computer site.
- A further need for centralization of the operations of the computer itself became evident.
- There was a move away from the accounting type of system (e.g., payroll, purchasing, or disbursements) toward a more operational type of system which effected current inventory, financial algorithms, and work-force scheduling.
- There was also a trend to make computer operation a kind of job shop, rather than part of overall system design. This was caused by using computers in a fragmented way; that is, they were to compile, sort, list, print and so forth, without becoming an integral part of the various systems in which they were being used. As a result many operations groups worked much like small tool and dye shops, with hundreds or thousands of small jobs passing through for some bits of either EAM or EDP work. A good part of this work would not have been passed through the mechanization effort if its cost had been known. Generally speaking, this was not a cost-effective way to operate.

- There was considerable growth at this time in various kinds of service organizations for processing. These ranged from independent organizations which would process data for rent, to organizations that would "design and program" an individual mechanization project, to various kinds of trouble shooting performed by management consultant and/or accounting firms.
- There was a trend toward a 24-hour-a-day computer operations group, operating 7 days a week. The theory was that a busy computer is a money making computer; hence, while all the rest of the operations of a company were shut down, the EDP department continued to grind out forms, paychecks, lists, and reports. This was caused in part by the way in which rental fees were established for the use of computers. Time has shown this scheduling to be of questionable value.
- There was also a trend to simplify the computer console operator's job by using various kinds of command and control language and software packages. The computer was used to schedule itself and the EAM operations around it.

With the business recession of the early 1970s, there was considerable concern in industry about the amount of money directed toward EDP operation. Many firms curtailed their plans for more computer systems. Many companies cut back on what they were then doing in computer operations in an effort to save money. In fact, in the minds of many chief executives, a whole rethinking of the computer process was required. Some overreacting executives threw out their computers in the interest of austerity and "better control" of their companies. The topic of conversation at executive luncheons was no longer what new computer had just been installed but ways and means of controlling expenses and cutting down on operational costs. It was natural, therefore, that poorly understood computer operations came in for considerable questioning. Also, the fact that computer applications were so poorly known, or were notorious money losers, caused industry to start to proceed more cautiously toward further utilization of computers. This was actually healthy. There had been approximately 20 years in which to learn how to use computers effectively during an era of considerable business expansion and inflation. In most businesses, very little accountability existed. Both "feasibility reports" and marketing programs by the various computer vendors could not have survived very close scrutiny. Many people who passed themselves off as various types of professionals within the system design world were merely pretenders; therefore, it was right and healthy for management to take a closer look at what computers and mechanization were actually contributing to business.

Adding to the confusion at this point were horror stories about computer sabotage, breached security, and massive errors or failure. Many multimillion-dollar efforts by various companies were aborted before they were completed.

The era of the catch words and elaborate but ill-defined plans for bigger systems was over. Operation groups began to look for new performance measurements to justify their existence within the corporation. Higher management was now saying, "Speak to me in terms of increased profit, better service, or improved managerial control. We are tired of hearing about potential and how great the benefits will be some day."

Another factor completely external to the computer room itself was also being felt at this time. This was the public's reaction to something it did not understand and exercised no control over—large computer-based information systems. There existed, at this time, fear and anxiety about having one's life be part of a large computerized data base, either in governmental organizations or in industry. Some fair-size student outbursts directed against the computer installations on various campuses caused considerable concern in government and industry. Program theft and unauthorized use of time-sharing computers became the themes of new scare stories. Security and control of internal files and records became almost a nightmare, particularly on real-time systems.

THE FUTURE OF OPERATIONS

The direction for future operations is toward dedicated computers as a part of large corporate systems. These will probably be located in certain secure, centralized locations. Data will be brought to the system and information taken from it by means of teleprocessing. Many smaller businesses will give up their EDP ventures in favor of using skilled service bureaus on a time-sharing basis. The way of the future indicates that these computer service types of companies will lead the way and pioneer in the use of new techniques. They will not be hidebound by all the organizational tradition that has kept EDP departments from functioning as smoothly as they might in many businesses. These service organizations will recruit personnel vigorously from the best that industry, research firms, and the campus have to offer.

Most operating EDP departments will find that a major portion of their problems are system design problems and are not of the operation departments' own making. They will make these findings abundantly clear to their management, thus taking the heat off operations and putting it on the designers of the computer-based systems. In this way, the operations groups will move out from under the domination of system design and become masters of their own destinies. They will require thorough documentation and certified testing of an entire system before accepting its conversion for their operation. They will demand that higher standards of reliability, maintainability, security, and control be designed into the system. This will cause systems to grow at a decreased rate, and most of the hectic pace and even frenzy associated with the late 1960s and early 1970s will be replaced by orderly and prescribed routines.

CHAPTER 14

EVALUATION PHASE AND
SUPPORT AND
MAINTENANCE PHASE

EVALUATION PHASE OVERVIEW

The evaluation phase and the support and maintenance phase are two
closely related system phases that come into play only after the system
has become operational. They continue for as long as the system exists.
Evaluation provides a continuing measurement of system performance
against the defined and designed requirements. Support and maintenance uses the information generated through evaluation to keep the
system performance within acceptable limits.

It is possible to confuse the concepts of evaluation with the process
of testing. Both are concerned with how well the system meets its
performance specifications. Testing, however, occurs before conversion and is part of the development process necessary to make the
system operational. Testing is acccomplished as a part of the development process to determine where the system fails to meet performance
specifications so that necessary adjustments can be made. Evaluation is
conducted on the operational system and is designed to determine how
well it continues to meet performance specification, and to determine
the effects of both internal and external environmental changes. Tests
are conducted under simulated and real conditions in order to predict
the performance of the system under actual operation. Because of the
pressures of economics and practicality, however, testing can only
approximate the actual conditions of operations.

Evaluation, on the other hand, is concerned with data from the real
system. It provides the information necessary to determine when the
system needs to be repaired, when a part must be replaced, whether a
major redesign is necessary, or whether a new major development

181

effort is required to meet changing demands. Data from the evaluation phase are the stimuli which initiate the support and maintenance activities or, in some cases, a new system development effort. There is probably no sharp line of demarcation between large-scale support and maintenance activities and small-scale system development activities. Both demand attention to all phases of system development, and both can involve the changing of objectives. Because support and maintenance are concerned with the operational system, provisions for their performance must be designed into the system as it is developed.

System evaluation is intricately tied to many of the subjects discussed earlier. Sometimes it may be difficult to distinguish system operation from evaluation, since many evaluative processes are designed into and integrated with other system processes. The evaluative criteria identified in the definition, preliminary design, and detail design phases are built into the system to provide continuous monitoring of important functions and to indicate when repairs or adjustments are required.

A loose analogy would be the various evaluative instruments that are built into automobiles. They provide ongoing monitoring of the well-being of the oil pressure system, temperature system, electrical system, and so forth. In the same way, the performance measures built into the system for administrative purposes also serve as evaluative criteria. The design documentation tells what the system should do; evaluation tells what it is doing. A comparison of the two may show that system performance is not up to design standards. The examination of this situation and efforts to correct it are called support and maintenance activities. One may think of support and maintenance activities as a sort of a system which usually has a related set of performance criteria and objectives such as the following: allowable downtime for preventive maintenance, limits on downtime for isolation and correction of malfunctions, and the portion of the system that must always be operational (particularly if there is a backup system).

It is easy to see the complex nature of the relationships among these ideas, from the development of the performance specifications, to built-in evaluation of these, to support and maintenance to keep system performance within design tolerance.

METHODS AND DEVICES FOR EVALUATION

Many evaluative techniques and devices for evaluation must be developed in order to protect the well-being of a large, complex system. And they must provide a means to compare what the system is doing with what it should be doing. These should be designed into the system to the greatest extent possible during its development. Some criteria specify the kinds of data that must be accumulated, and these in turn suggest the symbology and form. Among the many means available to secure evaluative data are the following:

- Reports, usually accumulated reports concerning system cost, productivity, quantity, quality, and utilization, may be generated by either the computer or manual controlling procedures.
- Meters can give useful data concerning the operation of certain types of system components, or utilization, or rate of processing.
- Check lists can be used to ensure completeness of information and to take sensitive readings at certain points in the systems. Osciloscopes and similar types of electronic measuring devices attached to the computer can provide measurements of circuit performance.
- Interviews can provide verbal feedback and can be designed to minimize subjective reactions.

The actual means and processes used for evaluation are derived from the nature of the system to be controlled. The form, organization, and kinds of measurements dictate, to a large extent, the type of information and the devices required for evaluation.

The concept of control, which was identified in Chapter 1 as a characteristic of the system, has a close relationship with evaluation. Detecting and correcting errors is a function of control. Measuring the number of errors and the amount of variation is a part of evaluation. Another characteristic identified earlier was system dynamics; both internal and external dynamics were discussed. It is generally external dynamics which cause the major problems in evaluation, whereas the internal dynamics of the system are responsible for the day-to-day type of evaluation. One must remember that the system is like a living thing; it changes as the environment around it changes. Therefore, no matter how well the system is designed, it will need evaluation, support, and maintenance.

EVALUATION WHEN IT HAPPENS

Evaluation actually starts on the first day of conversion or installation and continues throughout the life of the system. The more formal aspects of evaluation, however, are probably not in full play until the system is completely converted and is in operational mode. Some

184

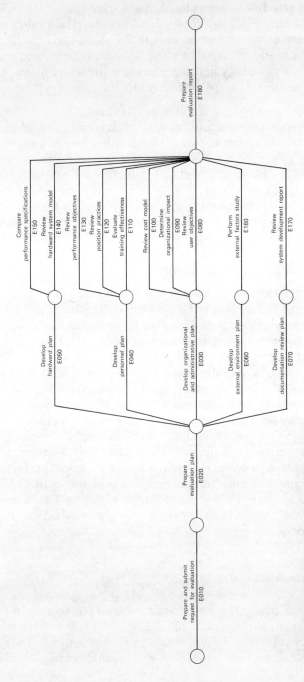

Figure 14.1 Activity network for the evaluation stage.

Prepare and submit request for evaluation
E010

Prepare evaluation plan
E020

Develop organizational and administrative plan
E030

Develop personnel plan
E040

Develop hardward plan
E050

Develop external environment plan
E060

Develop documentation review plan
E070

Review user objectives
E080

Determine organizational impact
E090

Review cost model
E100

Evaluate training effectiveness
E110

Review position practices
E120

Review performance objectives
E130

Review hardward system model
E140

Compare performance specifications
E150

Perform external factors study
E160

Review system development report
E170

Prepare evaluation report
E180

evaluation is routine and can be put on a time schedule, such as preventive measurements and periodic checkups for wear and tear. Other maintenance does not fall into any prescribed time frame and is dependent on conditions wholly outside the control of the system (e.g., changing government regulations, new products or services, changing organizational structure, and a different economic environment).

Broadly speaking, then, evaluation occurs after the fact, that is, after design and conversion are complete. It also occurs before the fact, before support and maintenance activities take place.

EVALUATION—WHO DOES IT?

The responsibility for the evaluation phase is probably best shared. Primary responsibility for ongoing evaluation lies with the using organization. Secondary responsibility for evaluation probably rests with some staff organization that has the time and the training to deal with the problem areas. These people determine the nature of the problem, the probable causes, and the appropriate actions that merit investigation. Such a group might be a quality control, an internal audit, or possibly a product assurance group. In any case, its members should be thoroughly familiar with and have access to all the design documentation on the system. They should also enjoy an excellent rapport with the using organization and its management. They will need to work in close liaison with the system support and maintenance group. Figure 14–1 portrays the activity sequence during this phase.

E010—REPAIR AND SUBMIT REQUEST FOR EVALUATION

Upon completion of the system, and periodically throughout its life span, the need for evaluation will arise. Some of the conditions creating this need are as follows:

- The necessity to quantify and qualify the impact of newly converted systems upon the working environment and to determine the efficiency of the system development effort in terms of user and corporate satisfaction.
- A performance analysis requirement triggered by a degraded system performance trend.
- Significant or unplanned changes in the system environment which affect user activities.

- Significant or unplanned changes in the external environment which affect system performance or objectives.
- Top management system status requirements. A request for formal evaluation may be submitted from any point in the using organization and should contain sufficent information to make the following determinations:

    a   Should corporate resources be committed to an evluation study?

    b   How do the conditions motivating the request impact on the system environment?

The request for evaluation must contain the following information:

- A general description of the originator's involvement with the system.
- A general description of the conditions that motivated the request.
- A quantitative and qualitative account of the factors characteristic of the motivating conditions.

The appropriate staff evaluation group will assist the originator in preparing the request. If the request for a formal evaluation of the system is approved, the following activities will take place.

E020—PREPARE EVALUATION PLAN

Generally two types of evaluating plans can be developed: a total or formal evaluation, and a partial or informal evaluation. A formal evaluation involves analysis of the total system and usually occurs for the first time shortly after system conversion. An informal evaluation involves analysis of a subsystem or group of subsystems.

An evaluation team prepares an evaluation plan consisting of the following elements:

- The type of evaluation to be performed.
- The time schedule and resource allocations required to complete the study.
- The area subsystem or subsystems to be evaluated.
- The specific objectives of the study efforts.

The evaluation team should establish the appropriate parameters of the evaluation study in terms of the following areas:

- Hardware, software, terminals, and network, that is, the machine aspects of the system.

- Personnel and training subsystems.
- Organizational and/or administrative impact.
- External environment.
- Development effort.

An informal evaluation consists of analysis of one or more of these areas. A formal evaluation covers all areas. The evaluation plan should be reviewed by the originator of the request and by appropriate management levels of approval.

E030—DEVELOP ORGANIZATIONAL AND ADMINISTRATIVE PLAN

During this activity, the evaluation group concerns itself with the effect of the system on the organizational structure and administrative procedures of the company. A plan should be developed to highlight the specific area of evaluation. The following activities must be included:

- A review and update of the system cost model.
- An analysis of how well the system meets its user objectives in quantified terms.

Other questions for consideration are these:

- Will the system facilitate or accommodate logical changes in the organizational structure?
- Does the system facilitate better interdepartmental or other inter-group relationships, communications, and so forth?
- How well does the system interact with the specific related administrative procedures?

E040—DEVELOP PERSONNEL PLAN

During this activity, a plan is developed to evaluate the personnel subsystem side of the system, which includes such areas as terminal and computer operating training and performance, work location layout, user and provider activities, and all other activities involving human beings as components of the system.

Generally, the plan considers three areas of concern:

- The behavior of individuals as they interact with the system in terms of performance, satisfaction, and motivation.
- The operational position practices, training packages, informational

materials, work layout, and human engineering (including forms design).
- The effectiveness of human orientation and adaptation to the system design.

E050—DEVELOP HARDWARE PLAN

During this activity, the evaluation group develops a plan to evaluate the hardware aspects of the system, which include such areas as all hardware at the site location, main frame, peripheral equipment, remote terminals, and all network and related communication equipment; all software and control programs; and any other mechanical or machine elements.

The plan contains a precise itemization of the aspects of the machine side of the system that are to be evaluated. In preparing the plan, it is assumed that the evaluation team will have collected sufficient data to provide a quantitative description of the conditions creating a need for evaluation.

A short illustrative list of items for evaluation might include:

- Rerun the hardware system model, varying certain conditions within the design parameters.
- Review the control monitor reports pertaining to input/output buffers, throughput, and transaction time.
- Review the system performance specifications regarding the central processing unit downtime and recovery procedures.

E060—DEVELOP EXTERNAL ENVIRONMENT PLAN

During this activity, the evaluation group attempts to isolate any factors external to the system which are having a probable impact on system performance and to determine this impact. Such factors might be a changing labor market, new government legislation, a change in competitors' shares of the market, development of new products, and technological breakthroughs.

E070—DEVELOP DOCUMENTATION REVIEW PLAN

The documentation review plan is developed to evaluate the system development effort, particularly with regard to the adequacy and completeness of the formal documentation.

This plan should itemize all activities which create documentation to be evaluated. Particular attention should be given to the activities of system development that bear a direct correlation to the condition motivating the request for the evaluation. For example, if user documentation is inadequate, it may suggest certain deficencies in the personnel subsystem, particularly in activities that relate to the development of position practices, job aids, or training materials. On the other hand, if the inadequacy is in the administrative and control procedures, the implication may be that the supervisory practices are at fault or that the control and administrative procedures were not adequately considered. A likely area for problems is the fallback, recovery, and reconstruction area. The specific activities which relate to these items will be isolated for a review of their documentation if this is the problem area.

This activity suggests that rather rigid standards should be used to control the documentation process.

E080—REVIEW USER OBJECTIVES

Note that this activity stems from developing an organizational and administrative plan. During this activity, the user objectives, as stated in a formation of objectives report, are reviewed and compared with current system activity. This is particularly important in the area of system output for determining whether this does, in fact, meet user needs. If deficiencies are found, the evaluation team attempts to determine whether they were forced, that is, the system objectives could not be accomplished, or whether the deficiencies represent inadvertent design errors. The latter might occur if the information were timely and accurate but improperly displayed or printed. This would be a major or serious deficiency if the operational system was not meeting user needs.

It will be recalled that not only is system output derived from user needs, but so also are input and functions. It may be that the expectation or need of a user has altered because of the passage of time or as a result of some condition not recognized at the time his original need was stated. If this is the case, the design organization is not at fault for designing the system to meet the specified set of needs given to it at the time.

In any case, the results of the comparison are documented in a quantitative and qualitative fashion to facilitate further discussion of the subject of system change, modification, or correction.

E090—DETERMINE ORGANIZATIONAL IMPACT

The following is an illustrative list of questions for consideration during this activity:

- Has management control and effectiveness been improved and enhanced in the areas affected by this system?
- Will pending or proposed changes in organizational structures be facilitated or complicated?
- Are existing, discrete administrative procedures assigned by the system?
- Does the system itself create an environment suggesting organizational change?
- What change does the system impose on the recruitment, selection, hiring, and training policies of the company?
- Does the system offer predictive or planning data to enhance management's control and decision making process?
- Does the system facilitate communications between departmental organizations, or does it tend to strengthen any barriers that already exist?

As a result of examining these areas and others, an impact summary should be prepared, including an analysis of the areas investigated and recommendations.

E100—REVIEW COST MODEL

During this activity, the cost model of the system is reviewed and updated. This activity consists primarily of the following:

- A review of the cost savings categories to determine accuracy and completeness.
- An update of all costs and savings, reflecting current information.
- A review and update of the intangible, noncosted benefits of the system.
- A current overall view of the budget affecting the cost and savings of the system, with all known information included.

All significant deviations from the design cost model are investigated, documented, and analyzed, and action is taken accordingly.

E110—EVALUATE TRAINING EFFECTIVENESS

By means of testing, interviewing, critical incident reports, and other types of data gathering techniques, the following aspects of training are examined:

- Does the training package cover all the aspects of the job it was designed for?
- Are the instructional materials available in sufficient quantity?
- Are training materials being used to their best advantage and in the designed fashion?
- Is training being provided for all appropriate aspects of the job?
- Is the training successful as measured by:
   a. The individuals' confidence in their ability to do their jobs well?
   b. Performance trends?
   c. The elimination of double checking or redundant activity?
   d. The implementation of work itself or other motivational programs?

If problems are found in any of these areas, an analysis of the behavioral change requirements must be made. This should go beyond the behavioral changes required, into the question of whether the training media and methods are truly cost effective. Both computer-assisted instruction and traditional programmed instruction are difficult to maintain and update. Therefore, the problem is likely to be one of neglect or obsolescence.

E120—REVIEW POSITION PRACTICES

During this activity, the review team examines the position practices or manual routines as depicted in the documentation to determine their effectiveness in operational use. Data obtained from testing, observation, and so forth should be supplemented by subjective evaluation on the part of the actual position practice users and their opinions on such subjects as ease of use, value in helping to prepare for the job, completeness of materials covered, specific criticisms.

The results of interviewing and data gathering efforts concerning the validity of the position practices should be compiled into an evaluative profile, which will guide the system support and maintenance group in making the appropriate changes.

E130—REVIEW PERFORMANCE OBJECTIVES

During this activity, the performance objectives relating to the human or personnel subsystem aspects of the system are reviewed and compared with current performance levels. Appropriate current levels of performance should be documented, along with all relevant influencing factors (e.g., employee turnover rate, changed entering repertoire, appropriateness of the job environment).

A comparison should be made between the actual performance and that called for in the system performance objectives. Significant differences should be highlighted, and a factual explanation provided. The result of this activity will be forwarded to the support and maintenance groups.

E140—REVIEW HARDWARE SYSTEM MODEL

During this activity, the hardware system model is rerun to help determine the effects of time, wear and tear, and system changes. Actual operating data are used to adjust the model to reflect its actual performance in the environment in which it is now operating.

In this fashion, the hardware system model is brought up to date and in alignment with the current actual system. Therefore, modifications (i.e., changes in certain parameters) can be made to determine the effect on customers, costs, or control features without affecting the live system. Factors such as cycle time, throughput, error rates, access time, and queuing time are examined. Particular care should be given to the factor of growth. It must be determined whether or not the system hardware will continue to be adequate to meet projected short-term and long-term growth.

If there have been new hardware offerings which might contribute sigificantly to this particular system, their parameters might well be fed into the model to analyze the results.

E150—COMPARE HARDWARE PERFORMANCE SPECIFICATIONS

During this activity the current performance specifications are assembled and then compared with the design specifications. These data are analyzed using the following perspectives:

- *Trend data.* Are the current data part of a significant trend away from the design standards, and will this continue?
- *Criticality.* How significant is the difference in data with regard to total system performance and well being?
- *Classification.* Can these data be subjected to an algorithmic manipulation for examination?

The results of this analysis will indicate to what extent change has degraded the performance of the system. Further analysis may be required to determine whether the operating system performance can deviate from specifications without significantly affecting the viability of the total system. The end result of this activity should be a precise quantification of the changes and their impact on system performance.

E160—PERFORM EXTERNAL FACTORS STUDY

During this activity the evaluation group attempts to isolate and study the factors external to the system environment which are having a probable negative impact on the system. The following is a list of some of these possible external factors:

- Significant changes in population distribution.
- Unexpected increase in volumes.
- Technological breakthroughs.
- Dramatic shifts in policies or regulations of governmental agencies.
- Unpredicted changes in the economy or the labor market.
- Changes in vendor policies or behavior.

This study should indicate which of these factors is affecting the system and provide a description in quantified terms of their impacts and consequences for system performance.

During this study, system expansion capabilities, as designed and documented during system development, are reviewed and checked for validity in the current environment. Any differences or changes are highlighted, and expansion capability is updated accordingly.

E170—REVIEW SYSTEM DEVELOPMENT DOCUMENTATION

In this activity the system development effort is evaluated in view of the current operating system. Conditions motivating the request for evaluation should indicate the area of development to be analyzed.

Generally, the development documentations should be examined for the following: clarity, completeness, accuracy, continuity, and conformity with standards. The review should not only highlight irregularity in order to facilitate corrective action, but also indicate where changes in standards or documentation format and filing schemes would enhance the documentation plan.

E180—PREPARE THE EVALUATION REPORT

This report should be prepared in a form suitable for higher management review and should contain the following:

- General comments regarding the results of system evaluation.
- Specific comments regarding the areas evaluated.
- Recommendations regarding the disposition of any problem areas.

In the case of a formal evaluation report, the document will be forwarded to the appropriate level of management (probably the executive systems steering committee) for review before being sent to the support and maintenance group. In the case of an informal review, the report will be forwarded directly to the support and maintenance group. The report will probably carry many attachments which will document and quantify the results of the evaluation.

SYSTEMS SUPPORT AND MAINTENANCE OVERVIEW

Once the diagnoses of evaluation are complete, planned treatment for corrective action can be started. Often the diagnostic procedures to isolate the problem consume more time than the treatment to resolve it. This is particularly true if the documentation is not as complete as it should be. The treatment procedures (support and maintenance activities) generally fall into four categories:

1. *Adjustment* is usually associated with equipment problems. Basically, it involves making equipment operate within the specified tolerance by using controls designed for this purpose.
2. *Repairing* refers to such activities as mending broken parts, fixing inaccuracies in the system, and patching up worn areas of the system.
3. *Replacing,* in the case of equipment, means subsituting a new part or assembly for an old or worn one.
4. *Servicing,* of course, can include anything from lubricating the machine to providing the system with the necessary supplies. This covers also the idea of inventory control for parts and supplies used in servicing.

During the first two decades in which computer-based systems were used, it was not at all uncommon to have more people involved in the support and maintenance activities than were required to build the system initially. Generally, this was caused by the fact that the development effort was not as comprehensive or complete as it should be, nor was it as well documented as is necessary for expedient support and maintenance. Many talks at professional associations, articles in magazines, and workshop seminars dealt with the excessive number of people required for the support and maintenance activities for almost any complex computer-based system. One other factor contributing to the number of people required for maintenance was the failure to recognize dynamics as a characteristics of the system; therefore, many systems were designed in a very rigid fashion which required constant adjustment because of faulty documentation. Also, an excessive amount of time was required to analyze, evaluate, and determine what was causing a problem and what was required to correct it.

If this trend were to continue, that is, using more people to support and maintain the system than were needed to build it, the outcome would be predictable. Therefore, a more thorough job of development must be done. Consideration of the dynamics, both external and internal, that will stress the system and its design must be reflected in comprehensive documentation which is easily accessible and understood by many, so that the job of supporting and maintaining the system can be scaled back and fewer people will be needed for these functions. This means allocating more resources to the development process and considerably fewer to the operations phase and the support and maintenance phase.

CRITICAL IMPORTANCE OF DOCUMENTATION

The great importance of system design documentation to the support and maintenance group cannot be overemphasized. Because of its nature, that is, its high intellectual content, the design of a system can exist for only a brief period without documentation. Also, documents are the only way in which much of the intellectual content can be retrieved for further use and for modifications to the system. The documentation is the physical record of the system and is required so that the system can be understood and modified to correct malfunctions or to accommodate changing conditions. Then the documents are changed to reflect the changed system.

Not only are the EDP machine and manual practices (position practices) important to system maintenance, but so also are the definition report and preliminary design report. They must be maintained to ensure that they reflect the changing objectives, criteria, and functional rationale of the system.

PROVISIONS FOR SUPPORT AND MAINTENANCE

An understanding during all phases of system development that support and maintenance will be required will help to ensure that the means for making adjustment and repairs are provided. Maintenance manuals must be available for each system component, whether it is purchased or developed in house.

All support and maintenance activities need not be generated within the support and maintenance group. Manufacturers of equipment usually offer some activities of this type for their own equipment or software packages. Actually, the terms and conditions of such an offer are often a major factor in the decision to purchase a given piece of equipment or software package. In these cases, usually a contractual arrangement is made with the equipment or software supplier to ensure that the support will be forthcoming.

PLANNING SYSTEM SUPPORT AND MAINTENANCE

The important thing to remember, in considering system evaluation and support and maintenance, is that the activities mentioned above will be required, and that there is a considerable degree of interaction among them. If these factors are not considered during the design, provisions for adjustments and preventive maintenance will not be built in, and this in turn will cause major problems in the maintenance and support phase.

A few years ago, reporter Keyes Beach, a *Chicago Daily News* correspondent in Saigon, told of a happening in Vietnam which was analogous to experience with some of our system and support activities in computer-based systems. The brief story went as follows:

The ups and downs of life in South Vietnam were vividly recorded Monday in a report by one Ny Yen Ven Toi, an employee of the U.S. Army in Saigon. He was requesting sick leave and his report read like this: "When I arrived at building T1640 to fix it, I found the rain had dislodged a large number of tiles from the roof. I rigged up a beam with the pulley at the top of the building and hoisted up a couple of barrels of tiles. When I fixed the roof, there were several tiles left over so I hoisted the barrel up again and secured the line at the bottom and went up and filled the barrel with the extra tiles. I then went down to the bottom and cast off the line; unfortunately the barrel of tiles was heavier than I was and before I knew what was happening the barrel started down and I started up. I decided to hang on and half-way up met the barrel coming down and received a severe blow on the shoulder. I then continued to the top, banging my head on the beam and getting my fingers jammed in the pulley. When the barrel hit the ground it burst at the bottom, allowing all the tiles to spill out. I was now heavier than the barrel and started down at high speed. Half-way down I met the barrel coming up and received severe injury on my shin. Then I hit the ground, landing on the tile and getting several painful cuts from the sharp edges. At this point I must have lost my presence of mind because I let go of the line. The barrel came down again, giving me another heavy blow to the head and putting me in the hospital."

CURRENT DEVELOPMENTS

Support and maintenance activities can, within certain limits, accommodate changes to the basic structure of the system itself. These types of changes are classified as current development. Current development can be as simple as redesigning a form to accommodate new information requirements, or as complex as accommodating a whole new CPU unit. As a matter of fact, the point at which accommodation to change ceases to be current system development and becomes a new system development effort is not too clearly defined. It suffices to say here that, if a change is of a type that will affect system objectives, it should be classified as a new system development effort.

SYSTEM CHANGES

As time passes, the dynamics of the system tend to be reduced because they are used up in filling the requirements for growth and flexibility. Storage space becomes filled. Forms cease to be able to accommodate all informational requirements. Eventually, there is a danger that, although normal operations are within the design specifications, all is not well with the system.

When a system is outgrowing its *planned and designed* dynamics, an unusual burden is placed on the maintenance and support group. At this point the system is becoming critical, and any minor malfunction may easily pyramid into a major breakdown. Therefore, time and energy should be devoted by the maintenance and support group to finding ways to increase system flexibility, particularly in areas that are sensitive or critical, to ensure continued operation without major malfunction.

ENVIRONMENTAL CHANGES

The environment in which the system operates can and will change, thus forcing alterations in system operation. A changing business or political climate may require modification of the objectives. Most external environmental factors which influence system performance will probably come from areas of competitive business and/or governmental regulation changes.

CHANGE IN THE STATE OF THE ART

Often, it may be argued that advances in the technological state of the art can present opportunities which might be worth exploiting. Exploitation of these advances can cause changes in the requirements of the system. They can cause the support effort to change to current development activities or even the design of a new system. For example, a new high-speed printer could allow a different reporting pattern, format, or form, or a whole new central processing unit might allow major changes in system operation.

Whether these items are considered to be system support and maintenance, or regarded as a new system development effort, must be determined by the impact of these changes on *system objectives and user needs*. If the changes can be implemented with the available support and maintenance personnel, rather than with additional employees, this criterion could represent a division between support and maintenance and new development.

Some of the proposed solutions to the high cost of maintenance and support are better languages, more flexible hardware, more versatile communications equipment, and more thorough debugging. However, despite all the new things talked and dreamed about for tomorrow, the solution does not lie entirely with technological progress. The trend toward costlier maintenance can best be checked through a more thorough development of the system in the first place. The job of supporting the system will be minimized by developing a sound total system with flexibility and thorough documentation.

TERMINATION OF A SYSTEM

When support and maintenance ends, the system ceases to function effectively and must be terminated or replaced. When support and maintenance or current development cannot maintain system operation within specified tolerances, a new or total system development effort will be required if there is a continuing user need for the system.

S010—EVALUATE REQUEST FOR SUPPORT

During this activity, requests for changes or modifications in the system are reviewed for their feasibility and practicality. Some questions for consideration during this evaluation are the following:

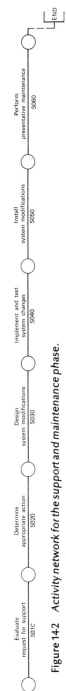

Figure 14·2   Activity network for the support and maintenance phase.

Evaluate
request for support
S01C

Determine
appropriate action
S020

Design
system modifications
S030

Implement and test
system changes
S040

Install
system modifications
S050

Perform
preventative maintenance
S060

END

199

- Is the proposed change consistent and within the system objectives?
- Will performance specification be adversely affected?
- How much effort will be required to implement the proposed change?
- What particular functions are affected by the change?
- Will the change require special training or behavioral modification for the people in the system?

The activities performed during this phase are depicted in Figure 14–2. A preliminary design of the change is prepared to aid in determining the appropriate action for the request if the change appears feasible. This preliminary design change is based on the information acquired during the evaluation phase. If additional data gathering is required, it is performed by the maintenance and support group. The preliminary design change may be tried out on the models of the system before the design is finalized.

S020—DETERMINE APPROPRIATE ACTION

During this activity, the support and maintenance group determines what action can be taken on the modification request. If the request is not considered feasible, the originator is so notified. If the request appears feasible but cannot be considered as a maintenance item, that is, it affects system objectives or user needs, it is referred to higher management.

For each request for modification considered feasible (i.e., falling within the scope of support and maintenance activity), a development plan is prepared, and manpower, money, and time are allocated to the accomplishment of the change.

S030—DESIGN SYSTEM MODIFICATION

During this activity, all the necessary detail design activities are performed for the approved modification. The nature of the change (i.e., change to manual subsystem, modification of the training package, change in program, etc.) will determine what must be done to complete this activity.

The support and maintenance group follows many of the same activities as prescribed in the preliminary and detail design phases for new systems work in order to complete its design activity.

S040—IMPLEMENT AND TEST MODIFICATIONS

During this activity, all modifications designed for the system are developed and tested for operational use. The nature of the modification, whether it be to change computer programs or to change position practices, will determine what actions are taken to completely test this activity. All affected and related system documentation should be updated as soon as testing is completed.

S050—INSTALL SYSTEMS MODIFICATION

During this activity, the system support and maintenance group is responsible for successful installation of the changes. This, in effect, is an acceptance test, which amounts to reviewing the changes with the using personnel involved. These persons should concur with the modifications and help to put them into effect.

During the accomplishment of this activity, the support and maintenance crew follows much the same outline as was given for the conversion phase activities.

S060—PERFORM PREVENTIVE MAINTENANCE

Preventive maintenance is an ongoing activity which begins as the system is installed and continues throughout its life. It consists of constant evaluation and fine tuning of the operational system to ensure that it continues to function as designed. This primarily involves regularly scheduled inspection and evaluation of the following:

- Wear and tear on all equipment used by the system.
- Degradation of personnel subsystem performance.
- Training courses necessary for system operation and use.

Preventive maintenance is performed in order to avoid more serious and costly breakdowns; therefore, it generally follows a time routine or amount-of-use cycle. If well designed and performed regularly, it prevents any serious malfunctions in the system.

Preventive maintenance is another one of the factors that should be designed into the system during the development phases. Therefore, when and where preventive maintenance is performed, and how the system is tuned and adjusted, should have been prescribed by the development team. Benjamin Franklin probably said it best years ago in the proverb, "An ounce of prevention is worth a pound of cure."

CHAPTER 15   DATA COLLECTION TECHNIQUES

DATA COLLECTION OVERVIEW

One of the major functions of any system development effort is to collect sufficient quantities of the right kind of data. As a general rule, the need for the collection of data may arise any time within the system development effort that there is insufficient information to support a necessary decision. If the sustaining or supportive information is lacking, it must be acquired. In many situations, planning, gathering, and analyzing the data so that they can serve as the basis for system development decisions involve major expenditures of time, manpower, and funds. The consequences of an error or of failure in data collection have major impacts on the system development effort itself. Invalid or insufficient data can result in the development of an ineffective and wasteful system, or at the other extreme, in aborting the development of a worth-while system. Therefore, each individual data collection effort must be carefully organized, effectively managed, and well executed.

In its own right, the data collection process will probably involve several decision points. Specifically, data should never be collected and/or analyzed for their own sake. Continuing surveillance should be maintained over the potential impact of the data being gathered on the system development decisions to be supported. At several points within the data collection process evaluation should be made of whether and how the procedures being followed, and the potential results, can impact the system development decision. At any time when it appears that the results of data collection are adequate, or will have no effect on the system development decision, the activity should be terminated. Data collection can be (and usually is) expensive and involved; therefore, when this process is begun, it should be done with the discipline and expertise which will help to assure success.

PLANNING THE DATA GATHERING ACTIVITIES

There is no single best way to go about gathering data in all situations. Generally speaking, however, one can follow a methodology similar to that just discussed for developing the system. The first phase of the data gathering effort is an objective requirement phase during which the problem is defined, the objectives for the data gathering effort are set, a definition and description of the required data are made, and a proposal for collection and analysis of the data and perhaps a sample design are determined.

The second phase, sampling, involves applying a statistical technique in which a mathematically validated subgroup of data and/or sources is selected and utilized to represent the complete body of information. The sampling phase includes all the steps necessary to identify sources of information and to determine the extent of the data collection effort. Under this interpretation, the sampling phase also covers situations for gathering information from all available sources rather than just a representative subgroup. During sampling, one determines the size and scope of the data gathering activity and the availability of the required data and respondents, and, finally, documents these results.

During the third phase, the collection phase, the actual data are collected and assembled in a form suitable for review and analysis. During this phase, one selects, designs, and pretests the data gathering instrument, administers the data collection effort, and conducts the collection activity.

The fourth general phase is that of analysis of the collected data. This involves the systematic organization and appraisal of the data, including such activities as receiving, organizing, preparing, and analyzing the data to evaluate their validity and usefulness.

The final phase is reporting on the data that have been analyzed. The extent and degree of formality of the data gathering report will depend on the nature, the organization, and the size of the data collection effort itself.

INITIAL PLANNING

It is usually true that the earlier in the development process that data collection and planning take place, the more valuable the results will be, and the greater the probability of return on the effort. By nature, the system development process involves a series of decisions, or choices between alternatives. In general, the bigger, more far-reaching decisions are made in the early phases of the system development process. To illustrate, the initial statement of objectives for the system under development establishes the scope, types, and level of service to be rendered. These factors, in turn, will guide the entire development process right up to determining the configuration and services of the implemented system. When such factors are considered, it becomes apparent that the early decisions are the most far reaching in terms of both cost and development efforts.

Traditionally, however, the early decisions within the system development project tend to be the least supported factually. For example, an early conference during the formation of objectives phase in system development might incorporate a desire by the user group that the system be capable of real-time response. The statement might even go so far as to specify an acceptable response time. In most cases, such statements should be treated at face value.

Even when a need for a factual basis for early decisions is recognized, the tendency has been to make the most far-reaching decision on the basis of a "guesstimate." This has been referred to as the "ask a friend" method of data gathering. Typically, a member of the system development management team recognizes the need for information as the basis for planning or designing decisions. He thinks back until he remembers the name of an associate who has some experience applicable to the current decision. A few telephone conversations later he has what he considers to be the desired data.

At the outset, then, a most important requirement within the system development process, as far as data collection is concerned, is an awareness that pertinent facts are going to have to be gathered, analyzed, and evaluated. Personnel associated with the system development project should be aware of this continuing need so that data collection requirements can be examined and acted upon as they arrive.

Three decision requirements are readily associated with the data collection effort supporting the system development process:

1. A basic, system-pertinent decision should be formalized in writing so that all personnel associated with the data collection, or the utilization of its end product, understand the criteria involved. The decision description should include the alternatives available and the consequences, both functionally and financially, of the selection and/or rejection of each. The com-

pleteness of the decision criteria is critical to effective data collection, because the initial description serves to provide a framework establishing the magnitude of the effort and expense which can be justified in data collection.

2. System development project management should stipulate the type of data needed as a basis for the decision at hand. These specifications should be as exact as possible, including factors of precision and accuracy in the end product, the presentation format, and the content.

3. The project management team should identify data sources. System development personnel will be closely familiar with their particular environment and operational situations by the time a need for data arises. In establishing an interdisciplinary activity like a data collection effort, it is part of the responsibility of the development project management to define supporting activities as specifically as possible.

PRINCIPLES OF SAMPLING

If asked for a definition of sampling, most people would say that sampling is a process of obtaining information about the whole of something by examining only a portion of it. Although stated generally, this definition is basically correct; a common ability to define the term stems from the fact that sampling, in one form or another, affects us all daily. For example, we might take a sip of coffee in the morning to determine whether the brew is too strong, too weak, or just right. Here a sample of one sip is sufficient because experience has shown that one sip is just like another.

In sampling, the aggregate, or entirety, of the items or units about which information is desired is usually called the universe. When information is to be obtained about the universe of items by examining the individual items, there are three possible methods of approach:

1. Examine all of the items in the universe.
2. Examine a portion of the items, using scientific sampling procedures.
3. Examine a portion of the items without using scientific sampling procedures.

The first of these three methods, examining all the items in the universe, is known as a census or making a 100% study.

The second method, scientific sampling, is a procedure in which the design and selection of the sample follow mathematical principles, in particular, probability theory. Two important features of scientific sampling should be mentioned at this point:

1. A scientific sample must be drawn by a completely objective method.
2. The reliability of the scientific sample can be controlled by the use of mathematical procedures.

The third method, nonscientific sampling, includes any kind of sampling procedure which is not properly designated as scientific. There are two common varieties of nonscientific sampling, sometimes referred to as judgment sampling and quasi-scientific sampling. In judgment sampling, data may be selected by one or more persons who choose or hand-pick the particular items which they feel represent the universe, or a segment of the universe may be arbitrarily selected as a sample. Sometimes this kind of selection is unavoidable or is necessary because of cost considerations, but two serious limitations should be recognized:

1. Judgment samples are subject to a personnel bias of the individual responsible for the selection.
2. The fact that the selection of items is not objective precludes the use of mathematical techniques to determine the reliability of the sample.

In quasi-scientific sampling, data are gathered by the same objective procedures used in scientific sampling, but the size of the sample taken is based on conjecture. No scientific procedure is applied to predetermine how large the sample should be or what type of sampling method would be most economical. The sample may, therefore, be larger or smaller than needed. However, this kind of sampling has one advantage over judgment sampling: after the sample has been drawn, its reliability can be computed because it has been selected by an objective method.

PRINCIPLES OF RANDOM SELECTION

Scientific sampling depends on the principle of random selection. In sampling, the term "random" is used in a special sense which differs from its commonly accepted meaning. Random selection implies selection governed wholly by the laws of chance. The selection of the individual sample items must be completely independent of human decision. In drawing a sample from a group of items, each item must have an equal chance of being selected. A truly random selection of items is not easy; therefore, tables of random numbers are now used in most sampling work to ensure randomization. These random numbers are produced by a machine. Although tests show that these tables are not perfect, the amount of error is too slight to be of any practical consequence.

THE IMPORTANCE OF VARIATION

Variation among the items in the universe is a very important factor in sampling. If all items in the universe were exactly alike, a sample of any one of them would be a true measure of all of them; but, as variation increases, the size of the sample required to obtain a specified reliability tends also to increase.

To illustrate the concepts of variation in sampling, suppose that we consider the individual incomes of two groups of five people each, assuming that the average incomes of the two groups are equal. The size of sample required tends to increase as variation increases. This can be understood if we consider the reliability of a sample of one person drawn from each of the two groups. A sample of one person from group 1 will be used to produce an estimate of average income. Actually, in this example the average can be as low as $2250 or as high as $5750 (the low and the high of the income in group 1). But a sample of one person in group 2 would be less reliable since it could produce an estimate as low as $1500 or as high as $6500, figures much further from the universe average of $4000.

RELIABILITY STATEMENT

The extent to which the difference between the sample result and the universe value is controlled is expressed in what is commonly called a reliability statement. This is basic in sampling, and it is important to fully understand its meaning. A reliability statement is composed of two parts, an assurance level and a confidence interval. The confidence interval is like the band around the sample average; it extends on both sides of it. The confidence interval expresses the range within which the universe figure will lie at the stated assurance level. It is somewhat similar to the tolerance factor which is present in any measurement. For example, a given dimension can be measured to the nearest foot, to the nearest inch, or to the nearest fraction of an inch.

Selection of the assurance level used in the reliability statement depends on how much risk we are willing to take that the universe value will lie outside the confidence interval. When we speak of a 90% assurance, it means that the universe value will lie within the confidence interval 90% of the time (i.e., there is only a 10% chance that it will fall outside the interval). The selection of the assurance level will depend, therefore, on a comparison of the penalty to be paid for a wrong answer and the cost of obtaining a more reliable sample. If the penalty is small, there is justification for using a relatively lower assurance level; if the penalty is large, a relatively high assurance level is necessary.

There are a number of different types of sampling procedures. Each procedure has its own set of advantages for certain purposes. The more commonly used sampling types are the following four:

1. Simple random sampling.
2. Systematic sampling.
3. Stratified sampling.
4. Cluster sampling.

When simple random sampling is used, the items in the sample are drawn completely at random from the entire universe. The common procedure for making this random selection is as follows: first, assign a serial number to each of the items in the universe, and then, using a table of random numbers, make a random selection of the serial numbers to be included in the sample.

Systematic sampling involves selection from an array of items in the universe in such a way that there is a uniform interval between each sample item and the next one. For example, if a sample is to include 1 of every 100 items in the universe, selection is made by first drawing an item at random from the first 100 items in the universe and then selecting every 100th item thereafter.

In stratified sampling, the items in the universe are first segregated into two or more classes called strata. Usually, these are chosen so that items that are generally comparable in regard to the characteristic being measured fall within the same stratum. Then each stratum is sampled independently, and the results for the several strata are weighed together to give an overall figure for the universe. This type of sampling is often appropriate when there is a wide variation among the items in respect to the characteristic to be measured.

With cluster sampling, the universe is formed into groups or clusters of items. The first step is to make a random selection of clusters to include in the sample. Then items within the selected cluster may be sampled, or a census may be taken of them. This type of sampling is often advantageous for cost reasons.

In designing the sample, then, one of the first and most important steps is to decide what kind of sampling procedures should be used. Each study has particular characteristics that make one type of sampling more appropriate than another. To use simple random sampling, for example, when stratified sampling is the appropriate type for the particular study, may either add greatly to the cost of the study or produce less satisfactory sample results. Selection of the proper sampling method is essential in developing an efficient and economical sampling design.

LIMITATION OF SAMPLING

Sampling methods have certain inherent limitations which under some conditions make their use undesirable. Broadly speaking, the cases when sampling should not be used fall into two categories:

1. Cases where exact figures or complete accuracy are essential.
2. Cases where the overall cost of sampling, including sampling and administrative costs, does not compare favorably with the costs of alternatives.

The first category of cases, that involving a need for exactness or completeness, requires no discussion. The inappropriateness of sampling in such instances is self evident.

In regard to the second category, sampling requires certain special costs not required by 100% studies. In designing the sample, some work is required to determine what kind of sampling to use, how large a sample to take, how to draw the sample, and so forth. There are also administrative operations, such as selecting the sample items and making the computations required for summarizing the results. Usually, the cost savings which result from having to examine only a portion of the universe far offset the supplementary costs incurred. But this is not always so.

VALIDATION

Two types of validation should be a basic part of every sampling effort:

1. After the sample has been designed, it should be checked with test data to see whether it actually gives the type of result that is being sought. The test data themselves can be hypothesized on the basis of what is known about the universe.

2. Once the actual sampling operation is ready to begin, it should be tested on a pilot basis to make sure that the data collected will fit the analysis plan and deliver the results specified.

DATA COLLECTION INSTRUMENTS

A data collection instrument is a document or recording medium for the orderly entry of collected data into a format compatible with the requirements for tabulation, processing, analysis, and reporting of results. Data gathering instruments can assume a virtually infinite number of forms. Critical criteria in these designs are the following:

- Pertinence of data requested to the goals of the study.
- Clarity in meaning, which is important for all questions or instructions associated with the data gathering instruments. Statements or questions must be clear in both intent and content so that they mean the same thing to the writer, project personnel, data gatherers, and respondents.
- Uniformity of procedure and format in the gathering of data.
- Convenience of use by project personnel, data gatherers, and respondents.
- Compatibility with tabulation, processing, analysis, and reporting requirements.
- Feasibility in terms of both gathering activities and project budgets.

Data gathering instruments applicable to system development projects can include the following:

1. Questionnaires.
2. Automatically recorded graphs.
3. Machine or computer printouts.
4. Photographic films.
5. Tabular forms.
6. Teletype transmissions.
7. Mark-sense or optical character recognition documents.
8. Audio, analog, or digital magnetic recordings.

Special requirements exist for the design of instruments for the collection of numeric data. Costs, including those of analyzing the data, depend heavily on such considerations as the use of boxes for numbers, line breaks, and formatting so that this instrument is easy to administer and process. The clarity of the meaning of each question is important to the reduction of errors. For example, if there is a misspelled word, it will probably be interpreted incorrectly. Moreover, every effort must be made to ensure that the numbers gathered are correct. In a man/machine interactive system where data are entered on on-line terminals, the computer immediately checks for validity, missing fields, parity, and so forth and may reply with further questions if problems exist.

Compatibility with optical scanning, magnetic media, and other automatic recording or reading devices is more frequently becoming an objective of data gathering instrument design.

QUESTIONNAIRES

Questionnaires tend to be the most complex data gathering instrument to design and implement. Questionnaires are special-purpose collection instruments for use in interviews or in situations where the subject matter lends itself to self-administration by respondents.

Personal interview questionnaires administered in person offer the highest potential in response rates and information yield. The personal interview, however, also involves the highest cost for the questionnaire type of data collection. Therefore, it is important to weigh against alternatives the relative cost and anticipated results.

Self-administered questionnaires must be particularly explicit because there will be no interviewer to explain the questions. This means that special care must be exercised in framing the questions. On the other hand, when applied well, self-administered questionnaires can provide a large cross section of data in a relatively short time and at an economic price, if the gathering is properly managed.

The response rate of self-administered questionnaires depends on the methods of distribution and the nature of the activity—whether voluntary or company sponsored. The term "response rate" refers to the percentage of completed and returned data gathering forms.

SELECTING QUESTIONNAIRE TECHNIQUES

Each type of questionnaire technique has both strong points and problem areas. There is no single best approach; rather, it is a matter of choosing a technique for the particular circumstances. In selecting the technique, it is also possible to mix the types of data gathering instruments within a single data collection project. It is entirely possible, for example, to use personal interviews, telephone interviews, and self-administered questionnaires on a single project.

TYPES OF QUESTIONS

There are two basic types of questions, open ended and closed. Open-ended questions are unstructured; they encourage free latitude and response. Closed questions, on the other hand, are structured so that one chooses between stated response alternatives, which can be tallied quantitatively. Open-ended questions are particularly useful when opinions or attitudes are being probed, or when it is difficult or undesirable to suggest possible answers to the respondent. Open-ended questions are often used in the exploratory phases of a study as a method of establishing alternatives for final questions which can be tallied quantitatively. In such situations, the open-ended question helps to establish final wording in terms used by the respondents themselves. Although closed questions can take several forms, they are all structured for quantitative tabulation and analysis within the framework of each data gathering activity.

There are several rules or guides that will help in the wording of questions:

- Use as simple and plain English as possible. Although technical language assists clarity if the respondents are equipped to deal with it, it can be a liability. Hence, if there is any doubt about the technical understanding of the respondents, use simple English and define any technical or other complex term within the context of its specific use.
- Avoid value-laden or loaded words. Words and phrases such as "Socialist," "demonstrator," or "only a clerical worker" mean more to most people than the simple dictionary definition. Furthermore, they mean different things to different people. The use of such words can bias the results of the data gathering effort.
- Avoid using questions that suggest the desired response—for example, "You read the newspaper every day, don't you?" The question almost forces the respondent to say yes; therefore, responses to such questions are statistically worthless.
- Be careful to word questions so that they do not embarrass respondents. For example, a question that makes the respondent appear poorly educated or inadequate for his job can produce a distorted response, refusal to answer, refusal to participate in the survey, and dissatisfaction.
- Do not place too great a burden on the respondent's ability to remember. Ask only for details that you are reasonably certain the respondent will know. If you want detailed information on specifics, use a different type of data gathering, such as observation,

mechanized measurement, quantitative processing, or file searches.
- Anticipate the context of the responses. For example, if you ask for an average, be sure that "average" means the same to all respondents and to you; otherwise, define the term in the question context.

The sequence and interrrelationships of questions and their parts also constitute an important aspect of the data gathering instrument design. The elements of the questions should be sequenced so that they carry the respondent through the instrument in a logical, easy manner. Organization of the questionnaire involves three separate levels of activity:

1. Logical topical order of questions, according to topical group.
2. Logical sequencing of questions within a topical group.
3. Ordering of response alternatives within individual questions.

QUESTIONNAIRE LAYOUT

The physical layout of a questionnaire depends in part on whether it is to be implemented by an interviewer or self administered. In both cases, the important thing is to make the instructions clear to the person executing the form. Although this requirement is more critical for self-administered questionnaires, the same general rules apply:

- Questions should be listed and numbered in an orderly manner so that the reader is easily led from one question to the next. Any complicated arrangement invites the omission of parts of the survey and/or errors in the recording of the responses.
- Where the question sequence calls for skipping questions or branching, instructions must be clearly written and, where possible, supplemented by arrows or other devices to assist the reader.
- The instructions on the questionnaire should be as complete as possible, even when the survey will be conducted by an interviewer.
- The face type for instructions should be distinct from the one used for questions. A common procedure is to use italics or capital letters for the instructions. Care should be taken with the use of italics, however, because some styles of italic type are hard to read if they are used for more than a few words.
- Adequate space must be provided for recording all responses. This is particularly true for open-ended questions. If the space is too small, only partial responses may be recorded.
- All questionnaires should include entry and exit statements. These

are to assist the interviewers or to enlist the cooperation of the respondent in the case of self-administered questionnaires.

Before a questionnaire is used for full-scale collection of data, it should be pretested on a selected, reasonably typical group of respondents. If the questionnaire is to be interview administered, a pretest should be done by an experienced interviewer who can pinpoint trouble spots.

Particular attention should be paid to such questions as the following:

- Do the respondents understand the questions?
- Are the instructions clear and complete?
- Are the response categories clear and distinct?
- Can the interview be completed in the planned time?
- Is there adequate space for entry of responses?
- Is the instrument usable?

GATHERING DATA THROUGH INTERVIEWS

The term "interview," as used in the data gathering context, denotes an activity aimed at gathering data through person-to-person confrontation. It is assumed that the interview is structured by questionnaires and/or special instructions to the interviewer. The respondent must be advised in advance of the interview activity and its subject area and agree to cooperate.

Interviewing is a standard technique for gathering data. It has valuable potential throughout the system development project. When time, budget, and other considerations permit, the personal interview offers the best chance of collecting the most complete and usable information through the use of the questionnaire. This stems from several reasons:

- Through persuasion, trained interviewers can elicit the highest attainable rate of response.
- By observing and controlling the interview, interviewers can obtain thoughtful answers to the questions.
- The interviewers can note possible disturbing effects on respondents and note them on the questionnaire for consideration when the data are received and edited.

The selection of interviewers is an important consideration in the successful use of this data gathering technique. As a general guideline, persons conducting the interviews should be as impartial as possible.

OBSERVATION AS A DATA COLLECTION TECHNIQUE

Some types of data pertinent to system development cannot be collected effectively, or even physically, through interviews or self-administered questionnaires. For example, if one wants to know how many employees come to work late, or leave early, within a given operation, it is too much trouble and comparably unreliable to ask individuals how often, or by how many minutes, they are off the job due to late arrival or early departure.

In such situations, it is far more reliable to run a tally of the time cards, or, if these are not available, to have a trained observer record the data. There is still another alternative; photographic observation, with time-lapse motion pictures, might be used to monitor activities at the beginning and end of shifts.

Data gathering through observation is a long-established, thoroughly proved approach. Job sequencing requirements associated with the input or output functions of a computerized system make this methodology highly practical in gathering data to support system development projects. Data gathering through personal observation follows the same general rules in terms of design and formatting of collection instruments as the preparation of questionnaires.

Observation has been used for the last 60 years or so in three main areas: the establishment of work standards, work simplification through re-evaluation and redesign of activity for clerical and craft functions, and the design of new manual procedures, including work space layout.

MECHANIZED GATHERING TECHNIQUES

Many data gathering projects are concerned with operations that involve mechanical, electrical, or electronic devices. There is usually a possibility that the needed data can be simply and economically extracted from the equipment. Where use of this technique is applicable, it returns a high yield of data with a small investment, particularly since the gathered data are likely to be in machine-readable format for direct automated processing and analysis.

When data within an ongoing computerized system are being processed by a computer, it is possible to insert counting and recording loops into the program so that the computer itself will perform the gathering function.

ANALYZING THE DATA

Analyzing the data includes the organization, numeric processing, and presentation of collected data in a form compatible with, and meaningful to, the decision situation which caused initiation of the effort.

The plan for data reduction and analysis should be established before any data are collected. The ground rules for analysis are first set out in the initial statement of objectives and requirements, which describes the content and the format for the data gathered and the end products.

Once the statement has been collected, edited, and checked for quality according to the original statement of objectives, analysis generally begins with an overall review of the collected data. This gives the analyst a chance to see the general characteristics of the data in the sample and to isolate any obvious problems before time and money are invested in further work. A device frequently used for this initial viewing of data is a scatter diagram, which is simply a graphic plot of the raw data. Using this plot, the analyst can find patterns in the data.

Once the analyst has examined the data and made any necessary corrections, the next step is usually to place the data in a format that makes numerical analysis possible. In other words, the data themselves must be processed and reported as statistics, that is, numerical renditions of bodies of actual data. In general, the techniques used for data representation and analysis are referred to as quantitative or analytical methods. These techniques take two basic forms:

1. *Tabular listings.* These include a variety of tables, such as correlation, matrix, and frequency distribution tables.
2. *Graphic representations.* Plotting a series of data such as frequency distributions results in presentations known as histograms. These presentations provide a pictorial view of the data.

An important way to characterize data is to find a point around which the numbers tend to concentrate. This point is called the measure of central tendency or, in every day terms, an average. However, "average" is too loose a term for the precision required in statistical work. Also, there are several different ways to calculate central tendency, each taking certain characteristics into account:

1. The *arithmetic mean,* also commonly called the average, is a calculated point based on equal consideration of every value in the distribution. It is found by dividing the sum of the values in the distribution by the total number of the values.
2. The *median* is the value of the middle term in a sorted series if there is an odd number of items. Otherwise the median is the arithmetic mean of the two middle terms.

3. The *mode* is the value of the data that occurs most frequently. By definition, the mode is the most common or typical value in a series.

Whatever measurement or combination of measurements is used, the resulting values will show the central tendency of the sample. These values are then tested as estimates of the central tendency of the universe to see whether they appear valid.

Obviously, measurements of central tendency indicate only the center or point of concentration of the values. In a distribution, however, this center or point is of little use without an indication of the degree of variation that occurs around it. This spread or scatter of items in a distribution around the central point is indicated as a measure of dispersion. There are two ways of measuring dispersion:

1. The *range.* The simplest measurement of dispersion is the difference between the minimum and maximum values in the distribution. Range can be expressed either in terms of actual value or high or low items, or as a difference between the high and low figures.
2. The *standard deviation,* which offers a more exact measurement of dispersion. It takes into account the differences between the mean and all the other values in the distribution and expresses them as the average difference.

From this point on, a variety of analytical tools are available for making determinations about the data in a sample and projecting the results to the universe. These tools include the following:

1. *Hypothesis testing* is used in cases where the data are gathered to test an assumption. These tests make use of a statistical method such as analysis of variance. An illustration of the use of this method would be to test the hypothesis that a residential telephone call in Birmingham, Alabama, lasts an average of 10 seconds longer than one in Chicago. The results of the test might be: there is a 1% chance that residential call lengths in Birmingham are an average of 10 seconds longer than ones in Chicago. In this case, the hypothesis would be rejected as not valid.
2. *Correlation* is used to explain the statistical relationships between two or more variables. In studying such relationships, however, the analyst must also consider the relevance of a particular relationship. For example, if analysis shows that there is a high positive correlation between the height and the weight of human beings, the analyst would accept this as fact because of his previous experience. On the other hand, if the data analysis showed that for a number of years the people participating in

scouting activities had a high positive correlation with coffee sales in the area, it would not be valid to conclude that scouters are drinking all the coffee consumed.

3. *Discrimination analysis* is used to separate two groups. An example would be the development of college entrance test criteria for selecting the applicants most likely to succeed.

4. *Factor analysis* attempts to pinpoint which factors are important within a process. One use for factor analysis is questionnaire evaluation, that is, to help determine the relative importance of specific questions.

5. *Modeling* is used to characterize a complex process by mathematically explaining the individual interactions in the process. By using this mathematical manipulation, it is possible to predict the results of all the parts of the process working simultaneously.

For many years the disciplines of physics and engineering have used models of physical systems to explain observed behavior. These well-known but sometimes imperfect models are accepted as valid, because they have been useful for a long period of time. In more recent times, the same method of scientific inquiry has been extended to solve business system problems.

One special modeling technique is forecasting. In forecasting, the analysis must extrapolate from observed behavior to predict future events, in contrast to the usual case in which the model explains observed interactions (interpolation). In forecasting there is a point of diminishing returns, where further refining of the model to fit past history reduces the model's ability to predict future events accurately.

DATA GATHERING DOCUMENTATION

The final report on the results of the data gathering effort provides the vehicle for measurement of the success and value of the project. Until the project team has completed its work, the report represents the data gathering effort and must communicate the needed information to the specific user audience. In effect, the entire data gathering effort will be judged on how well the report enables data users to assimilate the project findings.

When volumes of categorized figures are to be incorporated into the report, tables are frequently prepared. These are of two general types:

1. General-purpose tables are inclusive in nature, for example, population and area tables published by the U.S. Bureau of the

Census or economic data presentations by the U.S. Department of Commerce.

2. Special-purpose tables are used to present selected data to special audiences. By and large, reports of data gathering projects will make greater use of this type of table.

In any table, the data elements should be set off from one another. In printed tables this can be done by spacing, ruling, shading of lines or columns, color, type font, and type size. For typed tables, the options are more limited, but alternatives still exist through such techniques as spacing, underscoring, vertical rulings, and horizontal lines of periods or hyphens.

In special-purpose tables, it is better to keep only enough significant digits to serve the need of the analyst. Other things being equal, the more digits, the more difficult a table is to understand. There are seven basic parts of a statistical table:

1. The title should list such important factors as the kind of material presented in the table, its classification, and the time period covered.
2. The prefatory note is used to describe the figures in the table. This includes the units in which the figures are represented and any limitations or special characteristics that the data may possess.
3. The body of the table, that is, the rows and columns of actual figures, should be spaced or divided by rulings so that each figure can be found conveniently.
4. The caption (column headings) and stub (row identification, usually on the left) should be clear and concise.
5. The source note, usually placed at the bottom of the table, should give the primary source of the data and the place where the investigator actually found them.
6. The unit of measurement is used in the caption or as needed.
7. A footnote is used for further explanation of some specific part of the table if desired. It is placed immediately beneath the table, above the source note, and should be indicated by a symbol or a letter. If footnotes are numbered, there is a possibility for confusion with the data in the table.

GRAPHIC PRESENTATION OF DATA

Presenting statistical data graphically in charts, graphs, and so forth serves two broad purposes. First, a graph can be an interesting and effective device for recording and illustrating the essential features of a set of data and for pointing out the conclusions that can be drawn. For this reason, extensive use is made of such devices for presenting information to management or supervisory people who need a quick grasp of a broad situation. Second, technical diagrams which aid in the actual analysis of data are produced in the course of analysis. These are working, curved, structured graphs. They may be discarded before the actual report is written or included as working documentation in the appropriate section of the report, depending on the individual situation.

In order that charts can convey as much information as possible, quickly and effectively, they must be kept simple. The natural tendency to put unnecessary material on the chart must be resisted, or the result will be a complex presentation that defeats its own basic purpose. On the other hand, since graphs tend to catch the eye of the reader, they are often read out of context, making it extremely important that each one be complete and self-contained, with full information in the title, footnotes, and other parts, so that the casual reader will still get the true meaning of the data presented.

The rules for format and identification of charts and graphs are similar to those cited above for data tables, except for the following special cautions:

- Coordinate lines should be held to a minimum; conversely the curved line should stand out sharply from the background.
- Scales of value should be placed along the X and Y axis to give a general indication of the size of the variations represented by the coordinated lines in the graph.
- It is customary to put time measurements on the X axis.
- The zero point should be indicated on the Y scale unless the data being presented make this inappropriate.
- If more than one curve is drawn on the chart, each must stand out clearly. This is accomplished by using different designations for each curve (e.g., one solid and one dotted curve).

Lined or curved graphs use the line or curve to indicate variations in the data. This type of graph is constructed by graphing points whose positions are determined by their respective values in terms of the X and Y-axis scales. The points in turn are connected by straight lines, which are then, if desired, smoothed or rounded to give an even flow from point to point.

Two types of ruling are used to develop graphs:

- *Arithmetic rulings* have equal distances between the coordinate lines; thus, equal quantities are given equal distances on the graph. For this reason, an arithmetic gradation will plot as a straight line on arithmetic coordinates. Furthermore, since equal amounts are assigned equal distances, equal changes are shown as equal absolute differences. Since this makes comparison of change and difference easy on arithmetic graphs, arithmetic rulings are commonly used for general-purpose presentations.

- *Logarithmic* or *semilogarithmic rulings* are used when it is necessary to compare a percentage change rather than an absolute change. The reason is that in a constant percentage change between two pairs of figures the differences between the logarithms of the figures will be equal. This means that, if the logarithms of the values, rather than the values themselves, are plotted, constant differences will show a constant percentage change. However, it is very time consuming to convert the data to logarithmic rulings marked in arithmetic numbers so that the data may be plotted directly.

Special types of line graphs are used to emphasize certain aspects of the information being presented or to make the information easy to use.

- *Silhouette charts* are line graphs that show positive and negative deviations from the zero base line. For added emphasis, the area between the zero line and the curve is filled in.
- *Bar charts* are a form of line graphs which show variations in both the total and the component parts. These charts are built up by first plotting the amount for the largest component part of the total and then labeling or shading the area below the amount. Such charts are generally constructed with the line for the largest element plotted first and succeeding elements added in descending quantitative order.
- *High-low graphs* present the change that occurs over a period of time, and the fluctuation that occurs within each time period. These charts are constructed by first plotting the lowest value, and then the highest value, for each period and connecting the points to form either bars or curves.
- *Histograms* are charts that represent frequency distributions in terms of both the size of the class interval and the frequency in each class. In appearance they are similar to bar charts, but they are actually different because the widths of the bars are significant. In histograms, the width of the rectangle or bar represents the size of the class; the height of the rectangle, the frequency in the class.

Bar charts are an effective tool for visually contrasting or comparing quantities. They are constructed by representing the quantities as bars of equal width, while the relative length of the bar indicates the magnitude of the quantity it represents. Bar charts fall into several categories, including some modifications that involve pictures. However, there are four basic types:

1. Simple, absolute bar charts conform to the basic definition above. In these charts, rectangular bars of equal width are erected from the same base line. The lengths of the bars are scaled according to the absolute or actual data. The bars can be constructed either horizontally or vertically; however, when time is involved, it belongs on the X axis. This factor, in turn, controls the direction in which the bars will extend.

2. Subdivided, absolute bar charts are similar to band charts in construction; that is, the largest component of the chart is plotted as the base of each bar, and then the next largest component is plotted on top of the base. Thus, these charts are accumulated so that each subdivision is plotted as an addition to the subdivision below it. The result is that the overall length of the bars represents the total, while the various components of the total can be seen within the bars.

3. Simple, percentage bar charts are similar to simple absolute bar charts; the difference is that the lengths of the bars represent percentage rather than absolute values.

4. Subdivided, percentage bar charts are developed so that each bar represents 100%. The bars are then broken down into segments; the length of each segment represents the appropriate percentage of the total of the bar. The subdivisions are arranged so that they are in the same order in each bar, and so that the largest is at the base of each bar.

Area diagrams are used similarly to bar charts except that they contrast quantities by comparing figures of varying areas. For examples, circles of different sizes can be used to represent different quantities. Another type of area diagram compares subdivisions of a single area. The most common example of this type is the pie chart, which consists of circular shapes broken into subdivisions, with the relative size of each subdivision indicating its portion of the whole. Pie charts are usually arranged with the segments in a clockwise order, according to descending size. The largest segment starts at the top and continues around to the right sometimes for more than half of the circle. The next segment is the second largest, and so on. Returning to the top of the circle is the smallest segment.

If more than one pie chart is presented for the purposes of comparison, the sectors should be arranged uniformally in each chart. Also, whenever possible, the descriptive wording should be placed horizontally on each sector. An important fact about pie charts should be noted: It is difficult to estimate visually the portion of the whole that the size of a sector represents; hence percentages or figures that will help the reader to grasp the significance of the information being represented should be included.

Map graphs present facts about geographic distribution in a pictorial form. There are five basic types of map graphs:

1. Dotted maps are presented in two ways; dots of fixed or similar size are placed on the map to indicate density, and dots of proportionate size to indicate total number in a specified area.
2. Shaded maps use varying degrees of shading, ranging from solid black to white, to indicate proportionate quantities for particular areas.
3. Crossed-hatched maps are similar to shaded maps except that various densities and directions of cross hatching are used instead of shading.
4. Colored maps use different colors or various shades of the same color to indicate differences between areas.
5. Tack maps use tacks, flag pins, and other means to mark specific spots. They can then serve for such purposes as illustrating reports by photographing the map with the pins on it, or by drawing in the pins on a map.

16 HUMAN FACTORS
DESIGN CONSIDERATIONS

HUMAN FACTORS OVERVIEW

Human factors engineering, as used in this context, refers to all the considerations and activities required to develop a personnel subsystem, including those concerned with human engineering. Human engineering research centers on the determination of facts about human behavior by use of the scientific method. More broadly, human factors engineering in the system center involves the development of systematic methods for considering man's role in the design of systems, and the application of these methods throughout the design of the total system. To a large extent these methods directly employ the "facts" established by human engineering research.

Human factors engineering grew out of a cross pollination of many existing disciplines. These included such diverse fields as engineering, medicine, psychology, anthropology, sociology, physics, mathematics, biology, theology, chemistry, education, and operations research.

In the field of human engineering, there has been considerable investigation in seven areas:

- Sensory and perceptual capabilities.
- Motor skills.
- Information processing and decision making.
- Group communications and man/machine functions.
- Work space requirements.
- Performance under conditions of stress, speed, fatigue, and unusual environments.
- Methods of analyzing complex man/machine systems.

Some of the objectives of human engineering are to enhance performance, to enhance manpower utilization, to reduce loss due to accidents and improper use of equipment, to decrease training expenditure, and to gain better user acceptance.

It is significant that the organization and implementation of the first separate systems engineering function in which the systems approach to human engineering was used occurred at Bell Telephone Laboratories early in the 1940s. The problem there was (and still is) to plan and design long-distance communication systems. Two Bell Laboratories people contributed basic ideas still used in systems work. Claude Shannon published the basic mathematical theory for information processing and communication in 1948. In the same year Norbert Wiener published his book on cybernetics, in which he implied that the two fundamental principles of all systems, living or mechanical, are (a) informational systems and (b) feedback systems. Accordingly, he concluded that the most promising techniques for studying both living and mechanical systems, and for combining them to form integrated control systems, were informational theory and survey theory. Thus, the "system approach," as originally conceived and presently applied, is primarily concerned with how to best process information. All systems (commercial and governmental) exist to increase man's capability in some manner, and by doing so to improve his welfare.

A.D. Hall, also of Bell Laboratories at the time, states in his book *A Methodology for Systems Engineering* that the first formal attempt to teach systems engineering was made in 1950 at the Massachusetts Institute of Technology by Mr. G. W. Gilman (then director of systems engineering at Bell Telephone Laboratories). In the wake of Gilman the first writers to expand system engineering as a technical discipline, namely, Schlager (1956), Engstrom (1957), and Gooden and Michael (1957), emphasized the vastly increasing system complexity as a principal reason for the development of a distinct methodology for systematizing a "system" out of many discrete and technically different inputs to achieve a unified functional entity.

Hall identifies a significant causal factor in the need for an expansion in the system engineering methodology. He calls it the expansion environment. By this he means all the technical, social, economic, cultural, political, and even moral forces that create a demand for larger and more complex systems to satisfy human needs. In this connection Hall says:

Although applications of the new technology now occur more rapidly than ever, needs for new systems have expanded even faster. Expanding needs simply accentuate the tendency of new knowledge to outstrip its application. The increasing number of things wanted by a society of increasing complexity places a premium on the ability to choose only the most valuable projects for development. Many organizations have found that they cannot afford short-range developments which are valuable within themselves but fail to fit the well considered long-range plans. As a consequence of the expanding environment, the engineering systems started today exhibit increasing scope, urgency, and expense. When large-scale and expensive system problems are encountered, large numbers of people are required for their solution.

This inevitably necessitates highly technical decisions and high-level compromises in the organizations involved. These decisions are often made in the face of large uncertainties. The burden of such decisions and compromises has become so great that the system engineering function has evolved to help organize the factual basis for them.

EMERGENCE OF THE PERSONNEL SUBSYSTEM

In a report for the Office of Naval Research, entitled *Human Factors Methods for Systems Design* (1960), which was prepared by the American Institutes of Research and edited by J. D. Folley, the early human factors programs are described as follows:

As a professional endeavor, human factors got its start early in World War II, although work had been done in the field as early as the nineteenth century. Before the war, however, psychologists in industry and government had been busy with problems of selecting and training men to fit the machines. With the war, however, entirely new aircraft control systems, radar gear, submarines, gunnery systems and other equipment were being developed. Systems reliabilities were poor, and accidents and injuries were high. Careful manpower selection and training just were not enough. Man-machine combinations were not doing the jobs for which they were planned. One reason for this impasse was that man-machine systems were making impossible demands of their human operators.

What were some of these demands? They were the familiar problems of inferior console design, fatigue and monotony, unusual environments, and faulty visibility, interpretability, reachability, and suitability. These are problems that the layman commonly associates with human factors technology, but there were other, equally important problems as well. There was the problem of deciding early in system development what tasks should be assigned to man. There was the problem of identifying the information that should be picked off a machine for display to an operator performing a monitoring task. There was the problem of designing a servosystem with an intermittent, nonlinear human operator in the loop. There was the problem of measuring and controlling the variations in the day-to-day performance of a single individual within a group of individuals.

In approaching these problems, the human factors specialist had at his disposal two powerful tools. One was a detailed knowledge of human behavior that had been accumulated over many years of psychological, anthropological, and other types of behavioral research. True, there were gaps in this knowledge, but because men do not change in some ways from generation to generation, many of these data were of continuing value. The fact that the eye can resolve two points as close together as 2 minutes of an arc was of help in establishing the resolution requirements for visual displays such as cathode ray tubes. The knowledge that man can respond to a light as rapidly as 200 milliseconds after it appears on the set was useful in selecting the buffers needed between manual and high-speed electromechanical processes.

The human factors specialist also had at his disposal techniques for conducting research on human beings to learn new facts about their behavior or performance. Applications of such techniques resulted in data being accumulated on such things as man's ability to adapt to darkness and be able to see in it while wearing red goggles, his ability to withstand extremes of temperature, pressure, and humidity, and his ability to make precise settings on a scope display. Suitable sizes of hand wheels, cranks, and foot pedals, the effective locations for them, and the optimal forces that should be exerted with them were established. Similar studies were made for displays.

Two things are clear about findings such as these. First, they are not the products of common sense, although in some cases they verify common sense. Common sense, for example, does not tell you that a man cannot distinguish between a tone of 900 cycles per second and another of 905 cycles per second. It does not tell you that if you expose the eye to 50 bits of information per second you will lose about one third in transmission. These facts are known only after careful research.

The second thing that is clear about these findings is that they have little value to the designer unless he knows when to apply them in system development. Some kind of plan is needed to integrate human factors objectives and methods with overall system engineering. Just as there is a procedure for engineering development, there needs to be a procedure for recognizing and solving human factors problems as the system grows from requirements to blueprints, to prototype, and beyond.

In 1956 H. P. Van Cott and J. W. Altman published for the U.S. Air Force a report entitled *Procedures for Including Human Engineering Factors in the Development of Weapon Systems.* This was the first report to describe a process for integrating human factors considerations into the design of a system. It included procedures for identification and analysis of functions, descriptions of operator performance, work space layout and equipment design, and system evaluation, as well as data and references on human capabilities and limitations. Most importantly, this report first described how to carry out mission analysis by placing system requirements directly in the mission context, thus generating additional requirements where there are apparent gaps in the sequence of operations for carrying out the mission. Thus, the "mission analysis" approach, as a primary system engineering tool, is a direct contribution of human engineering research.

In 1958, W. P. Chase, J. D. Vandenberg, and C. T. Goldsmith wrote articles for engineering trade journals which attempted to present human factors and human engineering as part of overall systems engineering. They addressed the problem of allocating functions to man or to machine on the basis of the limitations or capabilities of each. This was expressed as a series of tradeoffs to come up with the best balance. These articles indicated an important realization that the human factors specialists had to break out of their own tight little circle, of talking among themselves about good equipment design from the human engineering standpoint, and to seek an effective avenue for communications with equipment designers about personnel performance requirements. The proper technical grouping with which to identify and to assign the responsibility for developing personnel sybsystem requirements was (and still is) "system engineering".

W. B. Knowles published his report, *Automation and Personnel Requirements for Guided Missile Grounds Support Facilities*, for the U. S. Air Force in 1959. It was the first report pertaining to aerospace (missile) systems which dealt with the requirements for true system design. Automatic test equipment had been designed for use in missile checkout and testing. The assumption had been made that its use would reduce overall requirements for high-skill-level personnel to perform trouble shooting in the maintenance of missile electronic guidance and control systems. In fact, experience was just the opposite: the requirements for highly skilled people increased. What was the reason? Knowles and a group of investigators at the General Electric Company's Advanced Electronic Center at Cornell University studied and analyzed the actual designs of the SHARK, BOMARC, and MACE missile systems. The following is quoted from their summary of the report:

These investigations lead to the conclusion that it is not automatic equipment itself, or simply the amount of automatic equipment, that leads to excessive personnel requirements, but rather the use to which automation is put within the overall support complex. In order to understand more fully the respective roles of automatic equipment and manual operations, the maintenance system concept was developed. It was argued that the design of the maintenance system centers in the detailed specifications of the testing logic, rationale or strategy. . . . It was further argued that a lack of attention to the programming of manual tasks is really the factor that leads to a high-skilled-level requirement.

This study was conceived and sponsored deliberately in the interest of furthering better methodological integration of hardware and personnel subsystem design. Furthermore, it was accomplished in an engineering frame of reference rather than as a human factors study. The difference in perspective which is achieved by doing it in this way is very important from the standpoint of contributing to the advancement of systems engineering methodology, which is managed exclusively by people who, by education and experience, are primarily hardware oriented.

Back in 1952, a dramatic event occurred which is generally considered to be the situation that initiated the personnel subsystem program for system development projects. The F86D aircraft was delivered to the Air Defense Command Bases for operational use with a new General Electric engine. It happened that the engine employed for the first time an electronic fuel control system. No one had bothered to consider whether the available engine mechanics had the proper knowledge and skill to maintain it. Of course, they did not, and the aircraft, although accepted and ready to fly operational missions, was grounded until mechanics were trained and qualified to maintain the new electronic fuel system. This situation led to the initiation of the development of qualitative personnel requirements information during the prototype development stage of an aircraft or missile, in order to identify what types of operation and maintenance personnel specialists would be needed. The requirements information also described the selection and training requirements for developing the special knowledge and skills to accomplish job tasks which existed solely because of the design of the equipment. To support the qualitative personnel requirements information effort, Miller, Folley, and others under contract to the U.S. Air Force made a series of investigations covering such subjects as the design of electronic equipment for maintenance, methods of man/machine task analysis, and anticipating job skill requirements and procedures on new equipment. They were also asked to develop a series of guides on how to structure positions, how to develop position-task descriptions, and how to prepare handbooks of job instructions.

The first system test plan to include detailed personnel sybsystem test and evaluation procedures was prepared in 1960 and implemented for the Atlas E Category 2 test program at Vandenberg Air Force Base. This included a human engineering evaluation of the hardware characteristics, using a check list based on published human engineering design criteria and standards for ground equipment. The test data were systematically collected and evaluated, and a test report was prepared. Very few of the equipment changes recommended in the report were ever seriously considered for adoption and equipment redesign. The excuse given was usually, "The equipment works, doesn't it?" The reason why the anecdotal history of the Atlas missile personnel subsystem effort is recounted here is that it was typical of a "system" development program for aerospace systems at that time. It illustrates the difficulties encountered by personnel subsystem specialists in attempting to implement a system engineering approach in their particular program when the rest of the development effort involved almost completely hardware engineering. The "systems approach" occurred when the equipment items were collected as separate pieces at the site and an attempt was made to get them to "work together". By this time, delivery schedules had slipped badly and cost overruns were skyrocketing. It is entirely understandable that the system engineering effort carried on by means of the U.S. Air Force Category II system test program was a "make-it-work" approach.

In 1960 A. Shapero, J. I. Cooper, M. Rappaport, K. H. Schaeffer, and C. Bates, Jr., published a historically significant report entitled *Human Engineering Testing and Malfunction Data Collection in a Weapon System Test Program.* This report discussed the lack of attention to, and the inadequacy of, a human-initiated failure reporting technique. A series of missile test program analyses of failure data revealed that human-initiated failures constituted 20% to 53% of 3829 missile equipment failures reported. The report backtracks from this evidence and argues for the inclusion of human factors engineering as an integral part of a system analysis, design, and test program. It indicates that the identification of human operations and the determination of pertinent man/machine parameters for design and subsequent testing are based on identification of critical operations in the system functional analysis before equipment is designed. Criteria for selecting critical items to include in the performance prediction and testing programs are listed. Requirements for satisfactory failure reporting forms and procedures to include critical human operations are outlined. This study is typical of the interest in system development in the aerospace industry during a period when the total system approach was barely understood.

The methodology for handling the allocation of functions and tasks to equipment and human components had not been worked out. Human engineering research was confined mostly to "knobs and dials" design. Functional and task analyses were in the process of being developed as technical descriptions of equipment and of systems operations and maintenance requirements after design was completed (and generally after hardware was selected). Complex systems were being put together as assemblages of individual equipment items. Checkout and test equipment was being designed first; subsequently, someone figured out how to connect it with the prime mission equipment. These practices are in sharp contrast to the modern, more advanced system engineering concept, which is to accomplish functional and task analysis in order to establish system and end item performance.

During the period from 1957 to 1964, as the understanding and skills of personnel subsystem people increased for handling system engineering problems, they were often accused by their hardware subsystem engineering associates of attempting to "drive" the system development effort. If, by that, these critics meant that the personnel subsystem group was trying to promote the system engineering viewpoint, the charge was correct. However, other specialist groups emphasizing such system design areas as reliability, maintainability, safety, and cost effectiveness were also attempting to use their objectives to force the achievement of a total system deesign approach.

There is one further significant contribution that the personnel subsystem people have made in the evolution of system engineering methodology in general. Since they are engineering psychologists by academic background and have a professional grouping as behavioral scientists, they are well qualified both to contribute to the development of system design and to organize and regulate the behavior of the human beings who are included in the system development team. It requires teamwork, proper communication, training, and motivational measures to get such diverse groups of scientific and engineering specialists as are employed in a system development program to understand, accept, and apply the uniform procedures required to accomplish effective system engineering.

Operability is an important consideration to the human factors engineering people. Their main concern under this heading is with the input-transform-output interrelationships for combining equipment and human components into effective and efficiently functioning units. Especially important are the provisions for sensing information and transmitting proper intelligence to the human components about the equipment operating status for effective decision making and ease of controlling the change in status. The effective utilization of human components in a system is the classical concern of human engineering. In a complex electronic information system or aerospace system it is essential that the input-transform-output interrelationship between equipment and human components be precisely determined and the resultant integrated performance requirements be engineered to produce a harmonious system.

Operability relates closely to the subject of maintainability. Maintainability is concerned with the characteristics and features of the design which contribute to speed, economy, ease, and accuracy in keeping or restoring the system to normal operating conditions. In the planned maintenance environment, the chief concerns are such things as accessability, handling, positioning, repairability, checkout, monitoring, fault isolation, calibration, adjustment, storability, tools, test equipment, and spare parts. The impact on overall system effectiveness of designing a system for ease of maintenance is more subtle than that of designing for direct operator/equipment interfaces, but it is nonetheless important. Unfortunately, errors in maintenance design can be concealed completely from inspection and checkout procedures before committing the system to fulfill its specified objectives. Resulting catastrophic failures are just as costly as those caused by operator errors. Achieving a design which facilitates error-free, human maintenance task performance requires a rigidly controlled discipline of system engineering methodology in which human engineering considerations of design for maintainability are an inherent step.

Because of the dramatic quality of catastrophic failure, especially if there is harm to human beings, safety engineering as a special technical discipline has become a convenient avenue for forcing the recognition of the importance of safety. After designs have been committed, and after tests or production qualities of hardware have been delivered, one of the best arguments to employ in support of a design change proposal is to show a need to correct an unsafe condition. Extra care should be taken during the design process to identify places where irreversible failures could occur, and to improve the quality of parts, materials, or processes where necessary to increase the safety factor. The possibility of a safety hazard can be an important argument for obtaining design features and characteristics to improve system reliability and effectiveness which would not be approved otherwise.

By now it should be apparent to the reader that the objectives of human engineering, maintainability, and safety are all the same, mainly to serve as a forcing function to obtain more comprehensive system design. Historically in military systems development, the reliability movement had to shoulder the burden most often for promoting effective total design. This is reflected in the definition of "reliability," which is usually given as "the probability that a system will perform the required functions under specified conditions, without failure, for a specified period of time." The performance of individual component parts of equipment in fulfilling system specification requirements was the first concern of reliability engineers. As collections of equipment were assembled in an attempt to make them function as a system, reliability analysis soon revealed that the test and failure data collected on the individual component parts of the equipment did not necessarily predict their performance when they were integrated with other component parts and used in an operational environment. "System reliability" and "operational confidence" naturally emerged as new concepts. In regard to system reliability the emphasis was on approaching the system engineering problem by "backing into it" from analysis of operational failure. The system orientation of contemporary reliability engineers is reflected in their concern with such things as simplicity, invulnerability to damage, redundancy of the functional active element, residual adequacy, accuracy, and proper personnel skills and proficiency.

As reliability engineers have increased their understanding of why systems fail, they have broadened the concept of reliability and accordingly have introduced the term "system effectiveness." This has been defined as the product of design adequacy, system availability (i.e., operational readiness), and reliability. Introduction of the more comprehensive concept of system effectiveness has been a big step toward achieving a total system design approach.

By 1967 it was apparent that personnel subsystem considerations had been started very early in some system design processes. Too little was known, however, about how these considerations interacted in the early phases of system design; therefore, Bell Telephone Laboratories let a research contract to American Institutes for Research to investigate the human performance considerations early in systems design. The resultant report, prepared by this writer, J. W. Altman, and S. J. Munger, served a significant need by determining the methodology to be used for human performance considerations from ground zero to the point where functions could knowledgeably be allocated. The activity networks as depicted in this book for the formation of objectives, definition, and preliminary design phases are based on this work.

In 1969 it became apparent that not enough was known about what the end products of thorough personnel subsystem development should be. Once again, Bell Telephone Laboratories let a research contract to investigate and determine what the end items of comprehensive personnel subsystem development in an informational system environment should be. This work was undertaken by Research Associates Incorporated, and the resultant report, written by this writer, J. G. Gardner, and G. E. McClure and entitled *Identification and Definition of Personnel Subsystem Analysis and Design Products and Services*, identified some twenty end products that would result from comprehensive design of the personnel subsystem in a man/machine computer-based information system. This report provided both the development information required to produce the products and services and the format specifications for each one. The results of this report were used extensively in the discussions of the preliminary design, detail design, and test phases presented earlier in this book.

By the year 1970, a great deal was known about the beginning, the middle, and the end of personnel subsystem design as it related to information systems. Most of the literature on this subject has been in the form of research reports, studies, and surveys, and most of these have involved either the U.S. Department of Defense or aerospace-related industries. Even in 1970 little application of this research was evident in industrial computer-based system development efforts, perhaps because the computer vendors still failed to recognize this whole body of knowledge.

HUMAN ENGINEERING PROCEDURES

As was demonstrated earlier, human engineering occurs throughout the development process and is integrated into the activity network discussed earlier. Human engineering is performed by human factors personnel in consultation with system analysts, equipment designers, equipment engineers, computer programmers, operations personnel, and managers. Human engineering considerations should be given to the allocation of functions and the specific design of human functions. Optimally, the relationship between the equipment engineers and designers and the human factors personnel is such that human considerations are introduced in the earliest phases of system development.

In order to be effective, human factors engineering people must analyze the data from task analysis and equipment requirements analysis to further delineate man/equipment interactions. In order to accomplish this, they must collect appropriate data on such factors as specific tasks, task relationships, and man/equipment task relationships. Task analysis charts, task descriptions, data characteristics, human requirements, and human attributes are required for each task and interface requirement.

Human factors personnel must also analyze critical design requirements, that is, the vital things that a system must do to a certain level of performance to meet its objectives. The purpose of the analysis of critical design requirements is to identify the possible choices and to choose among them in such a way as to obtain the optimal man/machine system performance. This analysis of critical design requirements includes the critical operations performed by the system, the activities for each critical operation involving man/machine interaction, the outputs of the activities for each critical operation, the critical operating variables in each activity, and the critical design requirements of the systems that affect these variables.

For example, human factors personnel should be deeply involved in the determination of display and control requirements so as to make certain that the human engineering inputs to the design requirements are fully considered. The human factors personnel would analyze the characteristics of the displays to be used by each operator with the following factors in mind:

- The human sense or senses used by the display; the load should be balanced among the senses.
- The form of display; the best way to display information for human use should be selected by considering such variables as:
  - a. Search time.
  - b. Complexity.
  - c. Information content.
  - d. Coding.
  - e. Density.
  - f. Size.
  - g. Methods of presentation.
- The accuracy, speed, and workload called for by the display; it is necessary to determine whether an operator can meet the requirements.
- Adverse environmental factors; noise, vibration, or other adverse factors which might influence the ability of an operator to read a display should be considered. Also, the controls to be used by each operator should be examined with the following factors in mind: task distribution among the various limbs, placement of controls, types of controls, hazards imposed by the equipment or layout, and overriding controls.

During design, controls should be made compatible with their associated displays through considerations of proximity, similarity of grouping, coding, framing, and leveling.

Some of the methods the human factors people use for analysis include the following:

- Motion picture camera. (This method is valuable for determining frequency of use, total time of use, and sequence of use.)
- Eye camera. (This method lends itself to the determination of frequency of use, total time of use, and sequence of use.)
- Direct observation of operators.
- Judgments. (This method is particularly useful in determining the relative importance of displays and controls. It is also helpful in obtaining judgments about the frequency of use, total time of use, and sequence of use.)
- Link analysis. (This technique is used to quantify visual, spatial, and operating relationships between displays and between controls in determining their optimal placement. The performance of link analysis requires some type of mockup or prototype.)

Frequently, the human factors engineering people need to prepare models and mockups. When they do, they should consider these kinds of things:

- The model should be kept current, reflecting design changes as accurately as possible.
- Effective mockups serve the following purposes: aid for design integration, testing man/machine interactions, design experimentation, three-dimensional conceptual aids, aids for training evaluation, presentation aids, and public relations tools.
- Dynamic simulation should be used, when appropriate, for the detailed design of equipment that requires critical performance.

Work space layout is another major consideration of the human factors people. In this regard they consider the human measurements of the population of individuals that will operate and maintain the system. Other work space layout recommendations might include the following:

- Determine whether a person will be sitting, standing, or moving about and then choose the appropriate measurements.
- When designing for reach, strength, or anything involving human limits, design for the smallest person in the population. If possible, design adjustable equipment, so that it will accommodate workers of various sizes.
- When designing seats, doors, passage ways, or anything else involving human size, design for the largest persons in the population.

Design should ensure capability and maintainability from the fifth through the ninety-fifth percentile group of user population. In using anthropomorphic data, the following items should be considered:

- Nature, frequency, and difficulty of related tasks.
- Position of the body during performance of tasks.
- Mobility or flexibility requirements imposed by each task.

Although this is not a book on human factors, the subject should be emphasized enough to bring it into complete balance with the other parts of the system development and to show its importance as reflected in the activities in the networks in previous chapters. In order to accomplish this, it may be well to go into some detail regarding one area thought to be rather simple, and to show what has been found out there by the human factors people. The area selected is that of seated operations. Some of the considerations and known quantified data for a person working at seated operations are as follows:

- When continuous monitoring or control is required of a seated operator, controls and displays should be mounted on a sloped console surface.
- For normal seated operations, the slope of the control display panel surface should begin at 31¾ inches from the floor, with the overall console height not exceeding 49 inches.
- Arm rests should be provided at all consoles as either a part of the console or a part of the operator's chair.
- Console arm supports should provide at least 8 inches and preferably 12 inches of resting surface, projecting horizontally from the front of the console.
- Arm rests should be a minimum of 2 inches wide by 10 inches long.
- If the operator must record data, a writing surface 13 inches in depth is recommended.
- Knee and foot room beneath the paneled surface should be provided. The minimum dimensions should be 25 inches high by 20 inches wide by 18 inches deep.
- All cabinets, consoles, and work surfaces requiring that operators stand or sit in close proximity to the front surface should contain a knee space 2½ feet deep by 4 feet wide at the base.
- Handles on cabinets and consoles should be reset when possible to eliminate projections on the surface.

At this point, the interested reader is referred to the bibliography, which lists the best human factors engineering books available today. They contain a wealth of data, and most of them have application to the design of man/machine information systems.

SUMMARY

Someone has said that human factors technology is "an ambiguously named multiscience approach to man/machine integration." This definition is not altogether accurate; human factors technology is a still-developing area where all the ideas have not yet been sorted out into a "cookbook" format that can be used under any conditions. Some of the technologies which have grown out of human engineering are now called by a larger family name personnel subsystem design. They are as follows:

- *Human factors* gives consideration to man and systems, including function allocation, equipment design, personnel selection and training, performance assessment.
- *Human factors engineering* emphasizes the application of human performance data through system development.
- *Human engineering* involves the application of data about man and his performance to the design of the physical part of the man/machine system (e.g., displays, controls, forms, and formats). Human engineering ensures that the physical part of the system will conform to man's abilities and limitations and be compatible with the tasks which he must perform.
- *Engineering psychology* is a field of specialization in psychology and is concerned with man's behavior (performance) while using machines and tools. It is academically oriented and mainly provides data inputs to human performance technology and personnel subsystem design.
- *Personnel subsystem development* is the complete integration of human factors considerations into the system design. It includes the application of human performance data to system design, the design and documentation of jobs, training, personnel planning, and test evaluation.
- *Ergonomics* is very much like human factors, but ergonomists tend to place strong emphasis on mechanics and human engineering. The term is used mostly in Great Britain and continental Europe.

Some terms relating to human performance technology have been developed in the aerospace industry and are widely used in the literature of the industry. Among them are the following:

- *Bioastronautics* deals specifically with human factors considerations in space travel.
- *Biotechnology* describes human engineering as applied to space vehicles.

- *Biomechanics* is the science of human body mechanics, including strength, work, and kinetics.
- *Life sciences* are somewhat similar to human factors, but with emphasis on human research with a strong medical, psychological, or biological orientation.
- *Life support* is an area of human factors concerned with the parts of the system requiring special attention to health, safety, or protection.

Those who make things for people to use have always been concerned with whether or not what they made could indeed serve the intended purpose. This level of concern is usually sufficient to ensure a usable product.

Even when it is not, people can adapt fairly easily to an improperly designed simple tool or machine. However, as individual machines and tools, along with the procedures to use them, become more complex, particularly when they are integrated into systems, simple concern on the part of the designer or reliance on the ability of people to adapt in most situations is not sufficient.

Soon after the start of World War II the introduction of many efficient and very complex weapons systems made it abundantly clear that, as one observer put it, "Machines do not fight alone. Radar does not see, people see; sonar does not hear, people hear; an aircraft does not guide itself to target, people do; a missile does not launch itself, people do." As various systems encountered difficulties or even failed as a result of exceeding human capability limits, or failing to utilize human capabilities effectively, something had to be done. Since the scientific area dealing with the human behavior of organisms is psychology, a number of well-known and highly regarded psychologists were asked to help. Unfortunately, their suggestions to the system designers for solving many of the problems which were encountered were largely ignored.

In postwar years these same psychologists and others, often engineers who were attracted to this new discipline, continued their activities and brought into sharp focus the fact that, just as machines do not fight alone, neither do they work alone, maintain themselves alone, or teach their operators to use them alone. These activities also made it clear that neither the common-sense approach or the retro-fit approach was a valid method of integrating people and machines into systems.

The common-sense approach is the name given to the attitude that anyone can design a person into a system solely because he is a person. Unfortunately, common sense has two major failings, one that it is not very precise. In designing a bridge, for example, common sense tells us that it must be strong, but not how strong, or what materials should be used. Other resources must be considered to answer such questions confidently. A second failing is that one person's common sense does not always agree with another's. As a result, the commonest common sense often belongs to the ranking person in the decision making process. The human performance technologists, recognizing the limitations of this approach, substitute the precision of determining and verifying data and logical analysis.

The tradition of relying on objectively determined data which the first human performance scientists brought with them has been continued through the years of evolution and growth. In addition to data which have been borrowed from other disciplines, such as experimental psychology, the specialty known as engineering psychology in human performance, specialists have generated a substantial body of data relating to particular parameters encountered in system development.

Since 1940 there have been published at least 25,000 articles and scholarly papers with direct relevance to human performance technology. Some of the major areas dealt with in these papers will be briefly discussed. The content areas may be grouped under two headings: human performance capabilities and limitations, and physical design parameters. Human performance capabilities and limitations include such factors as the following:

- Information processing: data under this heading relate to the amount of information in such things as a code or a display that a human being can assimilate and use. These data are useful in the design and evaluation of codes and in the determination of whether or not a given sequence, or group of tasks, can be expected to be performed successfully.
- Verbal and quantitative skills: data in this area relate to language manipulation and the learning and retention of verbal information. In the skill areas, such things as mental computation and concept formulation and use are included.
- Motor behavior: again, the learning of motor skills is an important area of concern. In addition, such things as hand/eye coordination, motor task compatibility, and reaction time are included under this heading.
- Sensory/perceptual capabilities: under this heading, all data relating to the functions and characters of the various senses such as vision and hearing, are included. Also covered are the ways in which patterns form and objectives are perceived.

Physical design parameters include such things as the following:

- Anthropometric measures: these data describe the various body dimensions, such as reach, standing height, seated height, or shoulder height. Anthropometric data are particularly valuable and important in the design of work space or of any equipment to be used or maintained by people.
- Displays/control characteristics: the area of human factors technology known as human engineering has produced a substantial body of knowledge concerning the design and evaluation of displays and controls of all types. This body of knowledge has, for the most part, been covered in the design standards and specifications and been made available in a number of sources.

The importance of the application of human factors engineering in system development varies as a function of the nature of the system. All systems have some manual involvement, even if it is only for the performance of maintenance functions. However, the degree of or need for human performance considerations, as well as their importance, can and does change, depending on the degree of manual activity necessary. Important manual activities may occur in the preparation of input, the operation of the system, or the utilization of output. The decisions as to the importance of these activities may be based on the volume or the criticality of the manual functions.

The overall objective of the application of human factors engineering is to purposely design the man/machine interaction and interfaces rather than allow them to evolve or develop by default. If this objective is met, then system performance is affected in several ways. First of all, there is a significantly higher probability of success on the first implementation of the system, since the involvement of people has been provided for and planned. Second, user acceptance of the system is enhanced, since the system has been designed to meet the needs of the user, taking maximum advantage of his capabilities without exceeding his limitations. Third, the skill level may be reduced, thereby enlarging the manpower available to operate the system and to reduce training time and cost. Finally, the time lost in the correction and processing of errors is reduced, since manual functions have been allocated in a logical fashion and the procedures associated with these functions have been designed in a specific manner.

CHAPTER **17**   STANDARDS FOR DESIGN
AND TECHNIQUES FOR
DOCUMENTATION

OVERVIEW OF STANDARDS AND DOCUMENTATION

The creation, use, and maintenance of adequate documentation are
critical for the development and operation of a total system. It is
important to recognize that documentation is the only tangible product
of the system development process. Since information systems do not
exist in stable, stationary forms, documentation is the only means we
have for capturing and reflecting the dynamics, requirements, and
parameters of the system.

Documentation serves a multiplicity of needs; the major one is probably the communication of ideas. Documentation communicates the
design and the quantification of the system from the designers to other
designers, users, maintainers, and so forth. System documentation also
reflects agreement among system developers, designers, management,
and users with respect to the intent of the effort. It provides a means for
highlighting discrepancies and for clarifying ambiguous or obscure
areas. In this regard, it is particularly important to document the
reasons for tradeoffs agreed upon during the development effort.

The kinds of system development efforts that we have been discus-
sing are complex. The number of developmental activities and the
potential relationships among them seem almost infinite. Without the
kinds of documentation indicated in the activity network, the task of
coordinating and integrating these activities would be nearly impossible. An example is the function flow chart, which is one manner of
reflecting the design responsibilities of the manual and machine
designers. With this chart, the designers can see how their particular
responsibilities relate to those of the other team members. Likewise, the

242

people who ultimately work on the system can use the completed chart to perceive how they fit into overall system operations.

In order to synchronize the development effort in meeting intermediate and final target dates, there must be a means of communicating time relationships and dependencies. Several kinds of descriptions were identified earlier in this book. It will be recalled that schedules and PERT networks were identified as particularly useful means for providing continuity.

Documentation is used throughout the development in briefing management, interfacing organizations, contracting groups, system workers, and the like. It would be impossible to capture the pertinent information, reflect it accurately, and retain it without some form of documentation. Reports, program documentation, and position practices all serve this end.

Most of the documentation cited above is formal and required. It should be recognized that each development team member also uses documentation consistently on an informal basis. These people continually record data, make up flow charts, sketch out designs, and use these to communicate to one another and to support their own memories. These rough notes and sketches are also useful to the designers for trying out new ideas on others. When this type of documentation record is finalized, it is included in the formal documentation.

System and user managements have a continuing need to be informed as the development progresses in order to secure their approval. They need information such as equipment requirements and agreements with manufacturers, and specifications for the kinds and numbers of people who will be needed to operate the system. They also need to know the training requirements for these people, the scheduling requirements, the production and quality results, and so forth. The personnel organization needs this information in order to select people; training people need it in order to develop training packages; maintenance personnel need it in order to make evaluations and repairs. It may be that operating management can use the same documentation that is developed for these other groups. It is more likely, however, that the same information will be more easily used by operating management if the documents are reorganized and reformatted to serve its specific needs.

The specifications for optimally useful management documentation are not yet known. Perhaps all system information should be pulled together in one place in order to highlight the complex interrelationships which exist. On the other hand, only certain types of information may be relevant and useful. In this case, only the pertinent information should be selected and presented to operating management. Whatever the appropriate quantity and blend of system information for management turn out to be, it is safe to assume that the most useful focus will be administrative implications for managing the operation.

Most developmental organizations have found it worth while to develop procedures for creating a development documentation library which will contain the information generated by the developmental team. Each member of the team contributes to the library through approved routines and also has ready access to it for his own informational requirements.

DOCUMENTATIONS AND STANDARDS TODAY

In the 20 years that computer-based systems have been built, marvelous means of documenting the machine logic portion of system documentation have been developed. Symbologies for flow charts, standards for decision tables, and specifications for design drawings have been drawn up; however, most of these were developed during the batch mode era and are now of questionable value in the real-time, random processing modes. Unfortunately, the computer field has not enjoyed the thousands of years of growth that have characterized the disciplines of engineering and architecture and, therefore, has not yet developed the most efficient ways of documenting. The designers of computer-based information systems seem particularly reluctant to document their results and findings, perhaps because they have too often had to fall back on long, descriptive narratives as a vehicle for documentation. Another compounding problem in the area of documentation is that too many attempts have been made to have one document serve too broad an audience. Not only would the system design team use the function flow chart, but using organizations were also expected to understand and apply it effectively. To complicate the matter further, it was frequently given to management as an explanation of how the system operated. It simply is not realistic to expect this kind of document to communicate effectively with such diverse audiences.

DOCUMENTATION AND STANDARDS—WHERE THEY ARE GOING

It will probably be a long while before an industry-wide set of documentations, symbols, and standards which communicate effectively is agreed upon. Although various vendors and large industries have formed a group to try to standardize in these areas, no immediate hope for solution is on the horizon. Probably documentation, standards, and criteria based on the activities discussed earlier in each of the stages in this book will be developed. This documentation will probably evolve after many revisions to a state of refinement where it can be said to be formal documentation for the twenty end products of personnel subsystem development. Also, certain standards and documents have been agreed upon for coding, depicting the logic, compiling and assembling, and some EDP testing functions.

Considerable work remains to be done in the area of documentation and standards. Without agreed-upon documents, the situation in regard to standards and acceptable performance within the design team is almost ludicrous because one does not have a set of requirements to work toward or be measured by.

Once again, the aerospace industry and government have a great deal to teach others about documentation. Since their efforts have been more complex in such areas as the development of the space system, they have required better and more thorough documentation. Therefore, other industries can learn a great deal by examining the kind of documentation requirements that have been developed for aerospace. You may remember the controversy about the supersonic transport jets. When the documentation was sent to Washington on the aircraft, the newspapers reported that it took five airplane loads to carry all the material. In other words, the documentation for these jets outweighed the actual aircraft by about 5 to 1.

Many of the problems in computer-based system design have been due to too little documentation, rather than too much. Designers are quick to state that they are not paper factories. This is a derogatory way to discuss documentation; however, the fact is that designers make their contributions through documented ideas. If the whole area of systems engineering or development is ever to grow into a profession, it must develop a language and a means for communication that is uniformly agreed upon and effective.

Documentation means the act or instance of furnishing or authenticating with documents. Generally speaking, documentation in systems work can be broken into three basic areas. First, the people who operate the system need job-relevant, concise, well-organized documentation of their jobs. This documentation could be called operating procedures or practices and might be likened to the owner's manual for an automobile. Basically, it tells how to operate and care for the system. The second reason for documentation is to give guidance to anyone wishing to maintain, correct, or change the system. This kind of documentation includes computer-run diagrams, program listings, files, and data layouts. It is similar to the technical or shop manual for an automobile. This documentation spells out in detail the requirements of a healthy system—how it operates, and how to correct, maintain, or change it. The third basic reason for documenting is to supply management with a basic policy, procedure, responsibility, and administrative reference about the system. It provides the insight that a manager needs in order to supervise and administer the system intelligently.

In summary, the three general types of documentation required are operational, maintenance, and managerial. It is important to remember that documentation is created for a specific use by certain individuals. These users and their needs govern the language, the depth, and the methodology for depicting the documentation information. Also, one must remember that, in order for documentation to be useful, it must be kept current. Therefore, a scheme for filing, retrieving, and updating the documentation for a system is essential.

CHAPTER 18 TRAINING TECHNOLOGY IN SYSTEM DESIGN

TRAINING OVERVIEW

Webster defines training as "a process or method to lead or direct growth; to form by instruction, discipline, or drill." This implies a result—growth or performance—and it implies a method and change. It should be understood that this, in fact, is the purpose of training—to result in learning, or a permanent change in the behavior of an individual so that he reliably performs in a certain prescribed manner. Training and learning, however, are not synonomous; unless learning (behavioral change) takes place, training time is wasted. It is interesting to note that, if performance can be specifically defined, answers as to training content and method can be obtained and learning measured.

Another way to look at training is to outline its components and the responsibilities of each. Training is generally thought of in a broad, inclusive sense, and its three basic components—development, administration, and instruction—are sometimes overlooked. The development component includes the design of job procedure preparation, development of media, and formulation of training materials. The administrative component consists primarily of establishing proper environmental conditions for effective training. This includes such factors as budget, personnel, time, equipment, training rooms, direction, control, and followup. The instructional component includes the imparting of information to the trainee within the confines of the developmental and administrative conditions established.

This chapter will consider two very different kinds of training problems. One is training the developmental or design team members in the skills and knowledge required to build the system. The second is training the operational personnel in how to operate the developed

247

system. For ease in dealing with these two, the training of designers will be referred to as developmental training, and the training of the operators of the system as operational training.

TRAINING DEVELOPMENT PROCESS OVERVIEW

The subject of training development underwent extensive research during the 1950s and 1960s. Although many variations on the process of developing training were created at the conceptual level, they do not differ very much. The one outlined here is a generalized model of the seven major steps in training development:

1. Determine and record job information. Job information details how the trained individuals must be able to perform; it describes the job. This information must exist in some form in order for the training to be job relevant.
2. Specify the objectives (or requirements) of training. In general, training requirements result from the differences between job performance requirements and trainee capabilities before training.
3. Identify and sequence appropriate units of training. Total training content is subdivided into units, parts, or lessons which can be efficiently taught together. These units should be ordered so as to best support learning.
4. Arrange the material to be taught within each unit in the order that will permit optimal learning. The order or sequence in which material is taught is most significant to effective learning.
5. Select the most effective method to teach each type of material. The method is the manner or technique by which the material is taught, for example, practice or drill, progressive (simple to complex) parts, and presentations.
6. Design appropriate training aids and materials. These include charts, slides, films, simulators, dummy media, and practice media.
7. Specify appropriate proficiency measures and their application within the training sequence. These are simply tests and other evaluative measures to determine the efficiency of training and the degree of learning at different points in the learning session.

OPERATIONAL TRAINING

Probably the most important thing to keep in mind is that effective training is a result. It results from thorough systems definition, optimal job design, complete and concise people-relevant documentation of jobs, preparation of instructional media, and training of instructor personnel. In simple terms, if jobs are not designed and documented, it is impossible to train personnel. It should be obvious that, in order to train people effectively, the subject must be attacked at its root, and that is in system design and documentation. This point rests on a fundamental educational fact: training must be based on thorough, clear information and knowledge about the job. It is the responsibility of the system development personnel to provide the amount and kind of job information required.

A system group cannot confine its responsibility to the development of the new system; it also has prime responsibility for seeing that the system is implemented and operates optimally. A vital ingredient in the implementation process is training based on thorough job design.

Perhaps a loose analogy will help to build appreciation for the fundamental concept of job design before training. If one were to build a car according to sound engineering principles rather than considering the job of driving the car, the throttle would be located at the carburetor, the fuel gauge at the fuel tank, the gear selector on the transmission, and so forth. If this were the case, a dozen or more people would be required to operate the automobile. However, job design indicates that these control mechanisms must be brought to a central place in the car for one person to effectively operate it. Similarly, in system design, jobs can be so poorly designed that effective training does not help. It is easy to design jobs that cannot be handled effectively by people; therefore, training must be viewed as resulting from thorough systems design and must be considered in the system development process. System designers should have the following questions uppermost in their minds during the development process: How am I going to get this subject across to the people who will operate this system? Can people, in fact, proficiently do the things I have designed for them to do?

Most of the research into the subject of training technology over the past two decades has concerned itself with developing training for existing jobs. B. F. Skinner, the eminent Harvard psychologist, probably said this as succinctly as possible when he stated, "Behavior that is rewarded tends to be repeated." Skinner, it will be recalled, is the father of programmed instruction. His contribution to training technology cannot be underestimated. Probably equally well known in training circles is Robert Mager, whose books on developing training objectives and instructional technology have changed the course of modern training development.

If one has defined, designed, and documented the new job in the system as indicated by the methodology put forth in this book, efficient training can result. On the other hand, if jobs were just allowed to evolve, efficient training would be nonexistent at the time the new system was put into operation.

Many studies indicate that training is an expensive solution, and that there are other, perhaps more desirable methods for achieving the desired behavior within the design of the system. Generally speaking, the easiest way to obtain individuals with the required behavior is to select those who already have it. If this cannot be done, the next easiest way to achieve effective performance is to select individuals who show promise and develop job aids to support them so that training is not required. Therefore, in any situation where a different behavior is required, the first thought should be, "Can I select individuals who have that behavior now?" The second should be, "Can I develop job aids, so that existing individuals can perform with these aids?" And, finally, one should ask, "If that cannot be, how and what training should be developed?"

In the process of system development, the most difficult part of training development is determining job requirements. Performance measurements and task sequences are, relatively speaking, easy to determine on an existing job and difficult to determine on a nonexistent one. In order to predetermine job requirements in the system development process, the designer has to use a combination of analytical techniques. These are generally called task analysis. "Task analysis" is a generic term used to denote a subset of analytical techniques, including input/output, decision analysis, contingency analysis, time line analysis, link analysis, and mission analysis. On the basis of this definition, input/output analysis is similar to what the training people call stimulus/response.

Perhaps a few words on the timing of training would be appropriate. The best training materials and design can be undermined by providing the training too far in advance of its use. Training that is not applied dissipates at a very rapid rate. Therefore, training for new behaviors should be given as close to their required actual use as possible. If the training is given months in advance of the cutover or conversion, the performance level achieved then will be degraded by nonuse.

The fundamental vehicle for the training of manual jobs in a new system is the position practice. This is not to say that the position practice is the training, but rather that it is the basis for the training.

Persons who are interested in clerical training should consult the bibliography of this book for publications on the research on training which has taken place in the last few years, and which is readily available to all who are interested.

TRAINING FOR THE DESIGNER

The kind and quality of training to be offered to system designers constitute a confusing subject. Hopefully, this chapter will shed some light not only on what training exists, but also on what training should exist. As stated in the preceding section, most research in training technology has been in the area of developing training for existing jobs. This is very frequently not the case in system development work, where new jobs are being created which did not exist before. Therefore, training technology which calls for job study including observation, interviewing, and data gathering from job incumbents does not apply in this situation.

It is fair to state that no college or university has yet trained a system designer. However, one must quickly add that various members of the design team, such as mathematicians, psychologists, and computer science experts, are adequately trained at many major colleges and universities. It is important to remember that the subject of system development is so broad and so deep that it encompasses many formal disciplines. It is for this reason that no schools are, as yet, training designers. Most industries and government have turned to the computer manufacturers or vendors for the type of training that they say is required to train system personnel. However, in the total system context of man/machine involvement for attaining corporate objectives, this kind of training leaves a great deal to be desired. Generally, it concentrates on how to make the computer operate or how to make it operate more effectively. Therefore, there is an abundance of courses in various languages, file design techniques, different types of control software, different hardware configurations, and so forth. Although these courses are needed for the design of computer-based information systems, they comprise only one small portion of the needed curriculum.

A recent review of all the courses offered by vendors, colleges, universities, and educational houses indicated that not a single course is taught in such subjects as mission analysis, contingency analysis, time-line analysis, or other task analysis techniques. These analytical techniques are used throughout the system development process; therefore, it is imperative for any system designer to know when and how to use a particular technique, and what can be expected as a result.

Also, in the early 1970s, few colleges and universities, and no educational vendor or computer manufacturer, offered courses in human engineering. To go one step further, only Bell Laboratories and the U.S. Air Force are currently offering courses directed toward the development of the personnel subsystem. Most of the workshops and seminars offered by the various system or EDP organizations still concentrate on techniques for making the computer run.

One should not conclude from this discussion that system developers or designers will be trained in a single curriculum in the future. The project development team should continue to remain interdisciplinary, as outlined in the earlier chapters of this book. Therefore, it is most appropriate to train psychologists, operations research people, computer scientists, and others much as we are doing today. Furthermore, within these fields there will be various kinds of specialization. Within psychology there will be behavioral psychologists, training psychologists, research psychologists, and others. Also, one might foresee such specialties as data gatherinng, modeling, and techniques for quantitative analysis within the operations research field. Within the field of computer science one can envision specialists in languages, data base design, communications equipment, and other areas.

How will the educational needs of the future be satisfied? Will the hardware vendors develop the kind of total curriculum that is required? The answer to this question is probably no. It is beyond the computer vendors' interest and capability to develop the kind of overall curriculum that has been suggested. Then will the colleges and universities produce the kinds of individuals who can manage systems and blend the different disciplines together effectively? Again the answer seems to be no. Although many colleges and universities would like to try to fulfill this role, they lag many years behind industry and government in the knowledge of what is required. Therefore, it is probable that in-house training programs, both in industry and government, will be the first to satisfy these needs. The various semiprofessional associations (e.g., The Association for Systems Management and Data Processing Management Association) will probably provide the avenue for sharing these training curricula. It now appears that the efforts of the military and of NASA will remain far in front of industry for some time to come. A coherent, overall approach to developing systems personnel of all types is probably 15 years away.

Meanwhile, industry and government must examine their specific needs for the training of system designers more closely. Course offerings by computer manufacturers, educational vendors, or colleges and universities must be examined for their behavioral objectives in the context of the total system development job. This examination should be made impartially and even ruthlessly, and all deficiencies exposed.

In conclusion, it is now possible to train many of the team members of a system development effort effectively, either at colleges or by means of courses developed by computer vendors or educational vendors. However, this is not nearly enough. Unfortunately, it will probably be a long time before enough research and effort have been expended to fully develop a comprehensive curriculum for system designers and ultimately for project managers.

TRAINING FOR THE PROJECT MANAGER

Generally speaking, the career path used to develop project managers in the past was a faulty one. Usually, a person started off in systems work as some sort of apprentice or junior programmer. After training and apprenticeship his experience allowed him to assume the title of senior programmer or a like designation. Often, if he was still found to be effective, he was promoted to perhaps a junior analyst role. Here the actual skills and knowledge required to do the job were quite different from those of the programmer; hence, many good programmers failed in the analyst role. If, however, a person was successful in making this transition, he was usually promoted again to some senior analyst role. Finally, if he was successful as a senior analyst, he became a candidate for promotion to project manager. By the time this person became project manager, he had acquired such a strong bias toward the hardware side of systems that he rarely functioned effectively in his new role.

It is in the crucial area of project management that the greatest training deficiency lies. One might well ask whether a business graduate would not be a likely candidate for a project manager. There is no inherent reason why a business graduate could not fill this role. However, his training has not been conducive to the job of managing the development of a complex system. He has not been taught the art and science of premanaging activities. Neither has he been given a reasonable appreciation for the various disciplines in system design and the particular contribution of each to the system development process. Also, he is ill equipped to deal with the specialized languages of the various disciplines and the languages of systems itself. The U.S. Department of Defense and some of the branches of service are closer to training project managers than is industry.

The term "project manager" is often misunderstood and misused.

Sometimes it is used to mean a particular technique such as PERT (*P*rogram *E*valuation *R*eview *T*echnique). At other times it is used to designate the supervisor of the programmers. Actually, the project manager is the single person who is in charge of and is responsible for the development of the total system.

In order to successfully discharge this responsibility the project manager must be able to lead the development team in the activities of planning, directing, organizing, and controlling. These management functions must be performed in a prescriptive, rather than a postscriptive, way. Most other management functions are performed after the fact. A project manager, however, must act before the fact. He must blend the various skills, knowledges, languages, and disciplines involved in system development into an effective whole. Therefore, the skill and knowledge requirements for a project manager are not the same as those for a programmer, for an analyst, or for a traditional line manager. The project manager's job is roughly analogous to that of a general contractor.

APPENDIX

This Appendix demonstrates the types of considerations that would take place during the formation of objectives phase. To provide examples, a mythical system was selected (a personnel resources system for a large company). The documentation given as examples of activity–generated products is not to be viewed as the ultimate or final resultant documentation; rather, it is suggestive of the kind of analysis, derivations, and information that would be depicted in the final documentation.

To understand these examples more fully the reader should refer to Chapter 7 and relate these examples to the activity network and activity discussions. Not all formations of objectives activities have examples given here. Rather, these examples are provided to give relative insight into the products of formation on those activities that seem to merit clarification by example.

ACTIVITY F010—CREATE LETTER OF REQUEST (AN EXAMPLE)

Mr. Systems Manager:

Our people constitute the most important resource our company has. We have not always been able to manage this resource as effectively as we should and, therefore, have not maximized its full potential. One of the reasons for not being able to fully maximize this resource is that we lack an accurate, complete, and easily accessible set of employee information. If we were to pull together all existing information and any other pertinent information into one easily accessible and very manipulatable file, we could plan, organize, direct, and control this resource much more effectively than we do presently.

We envision a system which will allow the company to assess potential candidates for a specific job opening on the basis of past experience, education, interest, and so forth. It will help in career path planning by scheduling educational courses and job assignments for each employee, and will allow immediate scheduling of personnel to care for any emergency situations which may occur, such as strikes, natural disasters, or other situations that require assigning personnel to temporary work tasks to keep the company functioning. The system will have the capability to select any information for reports for federal regulatory bodies (e.g., EEOC) or to select information on request by any authorized personnel.

We feel that this is an extremely important and timely effort because of its potential for almost unending return on investment to the company. This unending return will be realized by maximizing utilization of our personnel resource, decreasing turnover rate, and increasing production and should lead to a more efficiently managed company.

Therefore, we respectfully request that this project be given the highest priority for development.

Sincerely,

Requesting Department Manager

ACTIVITY F030—ESTABLISH FORMATION STUDY PLAN (AN EXAMPLE)

The objectives of the study are as follows:

ESTABLISH OBJECTIVES FOR A PERSONNEL SYSTEM
- The types of information included.
- The nature of the reports.
- The probable gains for the company.
- The areas for consideration.
- The needs of the users.

ESTABLISH THE INITIAL FEASIBILITY OF A PERSONNEL SYSTEM

PRESENT A FORMATION OF OBJECTIVES REPORT FOR MANAGEMENT

- Prepare documentation of all activities.
- File report on time.
- Prepare report, expending only resources allocated for study.
- Submit a sound recommendation for the system.

The study will be conducted in 2½ months by the four people in the study team.

The budget for the study will not exceed the sum of the salaries for the four study team members.

ACTIVITY F040—IDENTIFY USERS AND USER NEEDS (AN EXAMPLE)

USERS

1. Any management function involving personnel placement decisions, including:

    a. General personnel (new employee, placing/selecting established employees, placing inactive employees).
    b. Departmental personnel groups (staff offices in each department).
    c. Special assignments (strike, training, loans, civic activities, etc).

2. Any group currently maintaining or accessing a personnel file.

    a. Personnel Department—assist in selection of personnel for union contract negotiations.
    b. Public Relations—news media.
    c. Employment—fill position openings.
    d. Benefits—pension information, disability conditions.
    e. Comptrollers—payroll reports, issuing of checks.

3. Other users of personnel data.

    a. Those who need to contact/locate employees on job.
    b. Management personnel who may need to contact people at home—emergency list.

USER NEEDS

1. Information necessary to make more selective personnel decisions.

    a. Specific individuals.
    b. Cross indexes of individuals by specific parameters.
    c. All employee information that is currently available.
    d. Information not now available which will be needed.

2. Information currently found in personnel file.

3. Employee name, telephone number, address, and job.

4. Temporary assignments for personnel in emergency conditions.

ACTIVITY F050—IDENTIFY ASSUMPTIONS AND ITEMS FOR RESOLUTION (AN EXAMPLE)

ASSUMPTIONS

1. Much of the information required is available now.
2. Users want usable information to be more readily available.
3. Present information is not centralized.
4. Quality of the existing information is less than optimal.
5. We can do a better job if the information is centralized.
6. Information is needed to better utilize people.
7. We can build a better system than the one that now exists.
8. The system will be used to better utilize the people resource.
9. Employee payroll record information is available as a source.
10. A list of employees may be obtained from record files in the personnel department.
11. The data base will include all employees now in the company (approximately 43,000 employees).

ITEMS FOR RESOLUTION

1. What level of management should be able to send a request and/or receive information?
2. How will data be accessed?
3. How will data be used?
4. To what degree will the data in the system be confidential?
5. Does user need updated personnel records for each person periodically or just when personnel record changes? What changes would require update (e.g., new position or absence)?

6. Should inactive (pensioned or retired) employee records be maintained within our system?
7. How long should information be kept (how much past history included in record)?
8. How do emergency contingencies fit into our system?
9. What number of people should be included on our output list to be given to user?
10. Who selects fields within records—who codes document?
11. Where does maintenance fit in?

ACTIVITY F060—DEFINE TERMS (AN EXAMPLE)

EMPLOYEE. Any person, management or craft, currently employed by the company.

INACTIVE EMPLOYEE. Any person previously employed but still somehow associated with the company. This would include employees on leaves of absence, pensioners, early retirees, etc.

EMERGENCY CONTINGENCIES. Plans for continuing operations during events such as work stoppages, strikes, walk-outs; natural disasters such as fires, floods, tornadoes; sabotage and/or malicious damage to the company building, equipment, or records; power failure; and contaminated or destroyed records.

EMPLOYEE INFORMATION OR DATA. All information kept in data base on each employee. Included would be such things as name, address (home and work), social security number, closest relative, age, sex, marital status, date and place of birth, number of dependents, education, job assignments held previously and currently, and off-the-job interests and activities.

PERSONNEL FILE. Same as employee information data.

ACTIVITY F070—DEVELOP SYSTEM OBJECTIVES (AN EXAMPLE)

1. The utilization of all company personnel is to be improved.
2. A personnel system will be utilized to obtain a list of available qualified employees to fill positions within the system.
3. The output record will contain employees' names, qualifications, and background information.

4. The output report will be available upon request.
5. Management personnel will access the system. (Required level of management is to be resolved.)
6. There must be controls so that no input or data base records are lost and so that a manager receives the proper output.
7. All requests must be handled the day they are received.
8. Off-premises storage of information will serve as backup.
9. Management/employee relationships will be improved by:
   a. Providing management with an evaluative tool for personnel decisions.
   b. Providing suggestions to management concerning equitable treatment on personnel matters.
   c. Providing a systematic method whereby employees' records can be kept up to date in regard to changes in their status (such as salary increases and appraisals).

ACTIVITY F080—SET PERFORMANCE SPECIFICATIONS (AN EXAMPLE)

COST.

Not resolved; see cost view of system.

TIME/CAPACITY.

1. Must be able to handle volume processing:
   a. New employees (average of 5000 per year).
   b. Personnel treatment—between 10,000 and 50,000 per years.
   c. Inquiries—between 40,000 and 200,000 per year.
2. Periodic report (daily, weekly, or monthly).
3. Total capacity will be for 55,000 master records.

FLEXIBILITY.

Capacity for handling 10,000 employee records in addition to the number we have now.

SECURITY.

Access will be restricted to authorized personnel only.

ACCEPTANCE.

Will require some training for management to allow it to use the system to best advantage. Will require orientation to build trust and establish proper use of the system.

QUALITY
Periodic report data must be current and received before the time needed.

RELIABILITY.
No more than 4 hours of downtime per year.

ACCURACY/AVAILABILITY.
Accuracy level will be 98% or above. Control will be at least 99.5%.

EFFICIENCY.
1. All transactions will be completed daily; priority transactions will be completed within 10 to 30 seconds.
2. Operating cost per employee record per year will not exceed $40.

ACTIVITY F090—IDENTIFY RESOURCES AND THEIR PARAMETERS (AN EXAMPLE)

RESOURCES AND THEIR PARAMETERS (AN EXAMPLE)

RESOURCES

Employees currently involved in building lower-priority systems can be utilized without adversely affecting the company's overall goals.

Current financial condition of the company will support a developmental undertaking of $1 to 1½ million dollars per year of development to cover both salary of designers and supplies.

Our existing computerized facilities (environment) will accommodate three additional large-scale computers and ancillary equipment without modification.

Employee attitude surveys indicate that employees are eager and desirous of a new, more comprehensive method for maximizing their contribution to the company.

PARAMETERS

Union Agreements
a. Coordination with the unions is needed so that the system will

not violate any current contractual agreements without negotiations to provide for the changes.

b. Our system will not be bound by the traditional procedure of
promoting the employee with the most seniority first.

Company Policy

No person now in our employ shall be selected for a lower-level job
unless he so requests or such placement is authorized by a vice president of the company.

Regulatory Agencies

The system must provide for and adhere to all governmental agency
regulations.

ACTIVITY F110—EVALUATE RESOURCE PARAMETERS (AN EXAMPLE)

Resource Available	Resource Required	Difference Plan
Money—1 to 1½ million per year for development.	Estimate ¾ to 1 million dollars per year.	*No action* needed.
Employee attitude—60% of employees want to be managed better.	85% of employees need to accept the new system in order for it to receive a fair trial.	Start an employee education in 6 months to alter employee attitude.
Personnel—67 system designers available for work on this project.	Need 8 more behavior specialists (i.e., human factors and training specialists).	Contact special placement agencies to hire the required knowledgeable persons.
Environment— 5000 square feet of computer environment available in the DP area now.	Will require 3400 square feet to accommodate two large-scale CPUs and ancillary equipment.	*No action* needed.
Union agreements—will be renegotiated at least twice before this system takes effect.	Require fairly extensive realignment of con-tractual agreements.	Develop plan for a systematic rework and renegotiation of contracts.

ACTIVITY F120—ESTABLISH INITIAL VIEW OF THE ENVIRONMENT (AN EXAMPLE)

- Employee turnover rate is increasing.
- There is a trend toward earlier retirement and a 4-day work week.
- There is a trend toward increased and more complex employee benefits.
- There is a very pronounced trend toward increased governmental requirements for utilization of employee information.
- There is an increasing concern about people's lives being manipulated or controlled by "the computer".
- There is a trend toward decreased skill levels in people entering the job market.
- There is an increasing trend toward people wanting and demanding meaningful jobs in which they can feel they are making a worthwhile contribution.
- Increased information concerning the skills and knowledge needed for specific jobs, and newer techniques for teaching these skills and imparting this knowledge, should allow for better selection and training of employees to fill vacant job assignments.

ACTIVITY F130—IDENTIFY TERMINAL OUTPUTS (AN EXAMPLE)

1. PERIODIC REPORTS. These are issued on a regular (daily, weekly, or biweekly) basis to managers, showing where items such as the following apply to specific employees under their jurisdiction:

    a.   Salary increase (due, overdue, or possibly due).
    b.   Possible candidates for advancement.
    c.   Upgrade in job classification (as in b above).
    d.   Retirement eligibility.
    e.   Available jobs in the company to which it is feasible (on the basis of level, qualifications, and other considerations) to assign the employee.
    f.   Projection of what training an employee will be assigned to receive, and when.
    g.   Report of how many and what type of persons should be hired.

2. INQUIRY REPORTS. These are responses to valid requests for person-

nel data, whose content and form should be specifiable by the inquirer.

3. PAYROLL EMPLOYEE CHECKS. (Hold in abeyance.)

   a.   Monthly.
   b.   Biweekly.
   c.   Weekly.
   d.   On-demand.

4. NOTIFICATIONS such as:

   a.   Attend particular training course.
   b.   Appraisal—performance review dates.
   c.   Organizational change notices.
   d.   Service anniversary dates (on 5-year interval).

5. EMERGENCY CONDITION job assignments.

   a.   Job-to-employee match.
   b.   Location for employee reporting.

ACTIVITY F140—IDENTIFY INITIAL INPUT (AN EXAMPLE)

1. PERSONAL DATA. These include all pertinent records for each employee in the company. Input will be of two major classes:

   a.   Initial records.* All formal information available to the company at the time of hiring (or, for employees on the payroll at system turn-on, all available personnel information). This would include such things as physical and personal information, work experience, educational and training background, company test scores, and medical results.
   b.   Additional records.* All information on the employee after the initial record falls into this class. Included are such things as assignment, salary, training histories, performance evaluations, and absence records. This information will be added as it becomes available.

---

*All items in this category will probably become part of the data base.

2. INQUIRY REQUEST. This is an impulse-type input, triggering a specific response. It must be originated by an authorized person. It specifies delivery of specific personnel information, which should be available in accordance with virtually any "sort" or report generator specifications.

3. JOB AVAILABILITY AND SPECIFICATIONS. This item is added to the data base on a temporary basis. When a job must be filled, specifications are given which must be specific enough so that a check can be performed to eliminate from consideration all except the individuals (present employees) who are likely to be both interested in and qualified for the job. A method must be devised for removing this item from the data base when the job is filled.

4. UPDATE INFORMATION such as:
    a. New training classes.
    b. New job classifications.
    c. New benefits.
    d. All relevant employee change information.
    e. Wage and pay rates.

ACTIVITY F150—IDENTIFY FUNCTIONS (AN EXAMPLE)

1. RECEIVE—capture signals (messages, data) from the environment.
    a. *Observe*—maintain a posture of readiness to receive signals.
       (1) *Search*—actively seek out signals.
       (2) *Attend*—maintain readiness for signal reception passively or in a stable state.
    b. *Collect*—pass signals from the environment into the system.
       (1) *Sense*—pass some element or analog of environmental energies or forms into the system.
       (2) *Detect*—sense with filtering of noise or differentiation of signal and noise.
    c. *Discriminate*—distinguish among signals.
       (1) *Identify*—separate signals into messages and message units.
       (2) *Classify*—assign messages to categories or otherwise characterize their content in some general terms.

(3) *Measure*—assign some quantity to the message or one or more of its elements.

2. TRANSFER—direct and move messages within the system.

    a. *Filter*—sort, eliminate, and combine messages according to purpose or process.
    b. *Route*—assign destinations and/or routes to messages.
    c. *Convert*—modify the physical characteristics of messages to facilitate transfer.
    d. *Transmit*—move the message.

3. RECORD—prepare a message analog.

    a. *Write*—translate messages into a more permanent, transmittable, or storable form.
    (1) *Code*—translate messages into an arbitrary symbol system.
    (2) *Tag*—assign descriptors to messages to facilitate their retrieval.
    (3) *Format*—arrange messages into some standard form.
    b. *Read*—translate messages into a more accessible form.
    (1) *Decode*—translate messages into a more natural language.

4. STORE—retain messages in a static stage.
5. PROCESS—operate on or treat data.
    a. *Sort*—assign data to established classes.
    b. *Screen*—extract selected data.
    c. *Compute*—process data according to the formal rules of mathematics.
    d. *Associate*—bring into relationship items of discrete data.
    (1) *Collate*—juxtapose related data.
    (2) *Synthesize*—integrate discrete data into a cogent whole; create a meaningful array of data against some model or hypothesis.
    e. *Analyze*—order data according to its presumed underlying structure.
    f. *Evaluate*—interpret data in some frame of reference broader than its manifest characteristics.
    (1) *Value*—assign relative weights to data.
    (2) *Interpret*—attribute cause and effect relationships.
    g. *Act*—initiate further operations or terminate operations on the basis of results from processing data.

(1) *Chain*—follow a rote sequence or invariant program.

(2) *Follow* rules—execute a course of action according to general principles and objectives in situations where contingencies cannot be fully forecast and appropriate actions prescribed.

(3) *Decide*—choose among alternative courses of action in the face of uncertainties.

(4) *Solve*—integrate, adapt, or generate principles sufficient to resolve unique problems.

6. PRESENT—make information available to a customer.

    a. *Report*—translate information into a form compatible with the customer's needs.

    b. *Summarize*—select the most salient features of the data for presentation.

    c. *Communicate*—disseminate reports.

7. ADMINISTER—attempt to optimize system performance.

    a. *Plan*—prepare for future operations of the system.

        (1) *Sequence*—establish the priorities by which future operations will be carried out.

        (2) *Schedule*—determine when future operations will occur.

        (3) *Task*—assign responsibilities to elements of the system.

    b. *Program*—define the specific instructions or routines by which missions will be carried out.

    c. *Control*—establish expert direction over system operation.

        (1) *Command*—issue executive instructions to operating elements.

        (2) *Monitor*—observe, sample, or query the information flow to ensure quality.

        (3) *Correct*—initiate action to overcome the effects of past error and/or reduce the probability of future error.

    d. *Maintain*—prevent or correct failure of system elements.

ACTIVITY F160—IDENTIFY SYSTEM CONFIGURATIONS (AN EXAMPLE)

ACTIVITY F170—SURVEY TECHNOLOGICAL STATE OF THE ART (AN EXAMPLE)

HARDWARE. Existing 370 series or equal-in-size CPU hardware will accommodate both size and speed requirements.

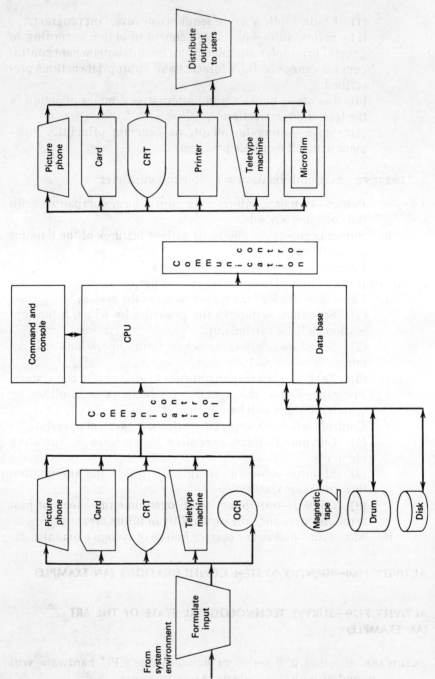

Activity F160—Identify system configurations (an example).

268

Microfilm (COM) or cathode ray tube (CRT or CDT) plus high- and low-speed printers will accommodate input/output requirements.

MANUAL. Less manual effort with more machine editing will make the manual system easier and more efficient. Therefore, operating procedures are within the state of the art.

CONTROL. Control of the manual procedures, communications network, and mechanized procedures offers a real problem. Additional measures and controls will be needed which are not now available. Hopefully, these breakthroughs will occur during development. If not, the system will be either infeasible or extremely vulnerable.

SOFTWARE. There are software languages, common routines, and algorithms advanced enough to build the system. However, its potential will be realized only through a very (not now available) humanistic language.

ACTIVITY F180—IDENTIFY USER IMPLICATIONS (AN EXAMPLE)

BUSINESS

- Less money in training, selection, recruitment.
- Fast manager access to complete employee record.
- Time saved in readjusting and reassigning work force.
- More accurate method of employee assignment.
- Better utilization of work force.
- Less turnover.
- Better job attitude due to more job confidence.
- Elimination of overstaffing.
- Better control (security) of employee information.

CUSTOMER

- Improved service because of better placed employees.
- Reduced errors because of better placed employees.
- Better employee relations caused by more "humanistic" treatment, planning, and rewarding.

ACTIVITY F190—PREPARE PERSONNEL SUBSYSTEM PLANNING CONSIDERATION

1. About 8500 to 10,000 people now access personnel records. These numbers include about 250 to 300 people who are full-time personnel workers. The new system will displace about 200 of these employees, and they will be available for other assignments.

2. Forms, reports, and displays generated by the new system will need to be readily understood (indeed, should be almost impossible to misunderstand) for the user audience of 8300 to 9800 people accessing the records.
3. Requests and inquiries to the system must be simple, unambiguous, and expressed in English-like statements in order that all users can readily learn to use the system.
4. Training must be largely self instructional and should probably consist of computer-assisted instructions which would be modular in form and directed toward specific sets of users.
5. System command and control instructions and requests must be designed for the president's own use.
6. With optional function allocation, personnel jobs in the new system will be designed to enrich employees' work experiences and to fulfill their expectations.

ACTIVITY F200—DETERMINE CONTROL OBJECTIVES HAVE BEEN INCLUDED (AN EXAMPLE)

1. There will be maximum security of records.
2. Duplicate records will be stored in a centralized place to provide secure off-premises backup storage.
3. The input of initial records, of requests, and of updates will be validated in order not to violate company and regulatory requirements and to be certain that a change or request is made by a properly authorized person.
4. Provision will be made for rejected information which was not properly entered.
5. The security department will be informed of repeated cases of attempted unauthorized entry.
6. A comprehensive audit trail will be built in for maintaining the integrity of the file.
7. System reliability will be achieved through built-in redundancy of all critical components.

ACTIVITY F210—PRIORITY RANK OBJECTIVES (AN EXAMPLE)

1. The system will improve utilization of the personnel resource by providing answers to inquiries from management the same day they are received.

2. The system will improve company/employee relationships by:

    a. Providing management with an evaluative tool for personnel decisions.
    b. Providing suggestions to management concerning equitable treatment on personnel matters.
    c. Providing a systematic method whereby employees' records can be kept up to date on changes in their status.

3. The system will have built-in control so that no data are lost or contaminated and so that the manager receives the proper output. It will further ensure control of the records by having off-premises storage of information which can serve as backup.

4. The system will provide, upon request, a list of available qualified personnel to fill vacant positions within the company. This report will contain all information on the candidates specified by the inquiry.

ACTIVITY F220—PREPARE DEVELOPMENTAL PLAN (AN EXAMPLE)

1. The system development standards will be adhered to in their entirety.
2. Formal quarterly progress reports will be issued—end of stage reports will conform to the standards.
3. Money requirements are specified in (Attachment A).

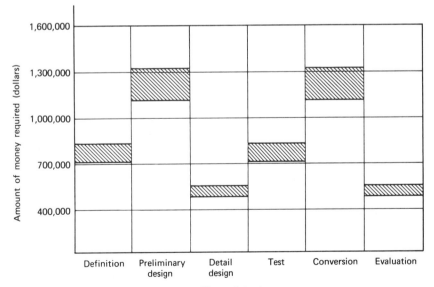

Activity F220—Attachment A: money requirements.

4. People requirements are specified in (Attachment B).

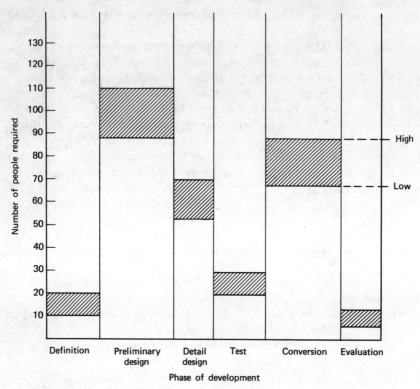

Activity F220—Attachment B: personnel requirements.

5. It is estimated that 4 to 6 years will be needed to complete the developmental effort.
6. Definition stage should start January 1, 1974, and last until about the 2nd quarter of 1975.
7. Preliminary design stage should start about the 2nd quarter of 1975 and extend through the 4th quarter of 1976.
8. Detail design stage should occur the 1st and 2nd quarters of 1975.
9. Test stage should occur about the 3rd and 4th quarters of 1977.
10. Conversion stage is to be in three phases with the 1st phase completed in the 3rd quarter of 1978.
11. Consultant services to be used for human engineering and for some system simulations.
12. Developmental staff to be housed in the company headquarters 125,000 square feet required, and 80,000 of this now available.

13. Project team method of development will be used with a division-level manager as the overall project leader.

14. All departments will be represented on the developmental team by either full- or part-time members or advisors.

15. The effort will require the authorization of approximately 2 million dollars to complete the definition and preliminary design stages.

ACTIVITY F230—DEVELOP COST VIEW OF THE PROPOSED SYSTEM (AN EXAMPLE)

Operational Costs: Annual CPU Rental		Annual I/O Equipment Rental	"Packaged" Software Costs	Annual Supplies and Materials Cost
Configuration A	800,000–1,400,000	350,000–600,000	80,000–140,000	180,000–240,000
Configuration D	800,000–1,400,000	700,000–1,200,000	40,000–70,000	90,000–120,000
Configuration E	800,000–1,400,000	500,000–950,000	80,000–140,000	135,000–180,000

Operational Projected Savings:	Displaced Salary and Wage Expense	File Storage Savings	Reduced Training Expense
Configuration A	2,000,000–2,500,000	45,000–65,000	75,000–105,000
Configuration D	2,200,000–2,500,000	45,000–65,000	80,000–110,000
Configuration E	1,500,000–2,000,000	25,000–40,000	65,000–95,000

Developmental Costs: People		Administration	Supplies	Space
Definition	495,000–525,000	75,000–90,000	3,000–5,250	37,500–45,000
Preliminary design	825,000–875,000	125,000–150,000	5,000–8,750	62,500–75,000
Detail design	330,000–350,000	50,000–60,000	2,000–3,5000	25,000–30,000
Testing	495,000–525,000	75,000–90,000	3,000–5,250	37,500–45,000
Conversion	825,000–875,000	125,000–150,000	5,000–8,750	62,500–75,000
Evaluation	330,000–350,000	50,000–60,000	2,000–3,500	25,000–30,000
Total	3,300,000–3,500,000	500,000–600,000	20,000–35,000	250,000–300,000

Depreciation of Development Costs:
   The two methods of depreciation used were:
1. Estimated life of the system (10 years) with straight line depreciation at 10%/per year. This comes out to between $474,000 and $549,500 per year.
2. Accelerated interest, where:

35% is written off the first year	$1,659,000–$1,923,250
30% is written off the second year	1,422,000–1,648,500
20% is written off the third year	948,000–1,099,000
10% is written off the fourth year	474,000–549,500
5% is written off the fifth year	237,000–274,750

The rate of return on investment was computed as follows:

$$R_I\left(\frac{T}{D}\right) = \frac{1}{E}\left[\left(C + \frac{1}{M}\right) - E_X\left(T_w - \frac{C}{M}\right)\right]$$

where RI = rate of return, T = Time, D = depreciation, E = earnings, E_X = Expense, C = capital, M = cost of money, and T_w = taxes written off. Therefore, the rate of return on investment = 28.3%.

Overhead Costs	Loaded Personnel Costs	Support and Maintenance Costs	Administrative Services
40,000–65,000	600,000–1,000,000	190,000–260,000	210,000–290,000
50,000–70,000	400,000–800,000	230,000–300,000	210,000–290,000
50,000–70,000	1,000,000–1,600,000	260,000–330,000	210,000–290,000

Reduced Recruitment, Selection, Placement Costs	Increased Productivity	Improved Service	Reduced Redundancy
50,000–70,000	400,000–500,000	300,000–400,000	70,000–90,000
60,000–80,000	400,000–500,000	300,000–400,000	80,000–100,000
40,000–60,000	400,000–500,000	300,000–400,000	60,000–80,000

Simulation	Test	Consultant Services	Training
1,500–6,000	27,000–45,000	12,000–18,000	60,000–90,000
2,500–10,000	45,000–75,000	20,000–30,000	100,000–150,000
1,000–4,000	18,000–30,000	8,000–12,000	40,000–60,000
1,500–6,000	27,000–45,000	12,000–18,000	60,000–90,000
2,500–10,000	45,000–75,000	20,000–30,000	100,000–150,000
1,000–4,000	18,000–30,000	8,000–12,000	40,000–60,000

10,000–40,000	180,000–300,000	80,000–120,000	400,000–600,000

BIBLIOGRAPHY

Air Force System Command, *Electronic System Test and Evaluation*, 1971.

Air Force System Command, *General Design Factors*, 1971.

Air Force System Command, *Handbook of Instructions for Aerospace Personnel Subsystem Designers*, 1966.

Aitchison, John, *Choice against Chance; an Introduction to Statistical Decision Theory*, Addison-Wesley, 1970.

Altman, James W., *Early Design of Information Systems: a Conceptualization*, American Institutes For Research, 1968

Altman, James W., *Management and the Early Design of Information Systems*, American Institutes For Research, 1968.

Amato, Vincent V., *Making the Computer Work for Management; Programmed Instruction Course*, American Management Association, 1967.

American Telephone & Telegraph Co., *The Bell System's Approach to Business Information Systems*, 1968.

American Telephone & Telegraph Co., *The Critical-Path Method; an Introductory Explanation of a Network Planning Method*, 1963.

Bennett, Edward, *Human Factors in Technology*, McGraw-Hill, 1963.

Brightman, Richard W., *Data Processing for Decision-making; an Introduction to Third-Generation Information Systems*, MacMillan, 1971.

Brinckloe, William D., *Managerial Operations Research*, McGraw-Hill, 1969.

Brink, Victor Z., *Computers and Management; the Executive Viewpoint*, Prentice-Hall, 1971.

Buzzell, Rovert D., *Mathematical Models and Marketing Management*, Harvard University Press, 1964.

Byrne, Brendan, *The Art of System Analysis*, Prentice-Hall, 1971.

Cleland, Davis I., *Systems, Organizations, Analysis, Management: A Book of Readings*, McGraw-Hill, 1969.

Corrigan, Robert E., and Robert A. Kaufman, *Why System Engineering*, Fearon, 1966.

Crowley, Thomas H., *Understanding Computers*, McGraw-Hill, 1967.

Cuenod, Michel, and A. Durling, *A Discrete-Time Approach for System Analysis*, Academic Press, 1969.

Davis, Gordon B., *An Introduction to Electronic Computers*, McGraw-Hill, 1965.

Defense Department, *Configuration Control—Engineering Changes, Deviations and Waivers*, 1968.

Demaree, Robert G., *Development of Qualitative and Quantitative Personnel Requirements Information*, Air Force Systems Command, 1962.

Dickmann, Robert A., *Personnel Implications for Business Data Processing*, Wiley-Interscience, 1971.

Farina, Mario V., *Computers; a Self-Teaching Introduction*, Prentice-Hall, 1969.

Farr, Leonard, V. LaBolle, and N. E. Willmorth, *Planning Guide for Computer Program Development*, System Development Corporation, 1965.

Fitts, Paul M., and M. I. Posner, *Human Performance*, Brooks/Cole, 1967.

Ford, Robert N., *Motivation through The Work Itself*, American Management Association, 1969.

Folley, J.D., *Human Factors Methods for System Design*, American Institutes of Research, 1960.

Gagne, Robert M., *Psychological Principles in System Development*, Holt, Rinehart & Winston, 1962.

Gardner, John F., F. G. Kirk, and G. E. McClure, *A Compilation of Format Specifications*, Research Associates, 1970.

Gardner, John F., F. G. Kirk, and G. E. McClure, *Identification and Definition of Personnel Subsystem Analysis and Design Products and Services—Phase I; A Compilation of Developmental Information*, Research Association, 1970.

Gellerman, Saul W., Motivation and Productivity, American Management Association, 1963.

Gleim, George A., Program Flowcharting; Holt, Rinehart & Winston, 1970.

Gordon, Davis B., *Auditing & EDP*, American Institute of Certified Public Accountants, 1968.

Greene, Keyon Brenton, *Systems Psychology*, McGraw-Hill, 1970

Haemer, K. W., *Making Your Meaning Clear; Six Steps in Effective Communication*, American Telephone & Telegraph Co., 1959.

Hall, Arthur D., *A Methodology for Systems Engineering*, Van Nostrand, 1962.

Hall, D. M., *Management of Human Systems*, Association for Systems Management, 1971.

Hartman, W., H. Matthes, and A. Proeme, *Management Information Systems Handbook*, McGraw-Hill, 1968.

Hitchcock, Robert, *The Computer and Business Unity*, American Elsevier, 1969.

Hopeman, Richard, *Systems Analysis and Operations Management*, Merrill, 1969.

Horowitz, Ira, *An Introduction to Quantitative Business Analysis*, McGraw-Hill, 1965.

Inaba, K., *The Underlying Concept of System Engineering*, Serendipity Associates, 1966.

Johnson, Richard A., J. E. Rosenweig, and F. E. Kast, *The Theory and Management of Systems*, McGraw-Hill, 1967.

Johnston, J., *Econometric Methods*, McGraw-Hill, 1963.

Kast, Fremont E., *Organization and Management*, McGraw-Hill, 1970.

Krauss, Leonard I., *Administering and Controlling the Company Data Processing Function*, Prentice-Hall, 1969.

Lehman, Richard S., and D. E. Bailey, *Digital Computing; Fortran IV and Its Applications in Behavioral Science*, Wiley, 1968.

Levin, Richard I., and C. A. Kirkpatrick, *Planning and Control with PERT/CPM*, McGraw-Hill, 1966.

Mager, Robert F., *Analyzing Performance Problems, Planning, or "You Really Oughta Wanna,"* Fearon, 1970.

Mager, Robert F., *Preparing Instructional Objectives*, Fearon, 1962.

McCormick, Ernest J., *Human Factors Engineering*, McGraw-Hill, 1970.

Meister, D., and D. E. Farr, *Designer's Guide for Effective Development of Aerospace Ground Equipment Control Panels; Preliminary Final Draft*, 1965.

Miller, R. B., *Manual for Man-Machine Job-Task Description*, American Institute of Research, 1955.

Morrison, Edward J., *Developing Computer-Based Employee Information System*, American Management Association, 1969.

National Aeronautics and Space Administration, *A Descriptive Model for Determining Optimal Human Performance in Systems*, Serendipity Associates, 1968.

Neuschel, Richard F., *Management by System*, McGraw-Hill, 1960.

Oettinger, Anthony G., and S. Marks, *Run, Computer, Run; the Mythology Of Educational Innovation*, Harvard University Press, 1969.

Optner, Stanford L., *Systems Analysis for Business Management*, Prentice-Hall, 1968.

Purifoy, George R., Jr., and S. P. Schumacher, *Guide to Preparation of Position Practices*, American Institutes for Research, 1965.

Raiffa, Howard, *Decision Analysis*, Addison-Wesley, 1968.

Rosove, Perry E., *Developing Computer-Based Information Systems*, Wiley, 1967.

Sackman, Harold, *Computers, System Science, and Evolving Society; the Challenge of Man-Machine Digital Systems*, Wiley, 1967.

Salzman, Lawrence, *Computerized Economic Analysis*, McGraw-Hill, 1968.

Sharpe, William F., *The Economics of Computers*, Columbia University Press, 1969.

Shurter, Robert L., and J. M. Reid, Jr., *A Program for Effective Writing*, Appleton-Century-Crofts, 1966.

Singleton, W. T., *The Industrial Use of Ergonomics*, Department of Scientific and Industrial Research, 1962.

Sippl, Charles J., *Computer Dictionary and Handbook*, Sams & Bobbs-Merrill, 1966.

Smith, Leighton F., *An Executive Briefing on The Control of Computers*, Data Processing Management Association, 1971.

Taylor, Herbert, *Management Information System: Purposes, Theory, Processes*, Structure, Hirschfeld Press, 1971.

Van Cott, Harold P., James W. Altman, Procedures for Including Human Engineering Factors in the Development of Weapons Systems, USAF WADC tech. Rept 56-488 1956

Vickery, B. C., *On Retrieval System Theory*, Butterworths, 1965.

Vroom, Victor H., *Work and Motivation*, Wiley, 1964.

Weinberg, Gerald M., *The Psychology of Computer Programming*, Van Nostrand-Reinhold, 1971.

Wiest, Jerome D., and F. K. Levy, *Critical Path Analysis—a Management Guide to PERT/CPM*, Prentice Hall, 1969.

INDEX